DISSEMINATING WHITMAN

Disseminating Whitman

Revision and Corporeality
in *Leaves of Grass*

Michael Moon

Harvard University Press
Cambridge, Massachusetts
London, England

Library of Congress Cataloging-in-Publication Data

Moon, Michael.
    Disseminating Whitman : revision and corporeality in
    Leaves of grass / Michael Moon.
        p.   cm.
    Includes bibliographical references.
        1. Whitman, Walt, 1819–1892.   Leaves of grass.
    2. Whitman, Walt, 1819–1892—Criticism, Textual.   I. Title.
PS3238.M66   1991   90-35138
811'.3—dc20   CIP

ISBN 0-674-21276-2 (cloth)
ISBN 0-674-21245-2 (paper)

Contents

Preface   *vii*

Acknowledgments   *ix*

Introduction: Whitman and the Politics of Embodiment   *1*

1   Rendering the Text and the Body Fluid:
The Cases of "The Child's Champion"
and the 1855 *Leaves of Grass*   *26*

2   Fluidity and Specularity in the Whitman Text   *59*

3   Dividing the Text and Crossing the Gaze in the
Second (1856) Edition of *Leaves of Grass*   *88*

4   The Politics of Nature and the Decomposition of
God: "The Great Construction of the New Bible"
in the Third (1860) Edition of *Leaves of Grass*   *123*

5   "The Blood of the World": Gender, Bloodshed,
and the Uncanny in the Fourth
(1867) Edition of *Leaves of Grass*   *171*

Notes   *225*

Index   *245*

Preface

Walt Whitman spent much of his career producing the successive editions of *Leaves of Grass*. Frequently announcing that he had left that book behind and was at work on another project, Whitman only gradually discovered that *Leaves of Grass* had a way for him of absorbing subsequent poetic projects. This gives his career, and the text that is its major product, an unusual shape, one formed by a long and elaborate process of revision. This book follows that process through the first four editions of *Leaves of Grass*.

In the Introduction I explore the meaning of Whitman's revisionary practice for *Leaves of Grass* and discuss how his lifelong commitment to revision is inextricably related to his commitment to representing the body and sexuality, especially sexuality between and among males, in his writing. In the first two chapters I consider Whitman's strategy in his early writing—including the first (1855) edition of *Leaves of Grass*—for eliminating differences between bodies and between bodies and texts by representing them as becoming "fluid," and I demonstrate how the "fluid" discourse of the first edition derives from (and tends to subvert) several contemporaneous discourses of the body in Whitman's society, especially those of temperance and anti-onanism, or "male purity."

Once *Leaves of Grass* had been published, the text itself became and remained for some time the primary context in which Whitman continued to write and revise his work. The relatively straightforward relation of the first edition of *Leaves of Grass* to the worlds of bodies and discourses-of-the-body it tries to bridge is complicated for the second and its successor editions by the significance for each of these of its predecessor-editions and its differences from them. In Chapter 3 I look at the ways in which the poetry of the second (1856) edition of *Leaves of Grass* manifests Whitman's strategies for coming to terms with difference, for not simply denying it and dissolving it by means of a metaphorics of "fluidity," as he had done in the poetry of the first edition. Not the least of the kinds of difference Whitman seems interested in discriminating in the second edition is what he presents as being the vital difference between this new edition of his text and its predecessor; finding terms in which to represent these differences is a central preoccupation of each of the early editions after the first (that is, through 1867).

The subject of the fourth chapter is the increasing tension in Whitman's writing for the third (1860) edition of *Leaves of Grass* between a desire to stabilize the text—he at one point expressed an ambition to establish in this edition the text of what he called a "New Bible"— and a desire to keep his revisionary project in play. Some of the stakes for pursuing either of these alternatives manifest themselves in Whitman's representations of the politics of male-male desire as he saw it, in the "Calamus" section of the third edition: should the subjects of such desire withdraw from society into the relative safety of its margins, or should they remain "within" it, retaining their radically revisionary relation to it, as Whitman had imagined himself and like-minded persons doing in his earlier work? The question is explored without being answered throughout "Calamus" and beyond it in other 1860 texts. Such tensions are exacerbated by the colossal violence of the Civil War, in response to which Whitman largely renounces his utopian designs for male-homoerotic desire, in the face of very different kinds of historical pressures from those that had impelled him toward the *Leaves of Grass* project as he had initially conceived it and pursued it through the first four editions. The final chapter examines the increasingly important role that representations of death and uncanny relations between living and dead bodies, between persons of different genders, and between one text and another come to play in Whitman's Civil War poetry and in the fourth (1867) edition of *Leaves of Grass* into which that poetry was incorporated.

Acknowledgments

I am very grateful to Sharon Cameron for the extremely high quality of her attention to my work over the past several years. Throughout our association she has provided an ideal balance of challenge, provocation, and warmhearted support. I also wish to thank Larzer Ziff for first getting me interested in American literature as well as for his help and encouragement with this project; Michael Warner for reading many of these pages with characteristic rigor and generosity; and Marcie Frank for sharing the gift of her unfailing good sense and good humor with me since we were both fledgling graduate students.

A grant from the Long and Widmont Memorial Foundation gave timely aid to an early stage of this project, and a Fellowship for Recent Recipients of the Ph.D. from the American Council of Learned Societies supported its latter stages during the 1989–90 academic year. Duke University generously made time available to me to carry out final revisions on the book. I thank Stanley Fish for his example, his relentless encouragement, and especially for helping me make time to complete this project expeditiously, and Jane Tompkins for first guiding me toward thinking about American popular culture and for always taking a friendly and enthusiastic interest in my work on it.

I might not have completed—indeed, might not have undertaken—this project were it not for the unstinting support of Bob and Jean Moon, and for the example of my loving and hardworking parents, Sy and Mary Moon; I was long sustained by their hopes for me, and I am delighted and humbled by their pride in me.

The process of writing several parts of this book has been inextricably

Acknowledgments

bound up for me with the pleasures of Stephen Orgel's friendship and hospitality over the past several years. Millie Seubert encouraged my first efforts to write about Whitman years ago, and she remains one of the best readers of my work. Nick Deutsch and Daniel Kaiser have also taken a lively, and for me enlivening, interest in this work from its earliest stages. Eve Kosofsky Sedgwick first informed and inspired this project through her brilliant work and then, later on, through her friendship and conversation, in all of which I delight. Jonathan Goldberg was often literally the first reader of the following pages, and they were substantially improved in many places by his suggestions. This book is dedicated to him in love and gratitude for the many kinds of help he gave me while I was writing it.

DISSEMINATING WHITMAN

Introduction: Whitman and the Politics of Embodiment

The Literary and the Political in Whitman's Revisionary Practice

Walt Whitman produced the first edition of *Leaves of Grass* in 1855. Within twelve years of that date he had produced three more editions of the work, each substantially different from its predecessor(s). These appeared in 1856, 1860, and 1867, respectively. Two more major versions appeared in 1881 and 1891–92. In each of these editions the author not only added substantial numbers of poems and deleted others, in whole or in part; he also generally reordered the poems and reclassified them into new kinds of groupings, which he came to call "clusters" and "annexes." In adding, deleting, interlineating, repositioning, and renaming poems and entire groups of poems, Whitman effectively redirected the patterns of meanings in each of the successive editions of *Leaves of Grass*.

Rather than asking which of the editions is best, as a number of Whitman's most influential critics have done,[1] or pursuing through his work the received literary sense of "revision" as rewriting at the local level of the text for the purpose of effecting stylistic improvements, I have chosen to focus my explorations of *Leaves of Grass* on what I would characterize as the "macro" level of the text. The very existence of a half-dozen different major versions of the text raises questions about Whitman's work that have not yet been closely investigated, and Whitman's revisionist career establishes a meaning for "revision" broader than that usually employed in literary studies. Although I shall be concerned in the following pages with numerous examples of local, line-by-line, word-by-word revisions by Whitman, and although I do not wish in any way to deny the great value of the textual scholarship on his local ("micro"-level) revisions carried out in the past thirty years principally by Fredson Bowers, Arthur Golden, and the editors of the exemplary and indispensable Variorum *Leaves of Grass*—for of all Whitman scholars, it is they to whom my own project is most deeply indebted—I have chosen in the present work to emphasize the possible meanings of Whitman's revisions from "book" to "book," that is, from one edition to the next.[2] Revision at this level is most strikingly evident in the first four editions, and I have therefore chosen to concentrate on them in this book, leaving aside the last two editions, where revision takes relatively local forms of the kind that have often been remarked in the critical literature on *Leaves of Grass*.

My rationale for emphasizing meanings at the level of the book over more local ones proceeds from my sense of the priorities of Whitman's *Leaves of Grass* project. Questions of *literary* revision are not the only— are not, I will argue, the most significant—matters of revision in Whitman's project. The revisionary *effects* which the texts of *Leaves of Grass* are designed to have on his culture's prevailing (or coming-to-be prevailing) conceptions of bodiliness manifest themselves most clearly when one follows them from edition to edition. I shall argue that it is such large-scale revisions of his society's constructions of bodiliness, and especially of sexuality, that make Whitman's micro-revision at the level of style cogent. I shall argue further that one primary effect *Leaves of Grass* was designed to have from its inception was ultimately to render various kinds of behavior which Whitman saw as potentially subversive—chief among these, both enacting and writing about proscribed forms of sexual behavior—indistinguishable from each other. However, even if the difference between sexual transgression and writing is repeatedly abolished at some moments in *Leaves of Grass*, it is important to recognize that Whitman does not achieve this result by simply proclaiming the equivalence of these two activities. Rather, he carries on in his writing a complex series of negotiations among the highly charged realms in his society which he desires to bring into contact, and ultimately to render in some ways identical, with each other: the literary, the sexual-political, and the political.

In the face of an increasing tendency in his culture to hypostatize and to idealize a limited range of types of writing as "literary" and thereby to separate them definitively from political and sexual-political discourses, Whitman insisted on the interconnectedness of these realms. Throughout his career he never tired of insisting that literary or poetic effects as such were at most a secondary consideration in his writing, but I wish to emphasize that there is more at issue in such passages than the mere diminution or devaluation of literariness. It is not simply the literary in itself that Whitman repudiates but his culture's increasing valuation of the literary in and for itself, in isolation from the political and sexual-political desires that impel what he sees as the writing most worth producing. In a representative statement on this matter drawn from the late essay "A Backward Glance o'er Travel'd Roads," he categorically devaluates attempts to understand his writings as essentially "literary" and "art[istic]" phenomena: "No one will get at my verses who insists on viewing them as a literary performance, or attempts at such a performance, or as aiming mainly toward art or aestheticism."[3] Rather than appealing primarily to the reader's intelligence or aesthetic sensibility as if these were isolated faculties, Leaves of Grass is designed to permit author and audience to effect more vital connections. Namely, Whitman wishes to disseminate affectionate physical presence from one to the other, fervently and directly. "I . . . sent out 'Leaves of Grass,'" he writes in an important note to his Preface to the 1876 version of the work, "to arouse and set flowing in men's and women's hearts, young and old, endless streams of living, pulsating love and friendship, directly from them to myself, now and ever."[4]

Whitman insists in such utterances that human feeling and bodiliness are the major concerns impelling Leaves of Grass. In the same note in which the lines just quoted appear, he speaks of "'Leaves of Grass' entire" as "not to be construed as an intellectual or scholastic effort or poem mainly, but more as a radical utterance out of the Emotions and the Physique."[5] Moreover, rather than being merely the transference of one isolated individual's (the author's) affectionate physical presence into the respective privatized solitudes of each of his readers, "emotional expressions" and the political are inextricably linked—as Whitman argues in a third contiguous passage from the note to the 1876 Preface: "[I]mportant as they are in my purpose as emotional expressions for humanity, the special meaning of the 'Calamus' cluster of 'Leaves of Grass,' (and more or less running through the book, and cropping out in 'Drum-Taps,') mainly resides in its political significance."[6] The long process of revisionary elaboration that *Leaves of Grass* gradually underwent produced a series of texts that powerfully articulate a politics comprehending ranges of experience as ostensibly disparate as the pleasurable and painful phases of male-homoerotic love ("Calamus") and the national trauma of the sectional division of the country over slavery. Moreover, as Whitman says, such concerns permeate the entire project and not just those subsections of it in which they are most extensively thematized.

Through his polemical elevation of this radical body-politics over the "merely" literary in his descriptions of his project, and through his integration of the two practices as he writes and rewrites *Leaves of Grass*, Whitman forces his readers to reconceptualize their ideas of the nature and limits of the bodily and of what can be written about them. This body-politics is designed to reconstitute the readers' very subjectivity in relation not only to the author's but to their own and everyone else's bodily existence—by critiquing and revising prevailing modes of conceiving bodiliness in relation to such primary forms of social practice as sexuality, gender, and writing. Whitman revises readerly subjectivity in the direction of a heightened, transforming sense of the constructedness and hence the dense politicality of all bodily experience, erotic and otherwise. Describing the dynamics of this process is the primary focus of this study. Whitman's appropriation of available discourses from the great mass movements of his time; his deft manipulation of literary/symbolic techniques for representing the social revisions of corporeality that he desired; his searching, albeit highly conflicted, critique of his society's prevailing notions of the nature and meanings of sexual difference—these will be the secondary foci of my account of the first four editions of *Leaves of Grass*.

GIVEN WHITMAN'S political ambitions for his project, it is not surprising that *Leaves of Grass* is significantly related to a number of major kinds of nonliterary writing that were contemporaneous with it and that concerned themselves with the discipline of the human body and its appetites, such as temperance and anti-onanist discourses. I examine these relations in the initial chapters of this study. Although I particularly emphasize changes in attitudes toward gender and sexuality in the United States in the mid-nineteenth century in my accounts of the ways in which the first four editions of *Leaves of Grass* attempt to revise predominant conceptions of the bodily, I have attempted to do so with an awareness of other, related historical changes which took place in the 1850s and 1860s, perhaps the period of the most intense political conflict and significant social transformation in American history to date. *Leaves of Grass* was continually engaged in the highly charged atmosphere of political and historical ferment from which it emerged and to which it passionately addressed itself. But as there are important connections between the early (that is, 1855–1867) editions of *Leaves of Grass* and the tumultuous social contexts that could be said to generate them, there is also, I believe, a no less impassioned dialogue between each of the subsequent editions and its predecessor-edition(s). Given the project's grounding in a double-edged practice of revision, directed both at the text itself and at the culture's predominant modes of constructing the human body and bodily experience, it should also be unsurprising that the various editions of *Leaves of Grass* themselves provide the richest context in which to consider the differences not only between but within these successive texts. Consequently, in my treatment of the first (1855) edition in the first two chapters that follow, I foreground what I see as the edition's "near-relations" among contemporaneous kinds of non-literary writings, such as temperance and anti-onanist tracts; in my treatments of the second, third, and fourth editions (1856, 1860, and 1867, respectively) in subsequent chapters, I emphasize what I see as each edition's particular relationship(s) with the other early editions.

The objects of the highly revisionary first four editions of *Leaves of Grass*, then, are both a historically specific set of political principles governing the disposition(s) of the human body in mid-nineteenth-century American culture *and* the cumulative, accretionary text(s) of the editions. In an attempt to exceed or "go beyond" the modes of representing human embodiment in the discourse of his age, Whitman set himself the problem of attempting to project actual physical presence in a literary text.[7] At the heart of this problem was the impossibility of doing so literally, of successfully disseminating the author's literal bodily presence through the medium of a book. As a consequence of this impossibility, Whitman found it necessary to undertake the project of producing metonymic substitutes for the author's literal corporeal presence in the text.[8] Out of this difficulty arises the generative contradiction in the text of *Leaves of Grass* as I read it: that which exists between Whitman's repeated assertions that he provides loving physical presence in the text and his awareness of the frustrating but ultimately incontrovertible conditions of writing and embodiment that actually render it impossible for him to produce in his writing more than metonymic substitutes for such contact.

As a result of this basic contradiction, Whitman's fundamental writerly strategy is one of substitution. The primary substitutive process in the development of the first four editions of *Leaves of Grass* is one which arises almost from the inception of the project, as the author continually represents his own divagations between perceiving and presenting the text as a successfully achieved vehicle for disseminating physical presence and, alternatively and substitutively, as a "merely" literary text, one formed under and to some degree *by* the constraints ordinarily operating on books (for example, that they do not serve as media for transmitting their author's actual physical presence in any direct fashion).

In practice, Whitman effectively destabilizes the reified relation between politicality and literariness. He undercuts in his poetry the very notion which he makes a primary article of the polemical theory of his project. Whitman's terms for this distinction are no doubt highly relevant to any attempt to understand why he kept producing edition after edition of "the same book"—not because he was trying to "perfect" it as a literary work, but because he of necessity kept having to redirect his radical body-politics program in relation to an explosive and protean political climate in the period 1855–1867.

Whitman's radical ambition for his writing was fundamentally a dual one from the beginning of his career: first, to continue and extend the public discourse of such matters as bodily states and products that were being more and more thoroughly relegated to the realm of the private or the unspeakable, and, second, to attempt to force recognition of them as possible subjects for writing, including literary writing. As a consequence of this, Whitman was always involved in a dual project of both cultural revision (rewriting notions of what the consequences of embodiment or the meanings of a body, its parts, functions, products, and states, may be) and literary revision at what I have called the "macro" level (rewriting notions of what a literary text may be). Extending the range of subjects considered possible for literature is one aspect of his project which exemplifies the manner in which writing can challenge the codes of literary convention at the same time that it challenges other cultural codes, such as those that govern which kinds of sexual desires and behavior are fostered by the culture's public discourses and which kinds are devaluated and repressed. There is consequently a double emphasis in my interpretations of *Leaves of Grass*, as I believe there was in Whitman's production of his text, on both what he manages to incorporate in the text, often in defiance of predominant forces in his culture, and the ways he partially reveals/ conceals what is being incorporated: desires, actions, physical organs and states which are generally excluded from literary writings and from all but a few kinds of public discourse.

Whitman's practice raises metonymic substitution and the indeterminacy which defines the relation in his writing between primary objects and their respective substitutes to a high level. The writing continually oscillates between and negotiates two fields, bringing into contact matters which the culture tends to hold apart or to render disjunct—for example, the "proper" citizenly body (an increasingly abstract and decorporealized one) and its bodily products (wastes, tears, sexual secretions). Hence the initial and in some ways persistent emphasis in Whitman's career on fluidity and parataxis in his writing, on its objects being brought into unobstructed contact with each other; hence also its interweaving of "safe"—ostensibly nonsexual—and "dangerous"—explicitly sexual—discourses (as I shall discuss below). Whitman produces texts in which discourses of the body and discourses of the literary interact in ways which extend readers' conceptions of both realms, and of the range of possible relations between these two realms. Ultimately, the critique of his culture which Whitman continues developing through the first several editions of *Leaves of Grass* addresses itself to the constraints the culture has placed on the categories of the bodily and the literary, and on the possibility of these categories' interacting in ways which exceed or overrule these constraints.

In continuing to carry out his project in the first several editions of *Leaves of Grass*, Whitman subverted conventional distinctions between "literary" activity on the one hand and cultural and political activity on the other in ways which many of his professional readers have refused to recognize, or to recognize in other than opprobrious terms. The primary reason why so many of the meanings of *Leaves of Grass* have to a large extent eluded much of what has been accepted as "standard" Whitman criticism is that the project that much of this criticism has made central to itself, that of undertaking the recovery of the "purely literary" value of Whitman's writing, is foredoomed by that writing's very design. This is the case because what is isolable in *Leaves of Grass* as its distinctly literary qualities is available for interpretation only to a limited degree apart from the cultural-revisionary project to which the "merely literary" is subordinated in the text. *Leaves of Grass* has been diminished—as Whitman insisted it would be—by having been read as if its "literary" qualities were not subordinate to other, primary, essentially nonliterary considerations, such as trying and inevitably failing to project actual physical presence in a text, and profoundly revising the culture's prevailing modes of representing the consequences of embodiment.

"Difficult as it will be," Whitman writes in "A Backward Glance o'er Travel'd Roads," "it has become, in my opinion, imperative to achieve a shifted attitude . . . towards the thought and fact of sexuality, as an element in character, personality, the emotions, and a theme in literature. I am not going to argue the question by itself; it does not stand by itself."[9] In the intervening century since these words were written, countless attempts have been made "to argue the question [of sexuality] by itself," with generally unsatisfactory results—a judgment in which I believe a number of leading historians of gender and/or sexuality (for example, John D'Emilio, Carroll Smith-Rosenberg, Christine Stansell, Jeffrey Weeks) would readily concur.[10] For Whitman—anticipating, as it were, Foucault's critique of the "repressive hypothesis"—simply taking a position counter to a dominant discourse on sexuality or literature and stating that position would be not to go far enough, because a crucial aspect of what he places under negotiation and in revision is the notion current in his culture that the range of both of these two fields is properly highly circumscribed, and that they bear little significant relation to each other.[11]

FOR ALL THE directness of Whitman's address to what he saw as the thoroughgoing devaluation of bodily life that his culture was in the process of imposing on its inhabitants, the ubiquity of substitution and the complexity of its functions in his texts signify a felt necessity on his part of sometimes concealing some of the real objects of the corporeal-utopian program of his writing. I want at this point briefly to consider an example of some of the functions of substitution in Whitman's writing in relation to male homoeroticism, perhaps the most fiercely proscribed of all the kinds of bodily transactions his work puts into revision. There is a good example of some of these kinds of substitution in the previously quoted note to the 1876 Preface, where, after asserting that he "sent out 'Leaves of Grass' to arouse and set flowing . . . endless streams of living, pulsating love and friendship," Whitman produces an elaborate set of terms which emphasize feelings of profound and widespread frustration and oppression with regard to relations between persons: "To this terrible, irrepressible yearning, (surely more or less down underneath in most human souls)—this never-satisfied appetite for sympathy, and this boundless offering of sympathy—this universal democratic comradeship—this old, eternal, yet ever-new interchange of adhesiveness, so fitly emblematic of America—I have given in that book, undisguisedly, declaredly, the openest expression."[12]

What is perhaps most notable about this passage is the rich diversity of vocabulary and reference with which Whitman here invokes the kinds of transfers or exchanges of affectionate presence he has designed his project to enable. What he initially calls simply "love and friendship" he goes on to rename five times in rapid succession as "this terrible, irrepressible yearning"; "this never-satisfied appetite for sympathy," and (conversely) "this boundless offering of sympathy"; "this universal democratic comradeship"; and "this old, eternal, yet ever-new interchange of adhesiveness, so fitly emblematic of America." The "[l]ove and friendship" which Leaves of Grass is designed to release into dissemination, then, are neither the mild and rational social pleasures endlessly fostered in the liberal, "philanthropic" rhetoric of post-Enlightenment humanism nor the social ideal of privatized domestic bliss that had largely come to replace it in the United States during Whitman's childhood; they are a "terrible, irrepressible yearning," unappeasable, yet nonetheless universal or at least widespread ("surely . . . down underneath in most human souls"). That these powerful desires are experienced, or at least viewed by his society, as being "terrible" and "irrepressible" may help one account for the terms in which Whitman goes on to claim that he has given in his book "the openest expression" of them, "undisguisedly, declaredly"—all terms which suggest that the "terrible . . . yearning[s]" which impel

9

Leaves of Grass have perforce moved or are in the process of moving underground, into disguise and disavowal or quarantine.

It is an assumption of this book (although not an unexamined one, as I hope to demonstrate in the following pages) that an epoch in American history marked by its own particular modes of intense homosociality had gradually come to an end during Whitman's early lifetime. Much, although of course by no means all, ordinary social activity, both labor and leisure, had traditionally been organized in single-gender groups, with at least potentially highly effective dynamics for integrating a boy or girl into his or her respective gender-community—for example, the apprentice-journeyman-master system of training boys to trades. Long-established modes of training young persons to inhabit gradually their respective gender roles as well as (in conjunction with) other social roles had become outmoded in Whitman's youth, and many persons seem to have found the perhaps no less homosocial but nonetheless very different modes that replaced them in the early industrial- and commercial-capitalist United States relatively brutal and unsatisfying, and, ultimately, destructive and deforming. It is a corollary assumption of my project that one chief design of the successive editions of *Leaves of Grass* was to counter the privatizing, standardizing, domesticizing, misogynist, and homophobic social arrangements of industrial, commercial, and (in the post–Civil War era) corporate capitalism that eventually replaced earlier arrangements. Without conservatively romanticizing "tradition," and also without absolutizing the difference between one of these dispensations and the other, I believe it is nonetheless still possible to say, based on recent work in the historiography of class and gender, that there was in the two or three decades preceding the appearance of the first *Leaves of Grass* a widespread sense that many types of social relationships had significantly declined in quality as a consequence of vast socioeconomic change in the United States. To specify only one range of these relations, the homosocial realm of officially approved modes of same-sex social relations significantly receded and the homophobic realm of proscribed and stigmatized modes of such relations correspondingly expanded during this period—according to both nineteenth-century testimony and recent historical studies. [13] Of nineteenth-century discourse on the urgency of reconstructing relations between men on bases more affectionate and bodily than those

Introduction

that the culture was currently fostering, there is no more eloquent testimony than *Leaves of Grass* itself—not only in the 1860 "Calamus" poems, where this program is most extensively thematized, but throughout the entire project.

The historical and political dynamics of the emergence of recognizable male-homosexual social roles in the modern period have received considerable scholarly attention in recent years.[14] Substantially more work has been done to date on the British than on the American context for this phenomenon. A significant point of contact between the two contexts occurred in August 1890 when John Addington Symonds wrote Whitman, pressing him—by no means for the first time—to respond to Symonds's interpretation of the "Calamus" poems in *Leaves of Grass* as both "encourag[ing] ardent & *physical* intimacies" between men and suggesting that the recognition and promotion of such relations might serve not only as the source of "private" pleasure and satisfaction but also as the basis for some kinds of social and political renewal.[15] Whitman's response to this is famous: in his reply he denounces Symonds's explicitly homophile sexual-political reading of his poems and (in desperate self-defense against the obvious "biographical" implications of Symonds's reading) makes his outrageous claim to having fathered six illegitimate children—no further evidence of whose existence has ever come to light. Rather than regarding this episode merely as an isolated biographical datum, as a semipublic outbreak of "homosexual panic" on Whitman's part, as Whitman's recent biographers have tended to do, I prefer to see it as one of many instances of the poet's lifelong practice of fiercely defending what he saw as a strategic necessity of his project.[16] At this and earlier points in his career, he insisted in practice on representing men taking pleasure (including erotic pleasure) in their own and in each other's bodies as a range of ungrounded possibilities standing in indeterminate relation to other, more firmly grounded and determinate discourses of embodiment abroad in his culture. By means of thus rendering indeterminate the full range of the metonymic substitutions his writing effected, Whitman—not with the proverbial stroke of the pen but with what one might call a stroke of the entire text—created a liminal space in his work of utopian potential in relation to perhaps the single most increasingly threatened and stigmatized mode of bodiliness in his culture, the male-homoerotic.

I want now to relocate the question posed in one form by Symonds—of Whitman's response to an emergent male-homosexual identity in their lifetimes—within a solely American context. Here, as one might expect, there was at least potentially a better "fit" between Whitman and his reader than there was between Whitman and Symonds, who brought very different kinds of social and political experience and expectations to *Leaves of Grass* than most American readers would have done.[17] A comparison of Whitman's anguished, angry, and defensive response to Symonds with an exchange of letters between the poet and the young American writer Charles Warren Stoddard allows us to see that Whitman was fully willing to recognize and acknowledge, to extend his blessing, as it were, to male-homoerotic readings of *Leaves of Grass*—provided the interpreter did not insist (as Symonds had done) on trying to undo the poetry's crucial equivocalities with regard to the nature of the relationships the poetry proposes between writer, reader, text, and body. (The exchange dates from 1870—around the same time when Symonds began his epistolary campaign for Whitman to "speak out" [one might say to "come out"] on the [homo]sexual meanings of his poems.) Stoddard's letter to Whitman begins impetuously, "In the name of CALAMUS listen to me!" He says he is writing to tell the poet that he is about to go off to Tahiti because he has become "numbed with the frigid manners of Christians" and longs to return to the "barbarism [which] has given [him] the fullest joy of [his] life."[18] He also submits for Whitman's approval a copy of his recently published "A South-Sea Idyl," a romantic sketch of his intensely homoerotic liaison with a devoted Polynesian boy.[19] Whitman responds by saying that he finds the piece "sweet . . . soothing & nourishing"; and as to its author, he goes on to say, "I do not of course object to your emotional & adhesive [Whitman's own term, appropriated from phrenology, for "male-homoerotic"] nature, & the outlet thereof, but warmly approve them." In conclusion, while offering his "emotional" young correspondent his heartfelt support for his "adhesive nature" and his preference for "barbarism" over "Christian" society, Whitman invites him to consider the "great value & even joy" to be found in the "American practical life" the younger man is so vehemently rejecting.

In strong contrast to his repudiation of Symonds, Whitman's response to Stoddard is sympathetic because Stoddard allows the terms of their exchange concerning their shared commitment to "emotional and adhesive" living and writing to remain fluid ones; he does not press the poet to specify whether the meanings of his poems extend to or "are really about" the celebration of (in Symonds's phrase) "*physical intimacies*" between males. It is crucial for my purposes to note in this connection, though, that the "fluidity" of the terms Stoddard and Whitman use in their exchange is not simply an evasion of the subject of the desirable limits of male-homoerotic behavior. There is nothing either evasive or coy in Stoddard's application to Whitman for his approval of his behavior or in Whitman's warmhearted response: engaging in an ardent romance with a "savage" boy and writing and publishing what Whitman calls a "soothing and nourishing" account of it are all activities he can "warmly approve"—with the caveat that in dismissing "American practical life" outright, his young correspondent may be rejecting "experiences and qualities . . . [of] great value and even joy."

I read much of Whitman's most powerful writing as an attempt to work out the by no means straightforward terms of the crucial relationship between what he here calls "emotional and adhesive [male-homoerotic] nature" on the one hand and "American practical life" on the other. Here, in his letter to Stoddard, as at most moments in his writing—except when he is being pressed for firmly grounded, determinate specifics, and denied strategic recourse to his substitutive powers of mind, by readers like Symonds—Whitman treats these two key terms and all they represent as by no means being in inherent conflict with each other. Similarly, through his literary and practical personal example, Whitman continually expresses his hopes and beliefs, in the face of increasing cultural pressure against doing so, that neither of the modes of embodiment (the 1970s term "lifestyles," some of the chief social contours of which emerged in the United States in the period here under discussion, 1870–1890, might be relevant in this connection) that the two terms denote—"emotional and adhesive nature," "American practical life"—need preclude the other. Indeed, he offers himself and his work as two different but related kinds of phenomena that integrate by embodying both possibilities simultaneously. The Whitman text defuses the increasingly negatively charged relationship between "adhesive nature" and "practical life" and opens a space (otherwise similarly increasingly unavailable in the culture) where they may stand in a paratactic relation in which one of them does not cancel the other out, whether or not they can actually be brought to reinforce each other.

As I have suggested, Whitman commits his work to opposing by appropriating and rewriting conceptions prevailing in his time of what a text is, what a person is, and what the consequences of embodiment are. These questions of text, person, and body are closely interwoven in Whitman's work. To summarize much of the foregoing: the energies that impel the grand revisionary project of *Leaves of Grass* for a decade and more after its inception in the 1855 text include the desire to locate a central place for the body in the practices of writing and reading; the desire somehow to open in the literary text a space in which the actual physical presence of the writer might come into loving contact with readers; and the desire to oppose the increasingly phobic attitude to men's taking pleasure in their own and in other men's bodies which Whitman's culture began manifesting in the 1830s and after, the years of Whitman's first youth. Whitman goes about the project of producing a text to serve as an ideal medium for the intermingling of (male) bodies by appropriating the chief discourses of (male) embodiment of his time and rendering the referents of those discourses indeterminate and fluid.[20] This fluidity—the fluid relations he imposes on the figures of (male) embodiment he takes over from discourses like anti-onanist and temperance ones—is from the inception of the *Leaves of Grass* project his writing's principal thematic, the fluid relations among his chosen topics serving as the "perfect" (a key Whitman term) means for representing in the text what the achievement of his desire would look like: relations among (male) persons/ bodies rendered totally fluid, all barriers to their merging "washed away."

The indeterminate relations of Whitman's figures of "fluid" embodiment to their respective "grounds" in contemporary discourse made it possible for him to produce texts with meanings more radical than his culture officially permitted writers to produce, because it allowed him to exploit the subversive potential inherent in the densely figurative public discourse of his time. For any term on the inadmissible range of meanings in Whitman's writing (such as the desirability of males' de-sublimating and de-repressing their erotic pleasure in their own and in each other's bodies), one could readily locate a comparable, "safe" term well within the admissible range ("philanthropic" love between men, "brotherly love," fraternal democracy) in relation to which the "dangerous" or prohibited meaning could be brought into some indeterminate relation, and thereby partly freed from its prohibited status—as is notably the case with "love and friendship" in the passage cited earlier, as it is successively and explicitly renamed "adhesive[ness]," "comradeship," and so forth.

As he discovered the potential of the conventional idealist and sentimental political and public discourse of his day for becoming "contaminated" with erotic, particularly male-homoerotic, meanings, Whitman also discovered a corollary potential in that discourse for "harboring" such officially proscribed meanings as the male-homoerotic ones which constantly play about the margins of antebellum public discourse. He frequently brings into "electrical" (another key Whitman term) contact in the language of his texts his culture's most cherished sentiments and ideals alongside its most highly charged figures for abasement and abjection—dung, filth, nakedness; the ejaculation of semen, sexual connection, and/or impregnation "outside" the sanctioned conjugal space to which these sexual processes were "supposed" to be limited; physical pain, deformity, mutilation, and decay. This repertory of bodily states and products serves as Whitman's image bank, as it were, for the most powerfully liminal points in his text(s): those moments which invite the reader to assume the subject-position of a stable self dissolving under pressure of overwhelming fears and desires.

There were well-established discourses of physical abjection in Whitman's culture, but they were in the main not literary ones. They treated of the alleged consequences of excessive drinking and sexual indulgence. In the next section of this introduction and in the first two chapters following, I shall explore relations between these discourses and the inception of the *Leaves of Grass* project.

"Kosmos" and Constitution: The Fluid
Politics of *Leaves of Grass*

Much valuable work has been done on the political history of Whitman's age, and, specifically, on his relation to the broad spectrum of political formations of his day.[21] His early activities as a radical Democrat ("Locofoco"), as a champion of workingmen's politics, and as a journalist-advocate of the Free Soil movement (which opposed the admission to the Union of new states which permitted slavery) have often been remarked. Biographers have commonly characterized Whitman's decision around 1850 or soon thereafter to abandon more conventional modes of political activism in order to pursue the *Leaves of Grass* project single-mindedly as having been simply a wholesale abandonment of political pursuits in favor of literary ones. As I have argued in the preceding section, the political and the literary interact in complex ways throughout Whitman's career, and to represent him as absolutely abandoning one and adopting the other before he even began producing *Leaves of Grass* is to give a highly reductive account of the real significance of either the political or the literary in his career. I want to begin my project of situating the *Leaves of Grass* project in its political and historical contexts by considering the relation of Whitman and his writing to a political formation which is prior to those with which he has commonly been associated. I am referring to the U.S. Constitution, the single most significant political "pretext" for the revisionary qualities of *Leaves of Grass*.

Whitman calls his idealized version of the (male) body as a potentially thoroughly "fluid" system a "kosmos." The term in ordinary usage in Whitman's time for the body considered as a self-inclusive system was "constitution." To use the same term to denote the U.S. Constitution and the (male) constitution (that is, the corporeal system) is not, in the case of Whitman, merely a play on words. The term "constitution" cuts across a whole range of antebellum discourses about the proper nature of political sovereignty as well as the proper nature ("health") of the body. In both cases the term addresses the politics of embodiment and writing, the preeminent concerns of the first four editions of *Leaves of Grass*.

The questions of what constitutes a text and what constitutes a self intersect in Whitman's writing in his representation of both text and self as pre-constituted entities, that is, as entities primordially subject to the revisionary processes I have described, prior to "individual" choice or intention. The model text for Whitman is the U.S. Constitution itself as he (and, among others, his hero Thomas Paine) read it, as a text that asserts its own profound provisionality and initiates the literally interminable process of its own amendment or revision.

From Paine to Whitman via a lengthy and politically crucial debate over the relation of this document to successive U.S. governments, the textuality (that is, writtenness) of the Constitution and its provision for its own revision in perpetuity were major concerns in American politics throughout the first half of the nineteenth century. When Thomas Paine wrote in *The Rights of Man* of one of the proto-constitutions of the United States (the Pennsylvania State Constitution) that it had been "published, not as a thing established, but for the consideration of the whole people," and that this "instrument" took as one of its chief purposes the provision for its own "revising[,] . . . alterations, additions, [and] abolitions," he could be taken to be describing proleptically the literary practice of Whitman.[22] "'The idea of incorporating, in the constitution itself, a plan of reformation,' enabling the people periodically and peacefully to return to first principles . . . was a totally new contribution to politics," Gordon S. Wood has written.[23] Wood goes on to quote the early American historian David Ramsay on the many defects of the early state constitutions: "But in one thing they were all perfect," Ramsay adds; "they left the people in power of altering and amending them, whenever they pleased."[24] The people, whose political involvement was otherwise mediated through their representatives, were, in J. G. A. Pocock's words, "constituent, directly engaged in the establishment and revision of constitutions, and there are passages of rhetoric that suggest that this too was seen as a continuous activity," "ongoing and perpetual."[25] The ultimate political power vested in the American people, as Pocock puts it, was "the power of constitutional revision," a power the exercise of which was regarded as being "always potentially imminent."[26]

Whitman writes in *The Eighteenth Presidency!* (1856) of "The Federal Constitution" that "time only is great enough to give it area," that is, it cannot be fully known or understood in the present because it is one of those verbal constructs, as *Leaves of Grass* is to be, the bulk of whose meanings remain provisionally unknowable or incomprehensible because "as yet" (and perhaps always) "unenacted."[27] Textuality that assures and invites revision rather than resisting or suppressing it; literal instrumentality that assures and invites the revision of lines of force and power in society rather than resisting or suppressing it: these are the political ideals of figures like Paine and Ramsay, and Whitman after them. With his long-held commitment to provisionality, revision, and popular engagement, Whitman modified his literary practice to make it responsive to the crucially important political lesson he learned from the Constitution: that writing, like other political acts, can, indeed must, be carried on in the face of the general deferral of its most urgent meanings.

Both the Constitution and the early editions of *Leaves of Grass* are texts which foreground their revisionary properties. Insofar as it vests sovereignty in the people via their potential agency in collectively exercising "the power of (constitutional) revision," the U.S. Constitution is (as I have called it) the preeminent pre-text for *Leaves of Grass*—not in the conventional sense that one literary text is said to "influence" another, but in the more complex way in which the Constitution demonstrated for Paine and his followers (a political group of which Whitman long remained a belated member) an ideal form for linking textuality and power in a literal instrument.

Paine invoked what was to become a commonplace in nineteenth-century American discourse when he drew an analogy between the power potential in adolescent males and in what he saw as the adolescent republic: "Youth is the seedtime of good habits, as well in nations as in individuals." Thus spoke Paine in *Common Sense* in the Revolutionary year of 1776. What is merely analogical in Paine became reified in the nineteenth century into a national preoccupation with the "waste" of America's "seed," meaning both the country's promise and potential and the "reproductive secretions" of its male citizens. Paine and Whitman, one might say, stand at the beginning and end of a period during which two kinds of political anxieties culminated in a prolonged crisis. The first anxiety was over the question of whether (on the national-political level) the United States had not emerged from its first youth—its "seedtime"—dissipated and doomed, possessing a "ruined constitution." The second was over the question of whether (on the sexual-political level) American youths were not dissipating what the culture represented as being their respective shares of the nation's "potential" or "energy" in a self-induced epidemic of wanton semination. One hundred and one years after *Common Sense* Whitman eulogized Paine (in a memorial address delivered in Philadelphia) in the by then belated and over-familiar rhetoric of insemination: Whitman praises Paine for having planted "the seeds of [the] character" of "the embryo Union."[28]

By the early 1850s, the political crisis in the United States over constitutional authority and the spread of slavery into the more recently settled areas of the country was at its height. The imminent dangers which were (correctly) seen as threatening the integrity of the American body politic gave rise not only to an extensive, explicitly political discourse but also (I would argue) to other widespread bodies of discourse of implicit political import; among these were the discourses of anti-onanism and anti-alcoholism, of the pollution and destruction of the (male) "constitution" by the practices of drunkenness and excessive sexual indulgence. "Constitution," "law," "laws of nature," "power," "mastery," "enslavement," "violation," "defilement," "ruin," "rebellion," "revolution"—the same vocabulary which informed the discourse of the constitutional crisis of the decades before the Civil War also informed the anti-onanist and anti-alcohol "crises" of the same period, years during which masturbation-phobic and alcohol-phobic discourse appeared in print in enormous quantities. Sylvester Graham, one of the founders and chief ideologues of the male-purity movement which took hold in the United States in the early 1830s and flourished throughout the antebellum period, employs many of these terms in a typical capsule "case history" of a reformed masturbator in his highly popular and often reprinted *Lecture to Young Men on Chastity* (first delivered in 1832; published 1834):

> C.N. commenced the practice of self-pollution very young; and before he was aware of its ruinous effects, he had nearly destroyed his constitution. As soon as his eyes were open, however, to his error, and the danger of his situation, he abandoned the mischievious [sic] practice with horror and remorse. By long perseverance in strictly virtuous habits, he regained a very good degree of health and enjoyment, but he was never able so completely to overcome the effects of his former error, as to give his system that constitutional vigor, and power of endurance and resistance, which belong to those who have never greatly violated the laws of their nature. [29]

Whitman would use many of the terms used by Graham and his colleagues to very different points. In order to clarify what is novel about these and other kinds of revisions Whitman makes of the forms of (male) embodiment in force in the major discourses of his culture, I want to summarize briefly the major features of the discourses of male sexuality current in the United States in the 1830s and 1840s.

American historians have come to agree generally that the year 1830 represents a watershed in public attitudes toward sexuality and its dissemination and "control" in the United States. According to Stephen Nissenbaum, the last of twenty-seven American editions of various parts of the so-called *Works of Aristotle*—four volumes of discussions of the physiology of sexual reproduction, midwifery, and so forth, epitomizing popular attitudes of the early modern period—appeared in 1831; in the same year the first of what was soon to be a flood of masturbation-phobic discourse, an anonymous booklet published by one J. N. Bolles entitled *Solitary Vice Considered*, appeared in New York.[30] The first book on birth control published in the United States, *Moral Physiology: or, a Brief and Plain Treatise on the Population Question*, by reformer Robert Dale Owen (son of philanthropist-reformer Robert Owen), appeared in 1830. At the time he published this work, Owen was a close associate in New York City of the Scottish political activist Frances Wright, who had come to work in the United States in 1829 amid a blaze of publicity; she was the first woman to deliver public lectures in this country. She and Owen produced a radical newspaper called the *Free Enquirer*, to which Whitman's father, farmer-turned-house-carpenter Walter Whitman, subscribed, as did many other freethinking members of the artisan class in the New York area during the early 1830s.

Works which represented a strong counter-tide against the at least potentially positive attitudes toward nonreproductive sexuality espoused by writers and lecturers like Owen and Wright continued to appear and reappear in large editions throughout the 1830s and beyond. In 1832 the first American edition of the seventy-year-old text *Onania: A Discourse on Onanism* by the Swiss author Samuel A. A. Tissot was published, and Sylvester Graham's *Lecture to Young Men on Chastity*, a founding document of the American male-purity movement, appeared in 1834. The following year Samuel B. Woodward, sometime superintendent of the Worcester (Massachusetts) Lunatic Asylum, began making his much-discussed reports to the Massachusetts state legislature and to the *Boston Medical and Surgical Journal* that masturbation "caused" insanity; in the same year Rev. John

Todd published *The Student's Manual,* another milestone in the male-purity movement. Graham claimed to be publishing his male-chastity lecture in response to the urgently felt need among young men for a counter-discourse to a type of book which had recently begun to appear, books tending (in Graham's words) "to encourage illicit and promiscuous commerce between the sexes." These are not explicitly "pornographic" works, as one might expect: Nissenbaum asserts that although Graham does not specify which books he means, "his list certainly included Owen's *Moral Physiology* and [the second work on birth control to appear in the United States] Charles Knowlton's *Fruits of Philosophy*" (1832).[31]

In his study of Graham, Nissenbaum entitles the chapter dealing with the male-purity movement "The New Chastity of the 1830s."[32] Whitman must have been pubescent during the years I have just reviewed, 1830–1835, when he was between eleven and sixteen years old, and he came of age in 1840, at the end of the decade which saw the efflorescence of public attention in the United States to the supposed necessity of limiting and controlling male sexual activity, especially among (and between) young and/or unmarried men. In engaging directly in the furor of the times over the increasing availability to young men in cities of novel spaces, both private and public, in which to enjoy the opportunities for pleasure ("dissipation") afforded by the brothel, the tavern, and the extrafamilial privacy of boarding-house rooms, Whitman was exceptional among American Renaissance writers. Read in the context of a proliferating mass of discourse which proscribed nonreproductive sexual activity as well as other kinds of non-"productive" behavior (such as recreational drinking), Whitman's insistence on the legitimacy of the (male) body and its pleasures in *Leaves of Grass* seems both less eccentric and less familiar than it does when read without benefit of its contemporary intertexts.

Anti-onanist titles continued to proliferate in the 1840s, the decade at the end of which Whitman made the transition from writing tales and conventional verse to writing the kind of poetry we find in *Leaves of Grass.* The phrenologist-publishers Fowler & Wells, with whom Whitman was to be associated for a number of years and for whose periodical *Life Illustrated* he wrote a series of articles on New York City in 1855, functioned as sole agent for the sale of *Leaves of Grass* during the first year after its appearance (Emerson, uncertain as to where to address his famous letter saluting Whitman "at the beginning of a great career," directed it to the poet in care of the Fowler & Wells store on lower Broadway).[33] Fowler & Wells had entered the anti-onanist field in the 1840s and continued throughout the next decade to produce books on sexuality in general and on specific topics such as "home treatment for sexual abuses"—the title of a book Fowler & Wells published in 1856 which was the work of Russell Thacher Trall, pioneer of the "water cure" (hydropathy) and another major ideologue of the male-purity movement. Trall was assistant editor of Fowler & Wells's *Life Illustrated* during the time the magazine published Whitman's series of articles; in 1856, when Bronson Alcott and Thoreau came to visit Whitman in Brooklyn, they lodged in Trall's Hydropathic School in Manhattan.[34]

Whitman cultivated acquaintances with a number of New York physicians during the 1840s and 1850s, including several who wrote anti-onanist works. Representative of these was Edward H. Dixon, author of a number of quasi-popular articles on "Onanism" and "Spermatorrhea" which appeared in book form in the years preceding the first *Leaves of Grass*.[35] As Harold Aspiz has pointed out, the phrase "he who works with the scalpel" among the roll call of men of "positive science" in what became "Song of Myself," section 23, may be taken to be an oblique compliment to Dixon, who edited the medical journal *The Scalpel*. Whitman frequently reviewed and reprinted Dixon's pronouncements on sexuality and hygiene during his editorship of the Brooklyn *Daily Times* in the 1840s, and he entered the addresses of the physician's home and office in a notebook in 1856. Dixon was a leading American "expert" on "spermatorrhea," a diagnostic category which commanded much attention in the medical literature (and patent medicine advertising) of the time. The sufferer of this "disorder" had supposedly (owing to excessive masturbation) lost any ability to control his seminal flow and become subject to continual debilitating seminal "discharges." Thousands of male victims of gonorrheal or other urinary-tract infections, as well as men who were simply anxious about experiencing "wet dreams," must have misdiagnosed their "complaints" (or been misdiagnosed by physicians) and relied on "spermatorrhea" remedies, which included such extreme and painful practices as cauterization of the urethra.

Some historians of nineteenth-century medicine have tried to downplay the significance of the campaigns against masturbation and the large body of medical and/or religious discourse on the "curse" of "spermatorrhea" by arguing that it was chiefly the work of quacks and that respectable, "mainstream" physicians did not hold the extreme views put forward by disreputable writers, many of whom were hawking "dollar cures" for "addiction" to masturbation. Whitman's associate Edward Dixon, however, is a good example of an American physician who held a prominent place in the medical establishment of his time whose opinions about the consequences of masturbation were identical with those promulgated by less reputable writers. [36] When Dixon writes about masturbation, he rehearses all the commonplaces of the anti-onanist discourse of the preceding two decades: "victims" of the habit can be easily recognized by "the pallid hue, lack-lustre eye, and emaciated form." A disposition to masturbate is aggravated by stimulating drinks (tea and coffee) and oily foods (meat and butter). As a deterrent to masturbation Dixon blandly advises young persons who can still break the habit to substitute for it "gardening, billiards, the lighter mechanics, etc." [37]

THE MALE-PURITY movement of the antebellum years and the extensive anti-onanist literature it generated have been the object of a substantial amount of interpretive analysis on the part of American historians in recent years. A number of recent studies of the history of industrialization, of the evangelical movement, of labor politics and the passing of the apprenticeship system in the United States, have given the student of the male-purity movement invaluable help in interpreting its meanings. [38] Masturbation-phobia per se is of course not a central concern (for example) of Sean Wilentz's history of the emergent labor movement in New York City or of W. J. Rorabaugh's history of the passing of the apprenticeship system, but changing modes of housing, training, educating, and disciplining young workers are among the matters this new scholarship treats in depth. Knowledge of such historical factors is of course highly pertinent to any study of what Whitman and his contemporaries were about when they took up (from various positions) the discourse of anti-onanism.

Whitman's putative uniqueness has been a constant theme in biographical studies of his work from the beginning. Much has been made of the emergence of this "genius" from a social background which scholars have generally represented as having been "unfortunate" or "unpromising" at best. [39] Whitman's family's emotional and economic difficulties have frequently been rehearsed by biographers and bio-graphical critics by way of "explaining" the ostensibly exceptional, even pathological, character of the poet's personality. In contrast to this strong tendency in the scholarship to privilege the notion of Whit-man's supposed uniqueness and to devalue his relationship to his social background, there has been relatively little work to this point like Wilentz's labor history, which situates the young Whitman in the historical context of his social class and political milieu. Whitman for the first forty years of his life was a by no means unrepresentative member of a number of the social formations on which recent Amer-ican historiography has concentrated: as a child of a family which moved from a rural area to a city during the 1820s; as a boy who left school at eleven and began at that time to work at a variety of apprentice-level occupations; and as a young man who lived on his own in boardinghouses in New York, where he worked as a printer and sometime newspaper writer and editor, and participated in party politics. Till well past his first youth, Whitman was in many ways a typical worker of his place and period. As a writer, he made himself one of the first chroniclers of such figures; the pages of Leaves of Grass abound with them. A carpenter, a mill girl, a printer, a machinist, a street-paver, a sign-maker, a canal-boy, a peddler, a photographer, a fare-collector, a mason: these figures, many of them depicted engaging in characteristic work activities, I take from a couple of pages chosen at random from Leaves of Grass.

Whitman's profound and lasting engagement as a writer with the vernacular culture of the social groups of which he was a member during his formative years is a many-faceted subject. At this point I want to consider only one aspect of this subject, and that is his relation to the male-purity movement which flourished during his youth.

Historians of sexuality such as Carroll Smith-Rosenberg and G. J. Barker-Benfield have directly engaged the question of the historical meaning of the male-purity movement. Barker-Benfield deals with the question by way of background to his central concern, nineteenth-century American men's attitudes toward women and sexuality in gen-eral. He relates nineteenth-century American males' anxieties about the catastrophic consequences of "losing" semen to a simple, closed, early-capitalist model of male sexuality in which "seed," the basic form of human "capital," must be hoarded, accumulated, saved, and withheld, rather than being spent or squandered.[40]

Smith-Rosenberg relates the male-purity movement to two major developments in Jacksonian America. First, drawing on the work of James Henretta, she argues that the unprecedented numbers of young men (especially newly arrived ones in the cities or on the frontier) living outside traditional restraining institutions—most notably the extended patriarchal agricultural settlement or the apprenticeship system—precipitated a crisis in the social control of young men, to which chastity lecturers and anti-onanist tracts were one kind of response. Smith-Rosenberg argues further that the widespread appeal of male-chastity writing can be accounted for on the grounds that the "masterless" state of the young man who had left traditional ties behind symbolized for many antebellum Americans the ungrounded state of their society in general: "[T]his was not simply a debate about containing the liminality of actual adolescents. It was a debate about the liminality of Jacksonian society poised between the traditional agrarian and mercantile social order and the new ways of commercial and industrial capitalism. The nationalistic orators were right. American society was itself the adolescent."[41] Smith-Rosenberg suggests that when writers like Sylvester Graham, Samuel B. Woodward, and Whitman's sometime associates L. N. Fowler, R. T. Trall, and Edward Dixon threatened their readers with disease, disgrace, and premature death for masturbating, they were inveighing—with varying degrees of awareness of their actual target—against a whole range of emergent social forms of male autonomy, including male homosexuality, for which "onanism" served as a general label. In his project of subverting the generally repressive discourse of male sexuality in his day, Whitman brought to bear on it the powerful compositional resource of collage (cutting up and rearranging received discourses "in bits") as well as the resource of encoding "forbidden" texts in "permissible" ones. In the following chapter I explore how these factors come into play in the cultural and literary revisions with which Whitman was experimenting from very early in his career.

I

Rendering the Text and the Body Fluid: The Cases of "The Child's Champion" and the 1855 *Leaves of Grass*

Self-Censorship, Literality, and Indeterminacy in Whitman

In this chapter I shall explore Whitman's strategies for rendering text and body "fluid" in the thoroughgoing manner that characterizes his practice in the first (1855) *Leaves of Grass.* Beginning by considering the meaning of the clear traces of self-censorship, a highly specialized form of writerly substitution, to be found in the successive editions of his very early story, "The Child's Champion," I shall go on to consider how even in the earliest published version of the story, in which self-censorship is relatively relaxed, Whitman practices a combined process of literality and indeterminacy of reference in his writing which permits him to incorporate into the story a wide range of otherwise proscribed meanings about power relations, including sexual relations, between men in his culture. In the remainder of the chapter I shall explore how these strategies of both practicing and evading self-censorship through simultaneous extreme literality and extreme indeterminacy have a formative effect on the representations of the fluidity of selves, bodies, and texts which are central to the 1855 *Leaves of Grass.* [1]

"THE CHILD'S CHAMPION"

Whitman published "The Child's Champion" in 1841, when he was twenty-two. It initially appeared in the *New World*, a mass-circulation periodical devoted to popular fiction, where Whitman was working as a compositor at the time. The tale was subsequently republished several times during his lifetime in various states of revision under the title "The Child and the Profligate."[2]

"The Child's Champion" tells a sentimental story about a twelve-year-old boy, the son of a poor widow, whose body and spirit are being crushed by the cruel master to whom he is apprenticed. This latter figure is nearly absent as a character from the story; the boy's father is entirely absent, except for a couple of oblique references to his having died years before. On the way back to his master's from a brief visit to his mother, the boy Charles stops to gaze through a tavern window at a rowdy drinking party taking place inside. He is hauled in through the window by a drunken, one-eyed sailor who attempts to force him to drink alcohol. When the boy refuses because he has promised his mother never to drink, the sailor begins to beat him. Fortunately for Charles, telling the sailor about his mother's wish rouses a dissipated but prosperous-looking young man named John Lankton to come to his defense. Having taken an instantaneous and strong liking to Charles, Lankton promises to rescue him immediately from his cruel master and further resolves to mend his own dissipated habits, all on the strength of his newfound tie to the boy. Charles is said at this point to require "little persuading" to accept Lankton's invitation to stay with him at the inn and share his bed. The story ends with the apparition of an angel who blesses and kisses the boy and the young man in turn. In the closing lines, the narrator invites the "loved reader" to linger over the "moral of this simple story."[3]

One of the most notable characteristics of "The Child's Champion" which is not apparent in my synopsis of the tale is that it is a narrative fairly awash in watery figures. The boy Charles and his mother live, we are told in the opening words of the story, in a village far from New York City "where the Hudson [the "beautiful masculine Hudson" of the 1855 Preface?] pours forth its waters" (p. 69n. 3); Lankton, we learn late in the story, lives on the west side of the city, very near the point where the Hudson "embouchures" (to borrow another term from the equally aqueous 1855 Preface) into the bay. Charles's mother realizes how his master overtaxes him when he comes to her from work and she discovers that his head and back are soaked with sweat; they commiserate over his condition with copious weeping. As he peers in at the tavern window Charles first sees and hears the one-eyed sailor inviting his companions to have a drink "on him" in terms that sound as much like an order to fellate him as an offer of a drink: "[C]urse me if you shant have a suck at my expense" (p. 72n.); the boy next sees the sailor becoming irate because so much of the liquor to which he is treating his companions is being spilled on the floor. (To quote in this context the line, "And liquor is spilled on lips and bosoms by touching glasses, and the best liquor afterward," from the 1855 poem "I wander all night in my vision" [later "The Sleepers"], is to foreground the possible erotic significance of all the spilled liquor and other liquids "poured out" in this early text.) The sailor tries to force Charles to drink a glass of brandy, but he refuses, invoking his mother's wish that he not drink. The sailor continues to coerce the boy in terms that once again sound more as though the sailor is demanding fellatio rather than merely pressing the boy to drink his brandy: "Placing one of his tremendous paws on the back of the boy's head, with the other he thrust the edge of the glass to his lips, swearing at the same time, that if he shook it so as to spill its contents the consequences would be of a nature by no means agreeable to his back and shoulders [which are also the site of the boy's abuse—of which sweat is the sign—by his cruel master] (p. 73)."

Here the boy is being "forbidden" to do with the proffered drink precisely what he might be "forced" to do with a proffered phallus, to "shake [or otherwise manipulate] it so as [in a sense] to spill its contents." But Charles follows his mother's order and refuses the older man's demands, striking the sailor's arm and spilling the brandy on his face, the sailor's clothes, and the floor. It is at this crucial point in the quasi-sexual exchange taking place between Charles and the sailor that the narrator describes Lankton's response to what has happened: seeing the sailor momentarily stunned with Charles standing before him, his face dripping with the liquor the sailor has tried to force him to drink, Lankton is said to feel Charles "touch[ing] the fountains of [his] love, and draw[ing] forth their swelling waters (p. 74n.)." Lankton is said to realize as he watches Charles being abused that "the wish to love and to be loved, which the forms of custom, and the engrossing anxiety for gain, so generally smother," has "burst forth" in him "in spite of all obstacles" (p. 74n.).

"Charles stood," Whitman writes, as if in the aftermath of having sexually serviced the sailor after all, "his [Charles's] cheek flushed and his heart throbbing, wiping the trickling drops from his face with a handkerchief." The sailor picks him up and kicks him hard, and

Charles helplessly "[hangs] like a rag in his grasp" as he prepares to kick him again; the gestures here are manifestly aggressive and violent, and suggest anal rape: "He seized the child with a grip of iron; he bent Charles half way over, and with the side of his heavy foot gave him a sharp and solid kick" (pp. 74–75n.). Here Lankton springs forward to rescue Charles, immediately just from the sailor's abuse but eventually also from his indenture to his oppressive master.

What are we to make of the preponderance of watery figures in this tale? I want to make more of its conspicuous "fluidity" than merely to trace it as an "image pattern." That the contradictory imperatives "drink/don't drink" impel the story makes it unsurprising that when Whitman revised it for republication in 1844 (three years after it first appeared), he turned it into a "temperance" (anti-alcohol) story. I read the first version of the story as a homoerotic "romance"; the many liquids which "flow through it"—the sweat, the tears, the liquor, the Hudson River, the "swelling waters" of "the fountains of [Lankton's] love" which are said to "burst forth" as he witnesses the sailor's assault on Charles—take on the function in the text of eroding and dissolving for Whitman and his reader the "sharp and solid" (as Whitman calls the sailor's phallic "kicking" of the boy's backside, p. 74) cultural boundaries along which the official proscription of erotic love between males is maintained. The sailor in this context is readily legible as an agent of the "dissipation" or dissolution of boundaries, between solid and liquid realms as well as sexual boundaries between males, in part owing to the simple homonymic equation of "seamen" with "semen." The sailor's one-eyed condition also links him with the "one-eyed monster" (the rapacious phallus) of male folklore. He is the demonic counterpart of the angel who is said to descend on the sleeping male couple at the end of the tale to "[drink] in the scene with his large soft eyes" (p. 78n.).

The most persuasive evidence that Whitman was aware of the strong homoerotic quality of "The Child's Champion" is that when he came to revise it for republication in 1844 (three years after its appearance in the form I have described), he did so by censoring it of a number of the pronounced and recurrent homoerotic references which the first version of the story foregrounded. In his revision Whitman expunges such references as those to "the young men of the place who were very fond of him [Charles]" (p. 73n.19), and to the sailor's attack on the boy's backside mentioned above. He also suppresses the entire climactic paragraph in which Charles's plight is said "to touch the fountains of [Lankton's] love, and draw forth its swelling waters," and Lankton's desire is said to "burst forth in spite of all obstacles" (p. 74n.). Similarly, the passage in which man and boy are said to sit and "[hold] communion" with each other is revised to read merely that they "converse[ ]" together (p. 76). Furthermore, Charles and Lankton, rather than sleeping in each other's arms as they do in the 1841 version, seem to have been removed into separate beds; the "close knit love" which is said to join them in the closing lines of the story becomes "friendship" in the three republications Whitman oversaw during his lifetime.

Not only is the date at which these revisions were first made (1844—eleven years before the appearance of the first *Leaves*) the earliest example of which I am aware of this kind of self-conscious self-censorship on the part of an American author for the apparent purpose of obscuring the homoerotic quality of his work; the story as initially published provides a quite early example of Whitman's engagement with one of his major projects, that of articulating and forcing recognition (even if shocked and disapproving recognition) of various forms of prohibited sexuality. In its first republications it also provides an early example of another of Whitman's major projects, that of confronting censorship and practicing self-censorship. Censorship was not merely an externally imposed phenomenon which Whitman encountered only, for example, in 1860—when Emerson tried to persuade him to bowdlerize the third edition of *Leaves of Grass*—or in 1882, when the Boston District Attorney, acting at the prompting of the Watch and Ward Society, threatened to prosecute the volume as "obscene literature." Censorship and self-censorship were crucial elements—were in a sense formative—of Whitman's literary practice from very early on.

Freud's discussion of the role of the psychic function of censorship in the process of "secondary revision" in *The Interpretation of Dreams* provides a fundamental statement of ways in which (self-)censorship can play not only an inhibitory but also a formative role on mental productions of all kinds. The effect of the psychic censoring agent in dreams, Freud writes, is recognizable not only in the "limitations and omissions" but also in the "interpolations and additions" it imposes. Psychic censorship is not merely subtractive; it has a role in the very formation of our thoughts: "[T]he censorship imposed by resistance, and representability, operates simultaneously in a conducive and selective sense" on texts in general, as well as on dream texts.[4]

"The Child's Champion" in its various versions provides an exemplary case of the dynamic relationship which may arise between the processes of revision and self-censorship and the perceived threat of external censorship. Nothing is known of the tale's reception when it first appeared in the *New World*; there is no evidence that adverse commentary regarding the story's marked male-homoerotic qualities caused Whitman to excise the more blatant instances of these when he republished it in 1844. In the absence of evidence that external censorship was either threatened or carried out, we can only assume that it was the author himself who decided to censor the tale of most of its candid references to the quasi-sexual exchanges which its boy-protagonist transacts, first with the sailor and then with Lankton.

Freud, in the ninth of the *Introductory Lectures* (1916–17), distinguishes between two different processes in dream-censorship by proposing an analogy for them from political and/or literary censorship. One kind of censorship that we encounter in dreams, he writes, is analogous to the blanks the government press-censor may introduce into newspaper accounts of "sensitive" matters. Here, the censor covers over or "whites out" the prohibited content in the text, leaving only blanks in its place. Such a straightforward mode of censorship, imposed "from above," as it were, leaves clear signs of its imposition. More difficult to try to recuperate are the objects of a second kind of censorship Freud describes:

> On other occasions the censorship has not dealt with the sentence in its completed form; for the writer, foreseeing which passages were likely to be objected to by the censor, has forestalled him by softening them down, making some slight modification or contenting himself with hints and allusions to what he really wants to write about. In this case there are no blanks, but from the roundabout and obscure mode of expression you can detect the fact that, at the time of writing, the author had censorship in mind.[5]

Although in Freud's analogies one kind of censorship is described as being externally imposed and the other authorially self-imposed, the psychic processes to which both these activities are supposed respectively to correspond are forms of censoring one's own dreams—that is, both of them are forms of psychic self-censorship. The revised versions of "The Child's Champion" bear the marks of both kinds of self-censorship. "Dangerous" or proscribed phrases and passages which occur in the first version have been elided, although of course the "blanks" which remain in their place are not literally visible on the page of the reprinted story; still, one can readily detect censorial strikings-out of this type by simply comparing the first text with the later one(s).

One must attend more closely to the relation of the story to its culture in order to perceive the effects in it of the second kind of censorship that Freud aptly describes as "forestalling" elisionary censorship. "The Child's Champion," even in its first, putatively "uncensored" version, is a text on which this second, anticipatory or strategic kind of (self-)censorship has already worked to a considerable degree. The story in its first published version forestalls further or external censorship by instituting its own censorial code at its inception, the most obvious signs of which are the tale's manner of representing the various specific kinds of sexual exchanges between males which are its impelling actions as being merely quasi-sexual or indeterminately sexual exchanges. Rendered indeterminate, these exchanges can be taken by readers hostile to their erotic components as being "essentially" nonsexual ones: for example, these readers are left free to deny that the meanings of the drunken sailor's behavior toward Charles include attempted rape, and that the meanings of Charles's and Lankton's behavior toward each other include erotic attraction and fulfillment. The text does not scant the erotic element, but because it does not isolate or disconnect the erotic from the other economies it represents, such as those of alcoholic sociability, the exploitation of child laborers, and the possible meanings of "philanthropic" impulses on the part of persons attempting to maintain or regain self-control or self-respect, the erotic need not be visible for the reader who prefers not to see it.

One notable characteristic of the revised versions of "The Child's Champion" (all of them entitled "The Child and the Profligate") which I do not wish to pass over is the fairly high level of concern with male-homoerotic behavior which the tale continues to manifest despite the excision in 1844 and after of a substantial number of its overt references to such behavior. Even after the numerous cuts I have described were made, the story still retains such fairly straightforward homoerotic references as the sailor's gloating over the good looks of the "catch" he has pulled in through the window. Charles, the narrator attests, is "not what is called pretty, [but is] fresh and manly looking" (p. 72). The sailor's liquor is figured as "the fiery enemy whose advances" he has been "court[ing]" all evening, and this dalliance is said to have "set busy devils at work within him, that might have made his hands do some dreadful deed" (pp. 75–76)—that is, his drinking, his flirtation with this "fiery" (male) "enemy" who finally nearly overpowers him, is at once a direct mirror image of his violent "courtship" of Charles and a demonic mirror image of Lankton's rescue and "courtship" of the boy.

How are we to account for the survival of some of these homoerotic gestures in the story after the excision of most of them? One notes that they are attributed for the most part to the demonic drunken sailor; after 1841, the tale has ceased to represent male-homoerotic behavior in any fashion other than the demonic. There is little likelihood of our learning whether it was during the period 1841–1844 in Whitman's life (when he would have been between twenty-two and twenty-five years of age) that he realized that "emotional and adhesive" relations between males had taken on a highly negatively charged character in his culture. How is one to explain the authorial change of attitude manifest in Whitman's revisions of "The Child's Champion" so as at least partially to soften its initially vividly male-homoerotic language? Was it Whitman's *awareness* of the prevailing view of such relations that had changed (that is, increased), or was it rather public attitudes toward male-male love that had changed substantially enough between 1841 and 1844 to make the young writer retrench to some degree in his representation of male homoeroticism? As with most questions that take the form, "Was it a change in the point of view of the individual, or social change, that made the difference?" the answer probably lies on both sides of the question. The young Whitman became more sharply aware of increasing homophobia in his social milieu during a period when it was notably on the rise on a mass scale. Whitman idealizes some aspects of male-male love in the first version of "The Child's Champion"—all those concerning Charles's relations with Lankton—and demonizes those of its other aspects that he represents as taking place between Charles and the drunken sailor. In other words, as his culture was increasingly tending to do from the early 1840s onward, the young Whitman "rewrote the script" of his story when he revised it in a way that de-emphasizes his earlier idealizations of male homoeroticism and intensifies its demonic characteristics.

Thus Whitman probably dropped his most overt references to erotic attraction between men from the post-1841 versions of his tale as a consequence both of increasing homophobia in his society and of an increase in his own awareness of this widespread hostility to male-homoerotic behavior. However, Whitman's apparently early discovery of the advisability and indeed the necessity of censoring certain kinds of erotic contents in his writing was not simply a defeat for his project. Instead, it may have served as an important lesson in the interdependence of transgressive writing and censorship. I would argue that Whitman discovered in writing texts like the several versions of "The Child's Champion" he produced in the course of the 1840s that overt reference to proscribed types of behavior was but one of the powerful ways available to him of "cutting into," challenging, and attempting to revise some of his culture's discourses of the meanings of (male) embodiment. Another way was, in combination with the first (that of "literality," or direct reference), to attempt in writing to produce a space, or what Whitman might call an "atmosphere," in which discourses more favorable to proscribed desires and behaviors, including but not limited to male-homoerotic ones, might be likely to emerge. The nature of this space or atmosphere is not in itself easy to describe because it is thoroughly liminal. Whitman sees it as being important to create such a space because it provides a site accessible to oneself and others where forbidden sexual desires can be explored without fear of persecution. He evokes such spaces in his writing from the inception of his career, asserting that his writing is designed (in the words of one of his self-reviews of the 1855 *Leaves*) to "exude[ ] an impalpable something which sticks to him that reads, and which pervades and provokes him to tread the half-invisible road where the poet, like an apparition, is striding fearlessly before."[6]

This formulation of Whitman's project provides the reader with terms for both of its strongest impulses: that toward attempting radical embodiment in the text, in the figure of the text as "exud[ing]" the "impalpable something which sticks to" the (male) reader—among other possible meanings, the semen which is one of the text's crucial metonyms for (male) corporeal presence—and the twin impulse toward projecting liminal spaces in the text to serve as paths for prohibited desires, here called "the half-invisible road" down which the reader is to follow the specular figure of the poet. This liminal path can never be rendered more than half-visible in the text because it cannot be grounded in more definite, less indeterminate discursive spaces than those which the Whitman text is designed to produce: for example, the "some where" where the speaker of "I celebrate myself" promises the reader in the poem's closing words that he awaits the reader ("I stop some where waiting for you," p. 54); or the "paths untrodden" or "margins" down which the speaker invites the reader to follow him at the opening of the "Calamus" poems ("In Paths Untrodden," 1860). "I seek less to state or display any theme or thought," Whitman writes in "A Backward Glance o'er Travel'd Roads," "and more to bring you, reader, into the atmosphere of the theme or thought—there to pursue your own flight." [7] Within such an "atmosphere" or liminal space, "faint clews and indirections"—Whitman's own terms for the constitutive indeterminacies of his project, in "When I Read the Book," 1867—are capable of bearing a considerably greater burden of signification than they would in conventional discursive contexts.

The Whitman text (of *Leaves of Grass* as well as of such an early work as "The Child's Champion") is consequently the site of an action that is always dual. Literality is one of the text's powerful modes of articulating its cultural-revisionary project: naming the body, its parts and ordinary activities, describing the ways in which the body serves as both the site and the object of prohibited desires, including erotic ones, which the author celebrates and names—that is one of its principal means of engaging and revising contemporary dispositions of the body. The other principal instrumental mode of the Whitman text is that of indeterminacy, of resisting the bases of official dispositions of the (male) body by rejecting the culture's strong tendencies to isolate and disconnect the erotic from other political economies of embodiment (labor, writing, anatomy, physiology) and thereby to render the erotic fundamentally meaningless or susceptible only of a greatly diminished range of meanings. Between the two poles of Whitman's writing in its instrumental mode, literality and indeterminacy, the text produces a relationship that one might call oscillative: it is always negotiating the passage back and forth between the two poles it brings into close contact. Together, these two principles provided Whitman with an effective means of exploring meanings that his culture considered "dangerous" while forestalling the worst forms of persecution imposed by the culture on persons who attempted to locate their projects in such "forbidden territory"—persecutions suffered by such figures as Whitman's counterpart in English Victorian culture, his onetime visitor Oscar Wilde. Between themselves, literality and indeterminacy render Whitman's text a Penelope's web, endlessly making and unmaking its meanings—meanings themselves densely interwebbed with the culture's economies (even when these meanings are antithetical to the culture's dominant versions of its economies). Whitman seems quite rightly to have perceived that to attempt to state them outright, as forthright discourse, would be to violate and to trivialize them. His culture considered meanings such as some of those he was exploring in his writing unspeakable. For different reasons, so did he—that is, he considered them unavailable to articulation by ordinary means. All this Whitman may have intended when he urged Symonds to consider the meaning of what he called his *"restraint"*: "I at certain moments let the spirit impulse, (?demon) rage its utmost, its wildest, damnedest—(I feel to do so in my L of G. & I do so). I end the matter [of Symonds's pressing him to specify the determinate sexual meanings of his writing, particularly "Calamus"] by saying I wholly stand by L of G. as it is, long as all parts & pages are construed as I said by their own ensemble, spirit & atmosphere."[8]

THE 1855 *LEAVES OF GRASS*

That *Leaves of Grass* was threatened with various forms of censorship, that Whitman occupied only a lower-margin position in the literary society of his time because his work was widely considered to verge on obscenity—these have been central articles of Whitman biography from its inception in the writing of William Douglas O'Connor, John Burroughs, and Richard Maurice Bucke. That in the later editions of *Leaves of Grass* Whitman came to compromise to some degree with public hostility to his mode of representing sexuality in his work is also an acknowledged fact. Felice Flanery Lewis, in her study of literature and censorship in the modern period, speculates plausibly that *Leaves* was never the object of an actual legal prosecution early or late because it seems to have been generally regarded as too abstruse a text to present a direct challenge to conventional morals.[9]

Few readers would deny that *Leaves of Grass* is in some ways a difficult text. I want to consider for a moment the relationship between its difficulties and the matter of censorship, self-imposed and otherwise. The 1855 edition seems even more difficult than the numerous subsequent editions because in it the author provides so few of the conventional demarcations on which readers depend in order to construe the relative status of the parts of a text, such as titles, stanza breaks, and rhyme schemes. The so-called 1855 "Preface" actually appears without a title, as do the poems that follow, the first six of which are headed "Leaves of Grass." Of the latter six, the four which do not commence at the top of a page are headed only with double rules. (Whitman thus enacts in literature Paine's pronouncement on the repudiation of aristocratic labels in the new republics of his time: "The . . . Constitution says *there shall be no titles.*")[10] The long lines of the 1855 text run on down its long pages almost unbroken, and the pages in turn proliferate almost without any suggestion as to how the reader is supposed to organize them. The *mise en page* of the 1855 *Leaves* is the volume's most striking manifestation of its program of aggressively drawing the reader into "contact" with the author (by forcing the reader to "cut into" the text without many directives as to where it may lead).

In these "complications" of the text, I believe, one can readily detect the kind of difficulty Annabel Patterson has identified as an unmistakable "sign of the hermeneutics of censorship" at work in a text. Patterson points out "the social uses of indeterminacy": it allows writers to develop practices which exploit the ungroundable quality of language in order to allow them to treat proscribed subjects with relative impunity. Such a practice is readily apparent in those passages in Whitman in which the ungrounded condition of the text's language permits him to treat censorable material in "permissible," because indeterminable, language.[11] "The Child's Champion" in both its initial and revised (that is, censored) versions manifests several of "the social uses of indeterminacy" for Whitman, permitting him to bring together in the story a whole range of contemporary notions of masculine abjection and deliverance, including such proscribed ones as sexual violence between man and boy and the expression of erotic affection between man and boy.

The indeterminacies of the 1855 *Leaves of Grass* also serve the purpose of rendering the text and the dispositions of the (male) body which it represents fluid, but its fluidity is more radical. Rather than

37

presenting a single liminal decor or "atmosphere" in which the culture's oppressive codes of (male) embodiment may be liquidated, such as the drunken frolic in "The Child's Champion," the first several editions of *Leaves of Grass,* while continuing to extend the project of evoking the (male) body "literally," also produce a whole repertory (a specular city, as it were) of the kinds of liminal spaces I have described.

I want now to examine some of the passages (to liminality) in the 1855 *Leaves* in which the dual impulses toward extreme literality and extreme indeterminacy manifest themselves most powerfully. For these I will look to the small anthology one could make of those passages in the 1855 *Leaves* in which nonprocreative sexual activity, and especially the ejaculation of semen in such activity, is indeterminately figured. Taken together, they would comprise most of what have come to be regarded as the interpretive cruxes of *Leaves of Grass.* Some of these Whitman allowed to stand through his successive revisions of the text; others he censored in the 1876 and subsequent editions. I shall begin by considering the one of these passages which is perhaps most obviously consonant with the terms that, in my discussion of "The Child's Champion," I have argued are paradigmatic ones for the first edition of *Leaves of Grass:* the "fluidity," substitutability, and indeterminacy of masculine identity and sexuality. This passage is the eighteen-line one from the 1855 *Leaves of Grass* which later became section 11 of "Song of Myself":

> Twenty-eight young men bathe by the shore,
> Twenty-eight young men, and all so friendly,
> Twenty-eight years of womanly life, and all so lonesome.
>
> She owns the fine house by the rise of the bank,
> She hides handsome and richly drest aft the blinds of the
>   window.
>
> Which of the young men does she like the best?
> Ah the homeliest of them is beautiful to her.
>
> Where are you off to, lady? for I see you,
> You splash in the water there, yet stay stock still in your
>   room.
>
> Dancing and laughing along the beach came the twenty-ninth
>   bather,
> The rest did not see her, but she saw them and loved them.

> The beards of the young men glistened with wet, it ran from
>   their long hair,
> Little streams passed all over their bodies.
>
> An unseen hand also passed over their bodies,
> It descended tremblingly from their temples and ribs.
>
> The young men float on their backs, their white bellies swell to
>   the sun....they do not ask who seizes fast to them,
> They do not know who puffs and declines with pendant and
>   bending arch,
> They do not think whom they souse with spray.[12]

The relation of this passage in "I celebrate myself" to the paradigm for Whitman's writing which I have derived from "The Child's Champion" can be described as follows. The poetic text depicts a group of male bathers who have been "merged" into a collective fluid identity, "all so friendly," like the sailors and other men in the early tale whom the boy Charles discovers getting drunk and dancing together. Early in the passage, as in the tale, a solitary figure, "all so lonesome," stands at a window and peers through it at the circle of "fluidly" linked males on the other side—Charles in the tale, the woman in the poetic passage.

As in the tale, the action of the passage is to bring the excluded figure through the window and incorporate him or her into the "fluid" circle. However, several significant factors differentiate the poetic passage from the tale. For one thing, male and female are placed in strong and direct appositional relationship from its opening lines: "Twenty-eight young men . . . / . . . and all so friendly, / Twenty-eight years of womanly life, and all so lonesome." Here, at least to begin with, masculinity bears a positive affective charge ("so friendly") and femininity a negative one ("so lonesome"). Moreover, insofar as they are both "twenty-eight," the large group of young men is made not only numerically parallel but also in some sense equivalent with the solitary woman and her life.

The various economies that determine the nature of the exchanges made in the passage are organized differently, again with regard to gender, from those of the tale. In the poetic passage, economic and class differences are aligned with gender difference in ways they are not in the tale, where all significant exchanges are represented as taking place solely between males. The young men are said to "bathe," but the woman to "own[ ]" and "hide[ ]," a contrast which suggests that while male homosociality can be untrammeled by economic constraints, bourgeois female domesticity ("She owns the fine house by the rise of the bank, / She hides handsome and richly drest . . .") is at least as much a privation as it is a privilege. Another way of putting this would be to say that while what the young men are represented as having they hold in common (each other, "twenty-eight young men . . . all so friendly"), what the woman is represented as having is private property, "fine" and "rich[ ]," but in some fundamental sense disjunct from herself ("Twenty-eight years of womanly life, and all so lonesome").

The passage makes two things clear about the "lonesome" woman's "fine house" and "rich[ ]" clothes: they are compensatory substitutes for her for what the twenty-eight young men possess in one another, and they are inadequate ones. What she proves to "have going for her," so to speak, is not her wealth or even her good looks (she is not said simply to be "handsome," after all, but to "hide[ ] handsome . . . aft the blinds of the window"), but the restless and frustrated desire she shares with Whitman's ideal readers as he describes them in the note to the 1876 Preface. Like them, she is subject to a "terrible, irrepressible yearning, (surely more or less down underneath in most human souls)," and it is this lack, rather than her wealth, that Whitman conceives of as impelling and empowering her to desire to plunge into the "endless streams of living, pulsating love and friendship" which *Leaves of Grass* was designed "to arouse and set flowing in men's and women's hearts."

In representing her wish to do so, the text releases this rich "lady" ("Where are you off to, lady?") from the constraints of gender and class which have hitherto relegated her to "[t]wenty-eight years of womanly [which in this text, at least to begin with, is to say "lonesome"] life." In the poem's liminal space, she can have her "fine house" to "hide" in, but also fly out of it, "Dancing and laughing," at the same time: "You splash in the water there, yet stay stock still in your room."

The speaker of the passage could be said to emerge from his strictly narrative role at this point, as he claims to see the "lady" not only maintaining her hidden position as she stands "handsome and richly drest aft the blinds of the window," but also (invisibly) passing out onto the beach and into the water to join the twenty-eight young men already disporting themselves there. However, it is also the case that the speaker's emergence into a more active role in the passage is set up perhaps as early as its opening lines, where the repetition of the words "Twenty-eight . . . / . . . and all so" to describe two very different entities and situations, the young men bathing and the woman watching them, may make the reader want to inquire of the speaker how these two entities can be said to be parallel.

The speaker in the passage assumes powers, derived from the watching-and-desiring position of the young woman, which include not only his phantasmatic powers of passing unseen among the twenty-eight bathers and touching their bodies at will but also the power to write about these pleasures. There is certainly a de-repression of desire being effected here, a merging of consciousness with unconscious desire on the psychological level, and a merging of "proper" and "improper" feeling and behavior on the social level. In a reading which *only* sees the male speaker appropriating the position of the female voyeur, Robert K. Martin reads the last three lines of this passage, where "[t]he young men float on their backs, their white bellies swell[ing] to the sun," as representing actual "*physical* intimacies," in Symonds's phrase, between them and the speaker, who "puffs and declines" over their bodies with "pendant and bending arch" until "they souse [him] with spray" (that is, they are fellated by him).[13] Whitman might have opposed such a literally "sexual" reading of these lines, as I have discussed in the Introduction, not so much because such a reading would be inaccurate or irrelevant as because limiting the determinate grounds for the exchanges which are represented in a passage like this one to specifically sexual ones is inevitably to produce a hermeneutic dead-end in a text which was designed to retain its fluidity and mobility of meaning(s). Various kinds of male-homosexual desires and interactions *are* being represented here, as they are elsewhere in Whitman's writing, and it is important to recognize them as such.[14] But there are also other kinds of highly significant factors represented as being at work in this passage, such as economies of gender (male versus female), age (young versus mature), general sexual epistemology (acknowledgment and acceptance of oneself as sexual subject and/or object versus repression of such knowledge and acceptance), and socioeconomic class (a "life-style" of private bourgeois

acquisitiveness versus one grounded in more egalitarian and com-
munitarian kinds of pleasure-taking).

Rather than attempting to ground the exchanges transacted in the
course of the passage unequivocally in a single sub-vocabulary, such
as that of the repertory of male-homosexual acts, one might do better
to attend to the often peculiar terms in which these exchanges are
conducted in Whitman's writing. Male-homosexual acts are, after all,
a set of behaviors which is itself not stable or closed, since most of
these acts (for example, fellatio, anal intercourse) are practiced by
"heterosexuals" as well—although I would not overlook the difference
that homosexual acts are symmetrically reversible in ways that corresponding heterosexual acts are not. In the passage in question, for
example, the crucial exchange effected may well be not the final one
(whatever it is) between the speaker and the young men, but that
between the speaker and the young woman. The nature of the exchange that takes place midway in the passage might be interpreted
as the speaker's appropriation of the woman's position for his own.
Leaving her standing at her window, he passes from one of its sides to
the other on the energy of her desire, as it were. To pursue this
interpretive line, one might argue that the feminine position invoked
and described in the first half of the passage disappears halfway through
it, or, rather, that the woman is dislocated from her position and
replaced by the (male) speaker. It would then be the (male) speaker
who assumes the privilege of becoming the "twenty-ninth bather"; in
a grammatically transvestite moment halfway through the passage
("Dancing and laughing along the beach came the twenty-ninth
bather, / The rest did not see her, but she saw them and loved them"),
he would briefly but consequentially pass through feminine identity.
Then, according to this reading, as feminine identity and feminine
pronouns disappear altogether from the passage, the figure of the rich
and lonely woman would vanish after having served as springboard for
the speaker's remarkable flight.

Rather than interpreting the passage as necessarily involving the
exclusion of the young woman and the femininity she represents at its
midway point, I want to argue that it would be more appropriate, in
view of the significant role the female figure occupies in the first half
of this section, to interpret her as being incorporated into the passage
at its crucial midpoint and for the rest of the section *as* a feminine

figure (and as a figure of femininity), and not merely as a transvestite "cover" or mask for the (male) speaker's prohibited and/or unspeakable desire for the male bathers he "spies" through the window. The speaker (in the interpretation I am arguing for) passes through the window and across the space between into the water with the twenty-eight bathers *along with* the young woman (both of them alike empowered by her desire), without necessarily ceasing to identify himself with her. Having merged with the young woman (but without necessarily having merged *her* into himself), the speaker (now in his merged state with the young woman neither determinately male nor female) extends his/her identification farther, partly with the young men and partly with the fluid medium in which they are immersed and enjoying themselves: the "wet" which "[runs] from their long hair" and "over their bodies" is represented as being homologous with the "unseen hand [which] also passe[s] over their bodies."

I shall have more to say in the context of my discussion of the poetry new to the third (1860) edition of *Leaves of Grass* about Whitman's ambitions of writing a kind of post-Scripture, a text designed to displace the Judeo-Christian scriptures in the moral and imaginative lives of American readers. At this point I want merely to note in passing how Whitman in the twenty-eight-bathers episode of the 1855 text definitively inverts the two canonical biblical bathing scenes—David watching Bathsheba and Susannah and the Elders. These narratives were doubtless burdened for Bible readers in his culture with several kinds of oppressive patriarchal significances, such as (from the point of view of the figures of Bathsheba and Susannah) women's being made the unwitting and/or unwilling objects of male voyeurism as well as other forms of male power, and (from the point of view of David and the Elders) scopic pleasure's (that is, pleasure in eroticized watching) necessarily taking the form of a stealthy and guilty voyeurism that inevitably carries the exposure and punishment of the watcher(s) in its wake. By contrast, the figure of "the twenty-ninth bather"—a composite of the young woman and the (male) bather—escapes traditional circuits of authority and desire which render the biblical bathers victimized women and their observers guilty evildoers, in order to enter and occupy a utopian space in which a figure representative of feminine desire and identity can effectively be incorporated into a scene of masculine *jouissance*.

43

Granted, the section may not represent female orgasm at all, and certainly does not represent it with anything like the directness and specificity with which it represents something like male orgasm ("They ["The young men"] do not think whom they souse with spray"). Still, there is a significant difference between not representing female orgasm in a given section of the text and excluding femininity from its representational program altogether. If this passage falls short of representing a woman (women's) attaining full physical sexual satisfaction, it does incorporate feminine sexuality to a considerable degree, and to a higher degree than most English-language texts contemporaneous with it that one might adduce; the female figure is, after all, represented with notable (and exceptional) straightforwardness desiring to join and at least in some way(s) to possess the young male bathers, and then passing out in tandem with the speaker into the water to do so.

The "unseen hand [which] . . . passe[s] over [the bathers'] bodies" is at least in part hers, a sign of the metonymic feminine agency she bears into what would otherwise be an uninflected scene of orgiastic male-homoerotic utopianism. That this key scene of male "fluidity," one of the most determinately and specifically erotic of all such scenes in *Leaves of Grass, is* inflected as it is with feminine erotic desire argues against the assumption that Whitman's privileging of male-homoeroticism in itself precludes his also representing feminine sexuality and feminine agency in his text. Literally almost from the beginning of the 1855 text, as this episode allows one to see, the figure of a woman's (women's) hand(s) is disseminated with other figures for physical presence and absence as well as masculine ones.

It is not to diminish but to confirm the real role of feminine agency in this representative section of the poetry of the first edition of *Leaves of Grass* that I also point out the female figure's role in the complex act of self-censorship the passage performs. It would be too direct a challenge to state censorship and criminal prosecution for Whitman simply to stage a scene (so to speak) in which a rich and handsome but repressed and lonely "mature" or "older" *man* gazes desirously out at a group of younger men bathing; the obvious tactical advantage of placing a woman in the voyeur's position is that in doing so the author does not outwardly violate powerful cultural proscriptions against (and against representing) erotic desire between men. Here, as at many other points in his writing, as I discuss elsewhere in this chapter,

Whitman uses self-censorship strategically, making it a means of extending rather than contracting the range of his writing's meanings. Rather than engaging in a simple, straightforward act of self-censorship and de-eroticizing the desirous gaze which the passage launches, he insists not only on its erotic quality but on the *commonness* (in both senses of the word, ordinariness and sharedness) of intense sexual desire ("surely more or less down underneath in most human souls"), "in men's and women's hearts, young and old." In merging without excluding either the (male) speaker and the woman into a composite "twenty-ninth bather," Whitman effectively destabilizes the genders of both the source and object(s) of the erotic gaze, projecting a space in which both women and men are free not only to direct such a gaze at (other) men, but also to fulfill the desires that impel the gaze.

What I am arguing here is that had he chosen to pursue a more common kind of self-censorship, Whitman might have represented sexual desire in de-eroticized and idealized forms, as his culture generally preferred to do—as a desire for "love and friendship" that excluded the corporeal to the degree that the erotic was conceived of as being antagonistic to, even actively disruptive of, "orderly" familial and domestic relations among people. Alongside the officially prohibited representation of a man feeling, enacting, and fulfilling his desire for other men, Whitman posits the hardly less transgressive representation of a woman doing the same thing.

That Whitman did not in this passage complete its eroticized representational program by somehow also figuring sexual desire and fulfillment between women may have less to do with any unwillingness on his part to do so than with the degree to which it was possible for him to subvert powerfully enforced cultural norms. [15] Just as the generally greater economic dependence of women during this period precluded the appearance of a visible lesbian subculture on the streets of New York City of the kind that came into existence for homosexual men, women figures are largely absent from the most highly erotically charged scenes of same-sex love in *Leaves of Grass*—except in liminal forms such as the "invisible" figure of the woman voyeur turned twenty-ninth bather. Foregrounding the male-homoerotic qualities that played around the margins of ordinary scenes of male homosociality in Whitman's culture is a major function of the first *Leaves of Grass*. Whitman readily turns such scenes—here, a large, rowdy, congenial swimming-hole party—"inside out," exposing their erotic linings to light, as it were. Because of the relatively low visibility of female communities and their general enclosure in domestic interior spaces in contemporary representations, it may have been difficult if not impossible for Whitman to come up with comparable scenes of ordinary female homosociality of the time that would provide anything like the flagrantly voyeuristic potential of the "twenty-eight bathers." Instead, the feminine is incorporated into the scene metonymically, as the actions of an "unseen hand."

The significance of this figure is one of intense indeterminacy, like others in the 1855 text, such as the "grass" that is turned into metonyms for numerous classes of persons and various parts of their bodies in what became section 6 of "Song of Myself," beginning "A child said, What is the grass? . . ." Supplementarity is a pronounced feature of the significance of such figures, signaled in the "twenty-eight bathers" section by the recurrence of the words "all so" ("also") in its opening lines. No unconsidered metonym, the "unseen hand" of the closing lines of this passage is also a sign of the poet's projected physical presence among the twenty-eight bathers as well as among his readers in general. It is a sign of the hand of the writer unseen by the reader, who has only the print on the page to signify the desire to provide affectionate physical presence which impels Whitman's writing—or, one might say, only the print on the page *and* the elaborate eroticized image of writing contained in the closing lines of the passage, where it is not (or not only) fellatio that is being figured but (or but also) the writer's "unseen hand[s]" in motion, "seiz[ing] fast" with one hand to the pages—the young men's "white bellies swell[ing]" in the light— and with the other covering them with the "pendant and bending arch" of his "flowing" script. Here is a point (by no means the only one in *Leaves of Grass*) at which the fluidity of writing (that is, *écriture*) and the fluidity of handwriting—and of Whitman's handwriting— intersect. Whitman has told us a few pages earlier in "I celebrate myself" that one of the meanings that his "leaves" (pages) includes is "the breasts of young men" ("It may be you [curling leaves of grass] transpire from the breasts of young men"); in the closing lines of the "twenty-eight-bathers" passages we learn that the pages of his book are intended to represent their bellies, too—and to serve as yet another metonymic substitute for the never more than liminal presence to the reader of these (male) bodies and their constituent parts.

Here, in the figure of the "unseen hand" and its activities, is also a point in Whitman's text where genders meet—both in the "un-seen[ness]" of the hand and also in the invisibility of its agency, a quality which does not necessarily lessen the reality of its agency ("Lit-tle streams passed over their bodies," then, "An unseen hand also passed over their bodies"). Woman and (male) speaker meet in the "unseen hand," which is also a sign of the substitutive relationship in which the poem *makes* seen what is unseen (hidden or proscribed desire) through the substitution for it of language and writing. Of this the hand is a doubly gendered metonym. In one sense a hand without a body, in another sense the hand is derived from both a woman's *and* a man's bodies. It is finally a figure for the metonymic text itself, and the kinds of exchanges it effects, which involve the mobilization ("pass[ing] over") of body parts and actions which are rendered as pairs of verbs which tend to denote discontinuous motions (for example, in the last lines, "float" and "swell," and "puffs and declines").

ANOTHER crucial passage that Whitman allowed to stand through all the editions of *Leaves of Grass* is the following, which has perhaps been the object of more critical commentary than any other in the book:

> I mind how we lay in June, such a transparent summer
>   morning;
> You settled your head athwart my hips and gently turned over
>   upon me,
> And parted the shirt from my bosom-bone, and plunged your
>   tongue to my barestript heart,
> And reached till you felt my beard, and reached till you held
>   my feet.
> Swiftly arose and spread around me the peace and joy and
>   knowledge that pass all the art and argument of the
>   earth . . . .   (p. 15)

Sexual exchange of an indeterminate kind is figured in these lines, and its consequences are described in profoundly positive terms (surpassing "peace and joy and knowledge"), but ejaculation is not figured in them in any direct way. What *is* clearly figured is the "turning over" of one body on another, the plunging of the top person's tongue into the "heart" of the person below, and the reaching by the top figure to hold the head ("beard") and feet of the recumbent one. Whitmanian literality and indeterminacy interact in this passage with particular intensity: a series of bodily, at least quasi-sexual, interactions are specified, but their precise nature (embracing? fellatio? penetration?) cannot be determined. One may say that whatever the text struggles to represent here repudiates representation in the conventional terms of earthly-versus-spiritual erotics (carnal love versus divine love). For this reason the note to this passage in Sculley Bradley and Harold W. Blodgett's "Comprehensive Reader's Edition" (the standard "reading" edition) of *Leaves of Grass* is precisely wrong in its import:

> The debate between the soul and the body, a fixed convention of medieval literature, influenced later writers. Generally the soul and the body were regarded as opposites and enemies, one good, one evil. But in this mystical union of body and soul, expressed in erotic imagery, the poet experiences immediate intuitive revelation. It is remarkable that the mystical state is achieved not by rejecting the physical senses but by their joyous consummation with the spiritual. [16]

That Whitman's lines continue to pose a threat to the sense of literary decorousness of many of his readers is evident in attempts like this one to "refamiliarize" or domesticate both the text's extreme literality and no less extreme indeterminacy at such points as the passage in question. Such an interpretation as the one quoted suppresses all of the text's literal specificity about the corporeal interactions of the two figures it represents (reduced by Bradley and Blodgett to simple "soul" versus "body"): the head, the hips, the turning over, the opening of the shirt, the action of the tongue on the "heart," the reaching of one figure for the other's beard and feet. At the same time, it also suppresses the indeterminate but nevertheless highly erotic "atmosphere" which permeates the passage: the authors of the note reduce the text's collage of intensely interactive persons, bodies, and parts of bodies to a literary-handbook notion of allegory, a simple variation on "a fixed convention of medieval literature."

If erection and ejaculation can be said to be figured in this passage at all (*pace* the "allegorical" interpretation), they may be said to be barely liminally present in the stanza break between the lines, "And reached till you felt my beard, and reached till you held my feet," and "Swiftly arose and spread around me the peace and knowledge that pass all the argument of the earth." Or perhaps the ejaculation suppressed at this point in the text manifests itself in one of the comparably "difficult" passages in the same poem. The one I have in mind is another passage which Whitman allowed to stand through the numerous republications of *Leaves* which he oversaw: "Something I cannot see puts upward libidinous prongs, / Seas of bright juice suffuse heaven" (p. 30). Here, the erection and ejaculation which are absent from or barely liminal in the "transparent summer morning" passage are figured as taking place on the outsize scale of a landscape; the male body in this case is not a human one, but a gigantic and invisible form ("Something I cannot see"). As orgasm temporarily obliterates (one might say "obliviates") ordinary consciousness or awareness, the "cosmic" orgasm figured in these lines temporarily obliterates the ordinary contents of the landscape; indeed, it obliterates everything but itself from the text's field of vision.

As an example of a passage from the 1855 text which seems to figure nonprocreative sexuality and which Whitman eventually excised from *Leaves of Grass*, I want to consider for a moment an example of one of the passages from the first edition of *Leaves of Grass* that seems to figure some kind of nonprocreative sexuality that cannot be precisely specified—and that Whitman excised from the text at a later point in its development (in this case, in the 1881 edition). The passage (from the poem we know as "The Sleepers") reads as follows:

> The cloth laps a first sweet eating and drinking,
> Laps life-swelling yolks....laps ear of rose-corn, milky and just
>   ripened:
> The white teeth stay, and the boss-tooth advances in darkness,
> And liquor is spilled on lips and bosoms by touching glasses,
>   and the best liquor afterward.   (p. 72)

I have already quoted the final line of this passage in the context of my discussion of the possible erotic significance of the spilled liquids in "The Child's Champion." The traces of ecstatic ejaculations of semen with which the 1855 *Leaves* abounds may be said to serve as the figurative adhesive with which the text would bind the poet and his readers in loving contact. The actual term "adhesiveness," which phrenologists defined as "male friendship" and Whitman as "manly love," does not enter *Leaves of Grass* until the third (1860) edition, in the Calamus cycle, but the notion of the text's "exud[ing] an impalpable something which sticks to him that reads" goes back at least as far as the self-review of the 1855 *Leaves of Grass* quoted earlier.

It is impossible to say with certainty why Whitman excised the "liquor is spilled" passage from "The Sleepers" in the sixth edition when he let stand other passages equally erotic in tone. Revisions like this one, made as late as 1881 (the year before *Leaves of Grass* was threatened with prosecution as obscene literature by the Boston District Attorney), seem to have been carried out as a compromise with those readers who were discomfited by Whitman's more direct de-sublimations of the corporeal. A passage from a pre-1855 notebook draft of a poem, stray lines and phrases of which appear in the 1855 "I celebrate myself," provides a striking example of the dynamics of revision and self-censorship in the first edition of *Leaves of Grass*. The draft reads:

> Fierce Wrestler! do you keep your heaviest grip for the last?
> Will you sting me most even at parting?
> Will you struggle even at the threshold with spasms more
>   delicious than all before?
> Does it make you ache so to leave me?
> Do you wish to show that even what you did before was
>   nothing to what you can do
> Or have you and all the rest combined to see how much I can
>   endure?
> Pass as you will; take drops of my life if that is what you are
>   after
> Only pass to someone else, for I can contain you no longer.
> I held more than I thought
> I did not think I was big enough for so much extasy
> Or that a touch could take it all out of me.[17]

Taken in themselves, these lines can be read as constituting a meditation on sexual experience, specifically on the shifting "threshold[s]" (line 3 above) of pleasure and pain in the kind of (male-homo)sexual exchange (between [male] speaker and "Wrestler") treated in these lines. The marked liminality of the passage is most apparent in the unlocatability or unspecifiability of the "threshold" at which the passage is poised, for the term in its context here is susceptible to a broad range of interpretations. One of these possible meanings is "the point at which a physiological or psychological effect begins to be produced"; that is, the "struggle . . . at the threshold" is an "internal" one which begins at the point at which erotic excitement commences (arousal) or at the point in which it culminates (orgasm). "Threshold" can also mean "boundary," here, between pleasure and pain and between male bodies; culturally enforced notions of both these kinds of boundaries are transgressed in this passage, in which pleasure and pain (delicious "spasms" and "sting[s]" and "ache[s]") commingle and in which two male bodies are figured as coming into intimate contact, even to the point of the penetration of one by the other. This brings us to a third possible meaning of "threshold," and that is "the point of physical entrance"; the "struggle . . . at the threshold" figured in these lines is a sexual exchange which takes place at the "point of entrance" to the body of one of the men, that is, at his anus. The passage conflates (by oscillating between) the respective experiences of the so-called "active" and "passive" partners in this sexual exchange: the speaker speaks at first of sensations which would follow on his being the "active" partner: the "Wrestler" is said to "grip" him (that is, his phallus) in a "Fierce" grasp, but then later in the passage the poet speaks as if he had been the "passive" receptacle of (the phallus of) the "Fierce Wrestler," of having "held more than [he] thought," and of having thought he was not "big enough for so much extasy."

It may seem unnecessary to insist as I am doing here on the physiological facts of phallo-anal connection between males as one conceivable ground for interpreting this passage when it is possible to read the phrases in question less literally than I have done: "I held more than I thought / I did not think I was big enough for so much extasy," are lines, after all, which permit entirely figurative or metaphorical readings. It is true that they are not "necessarily" about the anus's capacity for penetration by the phallus. But the primacy in Whitman's writing of his commitment to de-sublimating his (and our) culture's repressions of (male) bodies in their specificity inclines me to think that the literal sexual "level" must never be discounted or dismissed in interpreting his work. This becomes a more, and not less, crucial matter in reading his "revisions," that is, his published writings, even than it is in reading the kind of draft composition I have been considering. *Leaves of Grass* came into being in 1855 as already the product of a massive and thorough process of revision, and Whitman's treatment of the "Fierce Wrestler" passage quoted above in the 1855 "I celebrate myself" is a good example of this. The only clear trace of the eleven lines in the 1855 text is this couplet:

> Blind loving wrestling touch! Sheathed hooded sharptoothed
>   touch!
> Did it make you ache so leaving me?   (p. 33)

There are other lines in the poem which treat similar matters (the obscuring of the boundary between pleasure and pain possible in the experience of intense sexual pleasure), such as, "Thruster holding me tight and that I hold tight! / We hurt each other as the bridegroom and the bride hurt each other!" (p. 27) (Whitman excised these lines from *Leaves* after the first several editions as one of his apparent "small compromises" with the threat of external censorship in his later years), but such lines do not derive directly from the "Fierce Wrestler" notebook draft. Similarly, a line like the following, "To touch my person to some one else's is about as much as I can stand" ("I celebrate myself," p. 32), is obviously related to a line like the final one of the "Fierce Wrestler" draft passage, "[I did not think] . . . that a touch could take it all out of me," but, again, the former line does not directly derive from the latter. What we see in the revision of the eleven lines of the "Fierce Wrestler" passage, which gives a relatively straightforward monologic account of homoerotic pleasure/pain between two men, into the two lines of "I celebrate myself," in which the sexual partner of the draft is metonymically reduced to a "touch" ("Blind loving wrestling touch"—whether the poet's own or another man's is left unspecified)—is a representative example of the labor of metonymic substitution and constitutive self-censorship, of imbuing the objects of his text with the exemplary literality and the no less exemplary indeterminacy fundamental to Whitman's writing.

The dissemination through the text of Whitman's attempted recuperation of pleasure for males in their own bodies and in those of other men was a project designed both to challenge and to evade censorship. In this section I have discussed the constitutive role of a particularly effective form of culturally subversive self-censorship which Whitman exploited in his writing. The following section examines another of his most effective resources for deflecting external censorship while persisting in his project of writing, exploring, and celebrating possible revisions of his culture's dispositions of the (male) body.

"Unfolded Out of the Folds": Encoding Discourses in One Another

Unfolded out of the folds . . . .

—Opening words of Whitman's "Poem of Women" (1856)

I think there are truths which it is necessary to envelop or wrap up.

—Whitman to Edward Carpenter, quoted in the latter's *Days with Walt Whitman* (1906)

Whitman exploits to a high degree the capacity of language for allowing the writer to encode one discourse within another. A simple example of this is the encoding of male homoeroticism in what is on the surface a conventional sentimental narrative like the first version of "The Child's Champion." With its half-dozen leading references to male-homoerotic gestures excised, and a few lines added, the tale is "retooled" three years after its first appearance into a "temperance tale" with a still strong albeit now implicit male-homoerotic thematic.[18]

The encoding of abolitionist along with temperance writing is a common feature of antebellum writing; "The Child's Champion," for example, might have been revised into an abolitionist tale had Whitman been as invested (either personally or professionally) in writing abolitionist tracts as he was in writing temperance tales or homoerotic "romances" in the early 1840s. As it happens, he was not, but the tale still abounds in master-slave themes and rhetoric: the boy Charles calls himself a "slave" in his conversation with his mother (p. 70), and the narrator uses the quasi-biblical term "bond-child" to denote him (p. 76); the ostensible "point" of the tale is the boy's liberation

53

from bondage, and it concerns "a child [read "slave"] . . . being beaten," the (in our culture) primal sadomasochistic-autoerotic fantasy, according to the classic 1919 psychoanalytic essay "A Child Is Being Beaten." In this essay Freud adduces *Uncle Tom's Cabin*—and might have adduced much other American abolitionist fiction of the 1840s and 1850s had he known it—as an example of writing which draws some of its energy from childhood fantasies of being beaten and seeing other children beaten.[19]

Similarly, anti-onanist and male-homoerotic discourse are often encoded in temperance writing, so that it is impossible to say at many points "exactly" what is being signified by the writer's language, "for" or "against" inebriation, masturbation, or sexual connection between males: much moralistic antebellum writing—Whitman's early fiction included—exerts an ambiguous appeal because it provocatively "points beyond" the conventional moralism it ostensibly upholds toward a forbidden world which it in a sense takes as its "real," albeit deferred, subject. "From that moment," the protagonist of Whitman's temperance novel *Franklin Evans* (1842) says of his first drink of liquor, "I have an indistinct recollection of going through scenes which it makes my stomach now turn, to think upon—drunkenness, and the very lowest and filthiest kind of debauchery."[20] Obviously, this is in a sense an invitation to the reader to fill in the blank gesture the language makes with the fantasy of his choice ("his" since it is manifestly a male reader who is being invited to invest such referential gaps in the language of the text with his own fantasies). "Their friendship," Whitman writes in a similar vein of the pair of male protagonists of his unfinished tale "The Madman" (1843), "was not of that grosser kind which is rivetted by intimacy in scenes of dissipation. Many men in this great city of vice are banded together in a kind of companionship of vice, which they dignify by applying to it the word [friendship]."[21] Significantly, these sentences occur in the final words of Chapter 2 of a projected temperance novel or novella and are followed by the parenthetic phrase "To be continued," but they are actually the point where the narrative breaks off, never to be finished. Whitman is writing at intense cross-purposes at such moments. He can gesture toward his taboo subject, the ubiquity of intimate relations between men in his "great city," only by taking up the subject ostensibly in order to condemn it as "dissipat[ed]" and "vicious." These themes dead-end here, but Whitman will take them up again in quite different forms in the first three editions of *Leaves of Grass*—for example, to anticipate him once again, in two 1860 "Calamus" poems, no. 18 (later "City of Orgies") and no. 29 (beginning "A glimpse through an interstice caught," in which the poet and a male lover sit quietly holding hands in a squalid tavern, "amid the noises of . . . drinking and oath and smutty jest.") This latter poem rehearses precisely the situation of "the child" Charles and his "champion" Lankton when, after the altercation with the drunken sailor, they sit down at the side of the room to hold quiet "communion together" amidst the noise of the resumption of the drunken frolic; the appearance of the lyrical poetic version of the moment fifteen to twenty years after it is represented in "The Child's Champion" suggests that the configuration is a highly important one in Whitman's writing.

Whitman was first enabled to write about officially proscribed forms of sexual behavior by employing the vague, capacious, and flexible vocabulary which came to hand from the recklessly metaphorical public discourse of his time. "The fatal habit" is Franklin Evans's euphemism for drinking, but the phrase is ubiquitous in anti-onanist discourse to mean masturbation; there is inevitably some slippage between the two meanings in the use not just of this phrase but of many others like it in the writing of Whitman and his contemporaries.[22] The "morose habit" to which another of the young protagonists of one of Whitman's early tales is said to be addicted turns out to be neither drinking nor masturbation, as the reader of much of the discourse of the 1840s might well expect, but simply that of complaining about his lot without taking any active role in trying to change it; self-pitying passivity, a rather anomalous kind of behavior to dramatize in narrative, is here conflated with two of the period's major objects of prohibitionary rhetoric, the endlessly recycled, widely represented habits of excessive drinking and nonprocreative sexual indulgence.[23]

IT IS WORTH pausing over the question of the meaning of Whitman's early involvement as a writer in the temperance movement; most of his critics and biographers have been eager to follow his example in making the kinds of dismissive and dissociative gestures he made toward his youthful temperance writings later in life. The aged Whitman claimed, for example, that he had written the novel *Franklin Evans* cynically, that is, strictly for cash.[24] Yet as the historian Sean Wilentz has recently demonstrated, the temperance movement that was coming into being in New York City in Whitman's early years there had profound political significances which have long been lost sight of. According to Wilentz, the movement of the early 1840s was the first to declare its independence from the middle-class, missionary-style Christian-evangelical temperance movement and assert its commitment to lower-class autonomy and solidarity. The New York Washingtonians, a temperance organization which was founded in 1841 by a band of fifty-four local journeymen and small master craftsmen, disavowed all explicit religious motivations for their anti-alcohol stance and took as their purpose the relief of workers in the city who were suffering (specifically those who were drinking to excess) as a consequence of hard conditions prevailing among workers during the severe economic depression of 1837–1843. Within the first two years of its existence the group claimed to have attracted more than sixty thousand members among the working people of the city and had become the largest popular movement in the city's history to that point.[25] Much of Whitman's early fiction that did not appear in John O'Sullivan's prestigious *United States Magazine and Democratic Review* (such as "The Child's Champion," the unfinished tale "The Madman," and *Franklin Evans*) was directed at the large lower-class temperance-movement audience; "The Madman," Whitman's aborted novel about two men *not* joined by a friendship "of that grosser kind which is rivetted by intimacy in scenes of dissipation," appeared in the Washingtonian Temperance Society's official publication, the *Organ.* In the introduction to *Franklin Evans* Whitman writes, anticipating the radical democratic sympathies which will impel his departures from literary precedent in *Leaves of Grass*, "[M]y book is not written for the critics, but for THE PEOPLE."[26] In his apprenticeship as a writer for a mass lower-class audience, Whitman early became accustomed to directing his work elsewhere than at the literary establishment of the time.

There are several things about the New York Washingtonian temperance movement which warrant the attention of readers of Whitman. One of these is that the movement in its heyday (the early 1840s) brought the young Whitman into the kind of unapologetically, even aggressively, lower-class social (and potentially political) movement which he was later passionately to call for—without eliciting much response—in such texts of the mid-1850s as the radical pamphlet *The Eighteenth Presidency!* (a text which in fact remained unpublished until years after Whitman's death), and which he was to celebrate—as still an almost entirely potential phenomenon—in the Preface and poems of the first *Leaves of Grass*.

Another notable characteristic of the Washingtonians' movement for readers of Whitman is their so-called "experience meetings," occasions which sound as if they occupy a position historically midway between Puritan conversion narratives and Alcoholics Anonymous testimonials, in which members of the movement contrasted their sordid pasts with the pleasant lives they began to live (with the movement's support) after forswearing alcohol. From early on, the Washingtonian movement was roundly and repeatedly censured by the leaders of the genteel, evangelical American Temperance Union for the "vulgar tone" of the Washingtonians' "experience" testimony; according to Wilentz, the spokesmen for the Union took particular umbrage at the "spicy narratives of drunken orgies" which played a central role in attracting and holding the interest of new and regular attenders of the "experience meetings."[27]

This historical rupture between the middle-class and the lower-class temperance movements in Whitman's New York City in the 1840s is highly relevant, I think, to the questions I have been raising about the encoding of one kind of discourse within another in the period. In the face of a prudish social-control movement imposed from above, Whitman responds in much the same way his lower-class fellows in the Washingtonian movement seem to have done: with a discourse of temperance, self-restraint, "wholesome" sentimentality, "responsibility," "maturity," and sober domesticity that "cuts two ways"—that is, that undercuts the elements of dominant discourses it expresses by encoding in them a range of counter-discourses of "perverse," "orgiastic" sexuality, "morbid" sentimentality, the cultivation of "loafing" rather than utilization of the self as a marketable commodity, rejection of bourgeois models of respectability, and the espousal of radical social and political ambitions. These counter-discourses are not latter-day importations or inventions of the late-twentieth-century reader. As Wilentz's history reveals, they were recognized and attacked by genteel readers at their inception—in the "experience" testimony of the

Washingtonians, for example. The disapprobation of one such genteel reader of the 1840s, Benjamin Estes, is characteristic. Significantly, in lodging his complaint about the undesirable degree of detail into which lower-class temperance advocates go in depicting their sordid pasts, he fails to resist the temptation to rehearse once again just such details: "He [a Washingtonian] stated that for years he had loafed [crucial Whitman term] around the markets and wharves without any regular means of subsistence, sleeping in the markets and on the sidewalks, almost without clothes, or friends, and that all he sought was rum; and that his appetite was so craving that he would stoop to the meanest calling to obtain a little rum."[28]

This figure of a denuded "loafer" captivated by his desire(s) and detached from any defining involvement in the labor market or in the world of social competition is one on which Whitman will play variations in *Leaves of Grass*. Lifted from its context in temperance and anti-onanist discourse and resituated in one of Whitman's collagist compositions, the figure's oppositional potentialities multiply. In the following chapter I shall explore the career of this figure in the fluid medium of the text of the 1855 *Leaves*.

2

Fluidity and Specularity
in the Whitman Text

His [Whitman's] lines are pulsations, thrills, waves
of force, indefinite dynamics, formless, constantly
emanating . . .

—John Burroughs (with contributions from
Whitman), *Birds and Poets* (1877)

"The Dissipation of a Flowing and Friendly Life"

In the face of his culture's massive anxiety about the loss of boundaries
between mind and body, of erotic boundaries between males, of boundaries of gender between men and women, and of boundaries between
races and social classes, Whitman in the first edition of *Leaves of Grass*
espouses what I am calling "fluidity." This is a mode of consciousness
poised at the "washed-out" boundaries of mind and body in drunkenness
or in the latter phases of the cycle of sexual arousal. The 1855 *Leaves*
abounds with figures which embody this mode of consciousness: "the
friendly and flowing savage" of "I celebrate myself" (p. 44) succinctly
brings together Whitman's early ideals of a kind of identity and a kind
of sociability (homoerotic by definition) based on a mode of consciousness—"fluidity"—which in turn derives from Whitman's representations of the nature and sources of boundary-dissolving experience,
particularly intense sexual feeling. In the word "savage" the phrase
acknowledges that Whitman's culture insists on locating this mode of
consciousness outside itself.[1]

To consider a point of view which contrasts sharply with Whitman's
privileging of "fluidity," we might turn to an 1842 journal entry of
Emerson's in which he employs the same terms Whitman uses to describe his "savage": "friendly" and "flowing." Emerson uses the words
to (re)inscribe the general anxiety abroad in his and Whitman's culture
over the possibility of dissolving prevailing social or sexual boundaries:

"I have so little vital force that I could not stand the dissipation of a flowing and friendly life; I should die of consumption in three months. But now I husband all my strength in this bachelor life I lead; no doubt I shall be a well-preserved old gentleman."[2] We can situate this entry by noting that later that year, or perhaps the year after, Emerson responded to an invitation to deliver a temperance address in the village of Harvard, Massachusetts, and stressed the importance of temperate living in general and not just temperate drinking. The year before making the entry, he had made a small cash donation to the local temperance society and, around the same time, a rather larger cash payment for a small stock of Madeira.[3] His notion of "husband[ing]" his "strength," what he perceived as being his very limited reserve of "vital force," by leading a "bachelor life," lest he "die of consumption" in short order, brings into small compass a whole set of his culture's most highly charged categories (strength/disease, vitality/morbidity, husband/bachelor). As his journal entry suggests, "husband" and "bachelor" are options a man can pursue simultaneously if he is restrained enough in his pursuits in general—which is to say, in his strict regulation of his sexual and social "flows."

Emerson's anxious rejection of "the dissipation of a flowing and friendly life" could be paralleled in the writings of most of his (male) contemporaries. In the context of a cultural consensus which overwhelmingly privileges the solid, the stable, the fixed, the restricted, and the reserved over the fluid in its many modes, Whitman's claims in the 1855 *Leaves* for the personal empowerments proceeding, as he sees it, from the cultivation of just such a "dissipated" manner of living are exceptional, even extraordinary, assertions.

The first edition of *Leaves of Grass* can be read as a powerful attack on the culture's privileging of "solids" and as an exemplary enactment of a counter-cosmology which asserts the primacy of "fluidity" in the social, political, and "natural" realms.[4] The "waves" of de-repressed and de-sublimated homoerotic energy which flow through as early a Whitman text as "The Child's Champion" might be said to flood the 1855 *Leaves*. Signs of this flood in the opening pages of the text are such figures as the rich "fluency" which Whitman promises will adhere in the "very flesh" of the reader who embraces him and his program (p. vi), of the "most affluent man" who "confronts all the shows he sees by equivalents out of the stronger wealth of himself" (p. vii), of the "clean and vigorous children [who] are jetted and conceived . . . in those communities where the models of natural forms are public every day" (p. ix), of the poet who "flood[s] himself with the immediate age as with vast oceanic tides" and "plunges his semitic [that is, seminal] muscle" into his country. These figures from the 1855 Preface are homologous with those in "I celebrate myself" who are said "not [to] think whom they souse with spray" (p. 20), with the speaker who challenges the sea with the words, "Dash me with amorous wet....I can repay you" (p. 27), with the speaker who sees "seas of bright juice suffuse heaven" (p. 30) and salutes "rich showering rain" which is said to generate "recompense richer afterward" (p. 33)—a usage which returns us to the "richest fluency" promised early on in the Preface.

A literary formalist might be satisfied to read these and other passages like them in the first *Leaves of Grass* as mere thematizations of the topos wet/dry. As I have discussed above, fluid/solid seems a more useful set of categories in which to think about Whitman's writing, as long as we remain aware that one of the text's strongest tendencies is to poise itself at the point of obliteration or "wash-out" between conventional dualities of the kind I am invoking here for analytic purposes. In this chapter I want to consider what it means to be "solid" or to be "fluid" as these terms and other related ones are deployed in the 1855 *Leaves of Grass*. In the following section, I shall explore a liminal state the text generates which conflates "fluid" and "solid" to produce the intermediate state of the specular. Specular moments in the text are signs of particularly dynamic contact in it between "fluids" and "solids." I also wish to explore how the text aligns these terms with its representations of gender, particularly how certain notions of "solidity" and "fluidity" are made to constitute the text's ideal of masculinity and certain other notions of these qualities are made to constitute its ideal of femininity.

Looking into the Mirror of the Whitman Text

> You shall stand by my side and look in the mirror
> with me.
>
> —1855 Preface

> Even as a boy, I had the fancy, the wish, to write
> a piece, perhaps a poem, about the seashore—that
> suggesting, dividing line, contact, junction, the
> solid marrying the liquid . . . . Once at [Montauk,
> L.I.], (by the old lighthouse, nothing but sea-
> tossings in sight in every direction as far as the eye
> could reach,) I remember well, I felt that I must one
> day write a book expressing this liquid, mystic
> theme. Afterward, I recollect, how it came to me
> that instead of any special lyrical or epical or literary
> attempt, the sea-shore should be an invisible *influ-
> ence*, a pervading gauge and tally for me in my com-
> position. . . . .
>
> There is a dream, a picture, that for years at inter-
> vals, (sometimes quite long ones, but surely again
> in time,) has come noiselessly up before me, and I
> really believe, fiction as it is, has enter'd largely into
> my practical life—certainly into my writings, and
> shaped and color'd them. It is nothing more or less
> than a stretch of interminable white-brown sand,
> hard and smooth and broad, with the ocean perpetu-
> ally, grandly, rolling in upon it, with slow-measured
> sweep, with rustle and hiss and foam, and many a
> thump as of low bass drums. This scene, this picture,
> I say, has risen before me at times for years. Some-
> times I wake at night and can hear and see it plainly.
>
> —Sea-Shore Fancies, *Specimen Days* (1882)

The principle of specularity in Whitman's writing serves to mediate
the interactions between the fluid and the solid in their many modes.
The doubling and the shattering of specular self-images of the (male)
body and self is a process I shall consider first in the text I have been
employing as a paradigm of sorts, "The Child's Champion," and then
in the 1855 *Leaves of Grass*.

Attentive readers of "The Child's Champion" may well feel that they are looking at a text which perhaps to an uncanny degree (an uncanniness of a kind which Leaves of Grass will exploit and cultivate) seems to mirror—and thereby to expose to the common gaze, as it were—a position on the reader's part of intensely desirous subjectivity. This position is exemplarily embodied by such figures in the Whitman text as the child Charles and the woman who gazes out her window at the twenty-eight bathers. One has the sense in reading the story that it is at least in part impelled by a fantasy of being bodily drawn into a picture or mirror at which one has been gazing, as Charles is lifted up and drawn through the window into the scene at which he has been gazing in the story. Inventing a story which incorporates one's self/body into a compelling "picture" bears obvious resemblances to the process I have described as being fundamental to the Leaves of Grass project, that of attempting to provide actual (male) physical presence in a text—while actually being able only to produce metonymic substitutes for such presence. A desire for phantasmatic passage into the liminal space of a picture, and a concern with the means by which one's body might be "translated" or incorporated into the medium of a (visual or literary) text, is central to both "The Child's Champion" and Leaves of Grass.

One reason "The Child's Champion" may seem to produce the specular effects potential in all literary texts with particular intensity is that it quite possibly arose as a strong phantasmatic response on the young Whitman's part to an actual picture of a scene of debauchery in a rural tavern, one like that in a popular lithograph called Dance in a Country Tavern, engraved by George Lehman in 1835, after a drawing (no longer extant) by the German-emigrant artist John Lewis Krimmel. Like the scene of the "drunken frolic" in Whitman's tale, the lithograph depicts a black musician, a fiddler, sitting at one side of the public room of a rural tavern, who is providing music for a group of white revelers who are engaged in smoking, drinking, and dancing. The Lehman/Krimmel picture need not have directly "influenced" Whitman's tale, of course. What I am suggesting is, rather, that it may be useful in considering the conspicuous emphasis on the specular in the story to notice that as a depiction of a revel or debauch in a country tavern it may well derive some of its energy, and some of what may seem to be its peculiar emphases, from the popular pictorial tradition of such depictions which flourished in early-nineteenth-century America. The most famous of these is William Sidney Mount's *Rustic Dance after a Sleigh-Ride* (1830). It has been asserted that Mount derived much of the design of this painting, which also foregrounds the figure of a black fiddler seated to one side of a roomful of revelers, from the Krimmel drawing.[5]

Whitman mentioned Mount's work favorably, along with that of other less celebrated American genre painters, in his newspaper articles on contemporary painting from the early 1850s.[6] The works of Whitman and Mount, both Long Islanders by origin and both outspoken promoters and practitioners of "democratic art" in their time, have often been linked, most notably by F. O. Matthiessen in a general comparison of their art in *American Renaissance*.[7] Mount's numerous depictions of rural routs include several all-male dancing "frolics" (for example, the famous *Dance of the Haymakers* of 1845) which have obvious resemblances to Whitman's representations of antic sociability among male workingmen.

One interesting consequence of considering "The Child's Champion" in relation to two representative examples of the contemporary pictorial tradition of country-tavern revels like the Lehman/Krimmel drawing and the Mount painting is that in comparing the three texts one's attention is forcibly directed to the differing levels of "sordid" versus sentimental elements in them. In this case, Mount's work is the most thoroughly "sanitized" or censored to conform to the new canons of sentimental domesticity which were being more and more widely extended through the culture in the 1830s and 1840s.[8] Krimmel's work, on the other hand, depicts a scene of dissipation. Rather than the lively but "wholesome" group of village youths and girls who figure in the Mount painting, the white male revelers in the earlier *Country Tavern* give every appearance of being "swells," and their female companions of being prostitutes. The attentions the men pay the women appear for the most part to be gross ones, and in the right-hand corner of the picture a tapsman splashes one of his customers with a jet of drink from an overactive spigot.

The contrasting versions of rural sociability, one "sentimental" or "wholesome" and the other "sordid," which Mount's and Krimmel's

respective works convey help point up the extraordinarily mixed quality of the elements which compose "The Child's Champion." By the
time of its composition in 1841, "racy" depictions of rural life had for
a number of reasons become artistically old-fashioned, and more "sentimental" ones highly popular. In the tale, however, rather than being
separated as they largely are in the two visual works, the two modes
interact, the "sordid" standing in paratactic relation to the "sentimental" as its de-repressed and de-sublimated counterpart. "The Child's
Champion" represents a significant departure from either of the two
highly popular modes of representing "country pleasures" embodied by
Krimmel's version on the one hand and Mount's on the other. In order
to create one of his earliest experiments in male-homoerotic "atmosphere," Whitman replaces figures like Mount's village maidens and
Krimmel's female prostitutes with a group of drunken sailors, while
preserving, and to a degree celebrating, the air of dissipation and
incipient sexual transgression that predominates in the representational mode (the "racy" one) which was falling out of general favor
in the years before he wrote this early tale.

The project of creating male-homoerotic "atmosphere" in a text in
nineteenth-century America could only be (and, as *Leaves of Grass*
attests, in some senses could best be) accomplished in liminal terms,
in terms of what Whitman would call "a glimpse through an interstice
caught" in an 1860 poem of that title. The uncanny manner in which
"The Child's Champion" seems both to exert and to thematize the
exertion of powers by verbal texts which the reader may be more
accustomed to associating with visual texts is only one aspect (although I believe it is an important one) of the text's intense specularity. Some of this uncanniness no doubt arises from the text's claims
to deliver both the full physical presence of the author, which it of
course cannot actually provide, *and* the imaginary space it does extend,
in which the sympathetic reader may enter into partial or liminal
contact with the author/speaker of these texts.

Having looked at some of the ways in which the tale resembles and
differs from actual pictures of the kind of scene it depicts, I want now
to consider how specularity functions within the tale's own textual
dynamics. Its energies, one might say, pass from one major specular
object in the text to another, from the window through which Charles
is drawn into the scene to the glass of brandy that the sailor tries to

force him to drink. This glass becomes the focal point for the scene of corporeal and sexual violence which ensues between them. The boy passes through the specular plane of the tavern window without violence, one notices, but the violence suppressed at that phase of the narrative accumulates around the object of the drinking-glass. The displacement of energy in the story from the specular medium of the window to that of the drinking-glass suggests that specularity is as fundamental to the textual dynamics of "The Child's Champion" as fluidity is, and that the two characteristics are closely related to each other.

The Whitman text presents male bodies as being fundamentally interchangeable and masculine identity as being similarly commutable. Both of these processes depend on acts of speculation between males which are mediated by texts. This mediation *also* includes the reader. It does so because the reader occupies a position relative to the text analogous in some ways to the position the boy occupies relative to what is inside the window; the reader is thus implicitly pulled into the story. Standing on either side of the mirror of the Whitman text, author and reader jointly assume the roles of mutual specular doubles. The 1855 *Leaves of Grass* is designed to serve primarily as a site of male specularity, although, as I have discussed, Whitman begins negotiating ways in which he might stand in specular relation with women readers at several points in the first edition, through his use of such complex figures as the woman in the "twenty-eight bathers" passage of "Song of Myself." However, much of the energy of the 1855 *Leaves of Grass* is focused on making it an ideal text specifically for male specularization.[9]

In "The Child's Champion," the boy Charles and his champion Lankton exemplarily figure this relationship of mutual specular doubling between males. In Charles's eyes, Lankton has the economic power necessary to "rescue" him from his fatherless state and from his oppressive indenture to his cruel master. In Lankton's eyes, Charles possesses the very qualities—innocence and devotion to his mother—which the older man has lost, and the loss has rendered his life a chaos. In the story, it is specifically Lankton's seeing and hearing Charles invoke his promise to his mother that precipitates what the narrative represents as his fateful intervention in the boy's affairs. The older man's motives for intervening on the boy's behalf are thoroughly overdetermined: a whole system of impulsions is posited by the narrative as "driving" him toward Charles, beginning with Lankton's "[feeling] that he should love him [Charles]" on first sight, and including Lankton's strong response to Charles's voicing of his mother's will that he not drink. Lankton responds so powerfully because, according to the text, Charles's words "my mother has often pray'd me not to drink" (p. 73) cause Lankton to see "in his soul's eye the picture of *his* mother" (p. 74). It is notable that the boy's voicing of his mother's words is not said to awaken an echo of Lankton's mother's *words* in his soul's *ear:* Charles's mother's words stimulate a visual rather than an aural impression in Lankton's "soul." It is not literally Charles's mother's voice which speaks through her son in the tale, but a text about the son's voicing the mother and "reproducing" her in a way that commands the response of other men who produce themselves (and reproduce their mothers) in a similar way. When Charles reproduces his mother 's will/voice, he serves Lankton as a mirror in which to reproduce himself specularly in relation to *his* absent mother and thereby to recover partially his lost, "innocent" relation to her. Most important of the phantasmatic qualities that Lankton moves to preserve in the story is Charles's embattled innocence, which the older man sees as offering a kind of "last chance" for him to restore himself to some of his own lost innocence.

What the case of Lankton makes clear in the story is that innocence cannot be recovered absolutely. Once lost, any restoration is partial at best. The story represents being "innocent" as a term with two distinctly different meanings. In one sense the term means "guiltless"; in another it means being "sexually intact or inviolate." Lankton intervenes at exactly the point in the tale when Charles's physical integrity (his "innocence" as the object of male sexual possession) is under heaviest attack from the overbearing sailor. It is not physical possession or penetration itself which constitutes the "evil" from which Lankton intervenes to rescue Charles; it is possession or penetration of one male by another *by a hostile and undesirable force* like that represented by the drunken sailor. The absence of Charles's father, the oppressiveness of his master, the sailor's overbearing violence toward him—these are figures of "chaos" in Whitman's male-homosocial text for which an action like the sailor's attempted rape of Charles—as well as Charles's helplessness in the sailor's furious grip—are powerful and

67

highly charged representations. The economy of the text is to set these chaoses to rights by subjecting them to what it represents as being the compelling, indeed irresistible, forces of specularity and "fluidity," of boundary-dissolving between males, of masculine doubling and speculation. It is these processes which give rise to the figure of which Whitman's writing is designed to foster the dissemination, that of the "kosmos" (the opposite of a "chaos," according to traditional cosmology), the man who has developed a capacity for discovering the (male) figure in the text whom he can serve and at the same time be served by as mutual specular double. The text is designed to have an inexhaustible capacity for inducing and fostering this repetitive process of (male) mirroring and dissolving of mirror-images.

In recognizing how boy and man double and mirror each other in Whitman's story, I want to emphasize how it is the boy's doubling and mirroring of his absent mother, and Lankton's powerful mimetic desire to double and mirror *his* mother, that ultimately brings the speculating male pair together. In the following chapter I shall discuss another mother in Whitman's writing, in "Broad-Axe Poem," who is made to figure inviolable innocence. Later in the present chapter I discuss yet another mother, in what was to become a section of "The Sleepers," who is represented as a girl engaging with another woman in an intense and erotically charged exchange of gazes—surprisingly, to the reader who expects such behavior to take place only between males in Whitman's writing, especially that of 1855 and earlier, in which "fluidity" and "specularity" so often figure as male prerogatives.

It is important to notice the frequency with which specular relations among males are figured in Whitman's poetry of the early to mid-1850s, but it is also important not to overlook the ways in which, at some crucial moments in the 1855 *Leaves of Grass*, Whitman's practice exceeds the limitations of the male specularity he frequently exploits in that text to incorporate (at least partially or metonymically) female figures as *agents* rather than mere objects of exchange—as in the "unseen hand" that moves through the latter section of the "twenty-eight bathers" passage of "I celebrate myself." The 1855 text not only repeatedly produces but also shatters "smooth" or "fluid" modes of male-homosocial identification.

Fluidity and Specularity in the Whitman Text

It is in considering the relation in Whitman's writing between specularity and fluidity that we come closest, I think, to the point in his
project where we may most profitably seek some answers to one of the
fundamental questions it raises: what is the relation in the text between the fluidity it imposes on its subjects or discourses and the
fluidity it imposes on (male) bodies or persons? I believe these "fluid"
or boundary-dissolving powers which, according to Whitman, are
potential in both texts and persons stand in more than merely analogical relation to each other in his texts. They do so because fundamental to Whitman's project are the transformative equations between
"body" and "text" on which he insists: his own body *can* be successfully
projected through, and partially transformed into, his printed text,
and his readers in turn *can* engage in contact with the actual physical
presence of the author, at least in liminal terms, as they read his book.

I have already discussed the thematization of the scene of reading
in the relation of Charles and Lankton, and have interpreted it as a
figure for the uncanny power of "The Child's Champion" to compel
the reader to imitate the taking of a position of intensely desirous
subjectivity which recurs throughout Whitman's early writing through
the poetry of the first *Leaves of Grass*. A lonely and mistreated child
gazes through a window at a vision of a "wild party" into which he is,
after a while, "translated." Once drawn into the scene, he is first
reduced to abjection (he is beaten and nearly raped) by one dissipated
man and then delivered from it by another dissipated but nonetheless
kind and loving man who invites the child to join him in starting a
"new life" together.

This, I would argue, is the primary model or "allegory" of reading
which most of Whitman's texts project. A person engages in the private, privative, lonely experience of reading, "hid[ing] . . . aft the
blinds of the window" like the woman in the twenty-eight-bathers
passage, gazing through the text not only at the objects of desire it
posits but at the process of desiring itself as the text represents it. The
text first impels its readers into contact with abjection, and then delivers them into contact with the supposedly saving affectionate physical presence of the author.

The process of partially incorporating body into text can perhaps be elucidated by attending to Whitman's use of the term "model" in his writing during the years 1848–1856. His first significant use of the term occurs in two pieces he wrote for the New Orleans *Daily Crescent* during his residence in the city in 1848, in which he defends Dr. Colyer's troupe of "Model Artists" from charges of indecency.[10] These "model artists" apparently performed *poses plastiques;* that is, their bodies lightly veiled, they posed as "living" versions of famous sculptures of nude or nearly nude figures. Just as the language of Whitman's early stories frequently manifests not only the powerful attraction of "low-life" scenes of dissipation for the author (and presumably for many of his readers) but also the perceived necessity on the author's part of echoing the general condemnation of such scenes, so his defense of the "Model Artists" emphatically gestures toward the ease with which anyone in a city may see the "wrong" kind of these performances—those which appeal directly to prurient and lascivious spectatorship—while echoing "official" disapprobation of these: "There may be some petty attempts, in the low by-places, which all cities have, to counterfeit these groupings, after a vile method. Such, however, are only to be seen by those who go especially to see them."[11]

What is most pertinent about Whitman's defenses of this theatrical form to the rest of his writing is that *Leaves of Grass* is itself designed to be, if not a *performance* of nudity, something more unusual "along the same lines," as it were: an experiment in the textualization of it. This mode of "naked" self-presentation in a literary text is precisely what Whitman claims to be practicing in the 1855 *Leaves,* as when he writes in the self-review of the book which appeared in the Brooklyn *Daily Times* that his purpose in his new work is to "cast into literature . . . his own flesh and form, undraped, regardless of models, regardless of modesty or law."[12] According to Whitman, he presents not merely a mimetic version of a human body as a painter or sculptor of the nude does; more like the "model artists" he defended in his youth, he offers the reader "his own" exposed body.

The ambiguity of that "his own" (Whitman's own or the reader's own?) is a crucial one, since it is on such "folds" or reflexive indeterminacies of language that the Whitman text depends for making some of its fundamental gestures, for "turn[ing] over upon" the reader in a way uncannily like the way in which the body "turn[s] over upon" the speaker in the passage which became "Song of Myself," section 5. The indeterminacy in Whitman's account of the process in the self-review I have quoted or in "Song of Myself," section 5, signals that in "cast[ing]" his own nude body "into literature," the author is not simply making his body directly available to the reader: the author's "body," after all, cannot simply be reconstituted by the reader "at home" from the text into which it has been "cast." He is making the reader's own body available to him/herself in a way that it has not been available before, in the sense that he is providing "models" of bodiliness, here specifically of nakedness, that subvert the prevailing ones in his culture, which would link the unclothed state to scenes of humiliating exposure or abjection.

In noting how the attribution of "the body" in the Whitman text shifts between belonging to the author and belonging to the reader, I would not want to overlook how a second, related shift may or may not "work" for women readers. This second shift is the one that occurs when a female reader encounters the kind of crucial "fold" in the Whitman text that I am here taking the phrase "his body" to represent. Queen Victoria—perhaps in many ways not a representative woman reader, but a woman reader nonetheless—is said to have told Tennyson that during her first, most intense period of mourning after the death of Prince Albert she derived considerable comfort from reading *In Memoriam*—particularly the poem beginning with the words, "Tears of a Widower," which, she told the poet, she mentally modified to fit her own situation by reversing the gender of its pronouns.[13] Judging from the strong positive response of many, although by no means all, women readers of Whitman—from his contemporary Anne Gilchrist to our contemporary June Jordan—some women readers of *Leaves of Grass* have similarly reversed the gender of some of Whitman's crucial pronouns and *not* taken linguistic representations of characteristic male-homosocial forms in *Leaves of Grass*, such as the ambiguity or "fold" I am pointing out here in a phrase like "*his* own body," as signs of their exclusion from the principal actions represented in the text.[14] When the first female champion of *Leaves of Grass*, the Englishwoman Anne Gilchrist, characteristically writes to Whitman, of her attempts to read through the new fourth edition of *Leaves of Grass*, "I try again and again, but too great waves come swaying up & suffocate me," her terms suggest two things: that she is responding powerfully to the "fluid" energies of the text ("great waves"), and that these do not simply provide positively empowering and pleasurable experiences for her as reader (since they are "*too* great" [my emphasis] and "suffocat[ing]") as they seem to have been designed to do for male readers, at least at the beginning of the *Leaves of Grass* project.[15]

From the poet's point of view, he claims through his text to be empowering both men and women readers to reject to some degree the system of controls over their bodies that their culture enforces. Whitman suggests in his self-review that he intends that his "cast[ing]" of his body into a discursive formation ("literature") where it is officially not supposed to figure be regarded as an exemplary act, which can be repeated by the reader in this ("literary") context as well as in others. "Models," "artists," acceptable and unacceptable modes of presenting the nude body for public edification, and of presenting it in literature—Whitman produces a discourse in *Leaves of Grass* designed to cut across these proprietary codes of the culture for representing the human body. The word "model" remains a key term in his explanations and defenses of this original and disturbing characteristic of his writing; the word retains in his work not only its sense of meaning "a paradigm" or "an ideal example" of something, but also "a person who displays his or her body as an object for artists to reproduce in a plastic medium," or, in the case of "model artists" like Dr. Colyer's troupe, "a person who displays his or her body in performance for the edification and pleasure of spectators."

In the same self-review Whitman offers an alternative metaphor for the status of his body, his self, "his life," in the text of the first *Leaves*: "His whole work, his life, manners, friendship, writings, all have among their leading purposes an evident purpose to stamp a new type of character, namely his own, and indelibly to fix it and publish it, not for a model but an illustration, for the present and future of American letters and American young men." Here, the character of the first *Leaves of Grass* as in the main, but not entirely, a kind of textual conduit for affectionate physical presence between males is specifically stipulated. In these words, too, Whitman substitutes for his metaphor from the plastic arts a whole set of metaphors from what was for him and his practice perhaps the more congenial milieu of the printshop: he is to stand in his text "not for a model [that is, neither an ideal example nor an artist's nude model] but an illustration [that is, a *printed* model or example, for purposes of mere demonstration rather than to typify a status of ideality]," and as such he is to be "stamp[ed]," a "type," a "character," "indelibly . . . fix[ed] . . . and publish[ed]."[16]

Women's as well as men's bodies are incorporated into the 1855 texts at points such as those in "I celebrate myself" in which the poet writes, "This printed and bound book....but the printer and the printing-office boy?" (p. 47), and "The well-taken photographs.... but your wife or friend close and solid in your arms?" (p. 48). In such lines one sees that Whitman is making assertions not only about the *poet*'s but also about the *reader*'s body being enfolded in the text. I have called the desire to imbue a text with full physical presence and the recognition of the impossibility of doing so the generative contradiction at the heart of *Leaves of Grass*. The lines quoted here articulate this oscillation between the thought of the artifact-of-human-production ("this printed and bound book") or the textual-artifact-of-a-person ("the well-taken photographs"), on the one hand, and the thought of the actual body of the person which has been specularly incorporated into the artifact (as author or photographic subject), on the other. The reader of the Whitman text is continually put in the position of intensely and simultaneously desiring both aspects of what the text presents as the desirable, in its full physical presence and in its more readily accessible specular or liminal partiality:

> Come closer to me,
> Push close my lovers and take the best I possess,
> Yield closer and closer and give me the best you possess.
>
> This is unfinished business with me....how is it with you?
> I was chilled with the cold types and cylinder and wet paper
>   between us.
>
> I pass so poorly with papers and types....I must pass with the
>   contact of bodies and souls.   (p. 57)

Claiming that bodies can and should be successfully incorporated in texts, Whitman repudiates the gesture with the same motion, claiming to shiver with the "chill" of "cold types" and "wet paper." The discomfort of being a body pressed in an album (the album format of the actual book, the tall-and-narrow format of the 1855 *Leaves of Grass*) gives Whitman his poetic "cue" for pleading for "contact" with the

73

"bodies and souls" of his readers. That is, Whitman's rhetoric of the difficulties of embodying a self in a text gives way here to a more direct rhetoric of an authorial seduction of readers. In these lines (and in others like them), the poet pleads for the physical affection of readers as the only agency that can warm up and dry out the authorial body which has been imperiled in the process of text-making, exposed as it has been to chill and wet in the uncongenial ("I pass so poorly with papers and types") environment of the printed book. Passages in the early editions of *Leaves of Grass* like this one are emblematic of what one might call a kind of "advantageous shortfall" in the text: incapable of actually (re)producing physical presence, it repeatedly culminates in seductive gestures toward the reader to respond to author and text in ways that will bridge the gap between their announced intention and their inevitably incomplete achievement of this intention by fervently embracing the specular and liminal versions of affective possibilities that the text does succeed in providing.

THE 1855 TEXT makes a strong case for what it represents as the power and desirability of full physical presence, but it remarkably makes an equally strong case for the desirability and power of those aspects of embodiment it can represent only in specular or liminal form. The process of specularly figuring these aspects of embodiment begins in the Preface to the 1855 text, in a passage in which the poet represents himself as a mobile body of water disporting himself with American rivers and lakes and reflecting both the nation's coasts:

> His [the American bard's] spirit responds to his country's spirit....he incarnates its geography and natural life and rivers and lakes. Mississippi with annual freshets and changing chutes, Missouri and Columbia and Ohio and Saint Lawrence with the [Niagara] falls and beautiful masculine Hudson, do not embouchure where they spend themselves more than they embouchure into him. The blue breadth over the inland sea of Virginia and Maryland and the sea off Massachusetts and Maine and over Manhattan bay and over Champlain and Erie and over Ontario and Huron and Michigan and Superior, and over the Texan and Mexican and Floridian and Cuban seas and over the seas off California and Oregon, is not tallied by the blue breadth of the waters

below more than the breadth of above and below is tallied by him. When the long Atlantic coast stretches longer and the Pacific coast stretches longer he easily stretches with them north or south. He spans between them also from east to west and reflects what is between them. (p. iv)

Here in this syntactically overwhelming passage is a representation of the figure of the new kosmos "in action," literally embracing the "fluid" and male bodies with which he has immersed himself in the text—male because the figure of the kosmos is represented as being entirely a product of the male-homoerotic valencies of his culture's sanctioned male-homosocial institutions, formal and informal. In such passages as these, the text becomes the ungrounded medium in which he establishes his "new identity"—and that of any other man who cares to join him ("Is this then a touch?....quivering me to a new identity" [p. 32]). A relation of mutual specular doubling links "poet" and "geography": he "responds to his country's spirit" not only by "incarnat[ing] its geography" but by in turn endowing the country's "rivers and lakes and natural life" with specular male bodies, mirrors of his own and those of other "fluid" men (that is, "kosmoses"). Identity flows in both directions, from the man's body to the land's and water's, and from the land's and water's "bodies" to the man's. That the "beautiful masculine" bodies of water are said to "embouchure" into the poet just as they "embouchure where they spend themselves" not only suggests that the waters and the poets flow into each other but also indeterminately characterizes the media of these exchanges. "Embouchure" is, in its ordinary dictionary meanings, not only an outlet of a body of water but also the mouthpiece of a musical instrument. It is in this second sense that Whitman uses the term in "I celebrate myself": "I fling through my embouchures the loudest and gayest music" (p. 25). The quasi-sexual exchanges depicted as occurring here between rivers and poet, then, are (whatever else they are) fluid, oral, and seminal: he drinks the rivers and "spouts" them ("I fly the flight of the fluid and swallowing soul," he writes in "I celebrate myself" [p. 38]); his fluid "spoutings" are the lines he voices/writes as well as the "spirts of . . . seminal wet" (p. 45) to which he repeatedly likens them.[17] The specularity and homoeroticism in the poet's relation to the embodied waters become explicit in his "stretch[ing] with" the coasts to "span[ ] between them" and to "reflect[ ] what is between them." The man's body "stretches in company with the [bodies of] other" entities a couple of pages later in the Preface (p. vi) when "the greatest poet" is said to consort with (embodiments of) the qualities indispensable to his mission, "sympathy" and "pride": "The soul has that measureless pride which consists in never acknowledging any lessons but its own. But it has sympathy as measureless as its pride and the one balances the other and neither can stretch too far while it stretches in company with the other. The inmost secrets of art sleep with the twain. The greatest poet has lain close betwixt both."

Of primary importance in the specular dynamics of the Preface, and of the text as a whole, is the advance of the "stalwart and wellshaped heir" ("the greatest poet") toward his "equal," who is figured at several points as being his mirror image. "Only toward as good as itself and toward the like of itself will it [the soul of the nation] advance half-way" (p. xii), reads one of the climactic pronouncements of the Preface. This figure who reflects the corporeal figure of "the greatest poet" actually appears in the text near the end of the Preface, in the person of the strapping young man who is said to personify (embody) "the English language." He is represented in the Preface as arriving to "befriend[ ] the grand American expression" (p. xi), the "kosmos"-poet. The English (language) double of the "greatest" (American) poet shares the poet's ideal physique: his body is described as "brawny," "limber," and "full"; he is said to represent "the tough stock of a race" from which descend America's political ideals.

At the opposite end of the text from the Preface, on the next-to-last page of its final poem ("Great are the myths"), there occurs a secondary double of "the greatest poet" and another embodiment of the English language, this one (predictably) a maternal one—indeed, the mother of the entire Anglo-Saxon "race":

> Great is the English speech....What speech is so great as the
> English?
> Great is the English brood....What brood has so vast a destiny
> as the English?
> It is the mother of the brood that must rule the earth with the
> new rule,
> The new rule shall rule as the soul rules, and as the love and
> justice and equality that are in the soul rule.   (p. 94)

On its "universalist" or "philanthropic" level the text would "wash away" all boundaries between bodies, but in practice it tends to remove some of these boundaries while allowing others to stand. In considering the effects of fluidity in the first *Leaves of Grass,* it is necessary to acknowledge the limits the text itself imposes on the project: the paths the text opens up to fluidity—principally for white males—must be seen in relation to the barriers it tends in some ways to reerect for women and nonwhite males.

Fluidity at the Expense of Others? Gender, Race, and "Solid" versus "Fluid" Identity

There are two conflicting discourses of embodiment, sexuality, and identity at work in the 1855 *Leaves of Grass.* Through its appeal to what it advances as "universal" experiences of corporeality, the work ideally claims everyone (every"body") as its constituency—tautologically ("everyone who has a body"), since "the" body *is* the marker for a person's being "one," "individual." Implicit at many points in the 1855 text, however, is an asymmetrical "arrangement" or disposition of bodies with respect to gender and race. One of the text's characteristic modes of representing gender is succinctly articulated at moments such as (to glance ahead to a poem Whitman probably drafted during or soon after the time of the appearance of the first edition) the final line of the 1856 "Poem of Women": "First the man is shaped in the woman, he can then be shaped in himself." At such moments a woman, unlike a man, is represented as being not ultimately a self to be shaped, but (at least potentially) as merely a matrix for masculine self-shaping. The first *Leaves of Grass* is situated in a field the poles of which may be defined as follows:

mother	man
solid	fluid
cohesion	dispersal
matter	spirit

Although all these terms are according to the text supposed to hold equivalent status—"I am the poet of the body, / And I am the poet of the soul" ("I celebrate myself" [p. 26])—at numerous points the text does not succeed in aligning its primary terms, as following the poem just cited a few lines further will make clear:

> I am the poet of the woman the same as the man,
> And I say it is as great to be a woman as to be a man,
> And I say there is nothing greater than the mother of men.

The first two lines of this passage are parallel, but the third is not. Having asserted that the body is being included in the text on the same terms as the soul, and women on the same terms as men, the poet undercuts these proposed equivalences by skewing them in the third line into a hierarchical structure which privileges "the mother of men." If women and men are really equal, a feminist reader may well wonder, why this ostensible promotion of "the mother of men"—especially insofar as it is implicitly but unmistakably at the same time a devaluation not only of women who are not mothers but also of women who are the mothers of other women and not "of men"? In other words, the poet's alleged privileging of "the mother of men" reveals itself on analysis really to manifest a privileging of men—for it is the male gender of the mother's offspring, and not sheer maternity in itself (which is capable of producing offspring of either gender), which here attracts the poet's high valuation.

Having been "shaped in the woman," in the words of the "Poem of Woman," the man is then free "to be shaped in himself"—first, as the text would have it, by autoerotic activity and then by erotic arousal by other men, which brings him ("quiver[s]" him) to the "new" or second-phase identity which emerges in the middle of "I celebrate myself": "Is this then a touch?....quivering me to a new identity" (p. 32). There is a passage near the end of "I celebrate myself" which will serve as a representative moment of male self-instantiation ("standing on his own two feet" after having been preparatorily "shaped in the woman") linked to the launching by the (male) kosmos/poet into the "fluid" realm of "new identity"—first by saluting his own phallus and then being engulfed by the press of "lovers" to "touch" him:

> All forces have been steadily employed to complete and delight
>   me,
> Now I stand on this spot with my soul.

Span of youth! Ever-pushed elasticity! Manhood balanced and
   florid and full!
My lovers suffocate me!
Crowding my lips, and thick in the pores of my skin,
Jostling me through streets and public halls....coming naked to
   me at night. (p. 50)

"Perfect and clean the [male] genitals previously jetting," the poet
writes in "I wander all night in my vision," "perfect and clean the
womb cohering" (p. 76). "Cohering" (which is what, according to the
text, female genitals properly do) and "jetting" (what male genitals
properly do) might be taken as two further terms for "stable" or maternal identity and "fluid" (primarily male) identity, respectively. So
stated, the phallocentrism of such a model of the origins and nature
of identity and the self becomes patent; in the text's most exorbitantly
masculinist moments, males are represented as the only persons being
capable of exceeding the limits of "solid" identity and achieving identities that can be disseminated: "On women fit for conception I start
bigger and nimbler babes, / This day I am jetting the stuff of far more
arrogant republics" ("I celebrate myself," p. 45). The poet's primary
means of self-dissemination through the text is represented as being a
form of lovemaking, not between any mother and father but primarily
between the poet and his specular double: "Out of the dimness opposite
equals advance....Always substance and increase, / Always a knit of
identity....always distinction....always a breed of life," reads a pair of
lines early in "I celebrate myself" (p. 14).

That the "opposite equals" who knit themselves and their bodies
into a "breed of life" here are both male—this is conceivable only as
a scandalous possibility for many of Whitman's readers, in his time as
well as ours. Nonetheless, as I have been attempting to show in these
first two chapters, Leaves of Grass from its beginning may be said to
be saturated with representations of male-homoerotic exchange, some
of them relatively straightforward, some of them relatively occulted in
the text. The exorbitance (by his culture's prevailingly homophobic
standards) of Whitman's lavish representational program in the 1855
edition of male-homoerotic "fluidity" may go some way toward explaining certain other passages in Leaves of Grass in which the poet represents himself—apotropaically, with the hope of "turning aside [homo-

phobic] evil"?—as a swaggering model of paternal potency and fecundity, as he would thirty-five years later in his desperate letter to Symonds.

The "opposite equals" who advance toward each other early on in "I celebrate myself" are the "fluid" male subject who occupies the central position in the 1855 text and his specular double, the couple who figure in the Preface as the newly arrived greatest American poet and the "brawny" and "limber" youth, the English language, who "befriends" him (p. xi). It is primarily in relation to this ambiguous figure, the linguistic self/other, that the poet binds and unbinds the threads, the "knit of identity" and "distinction," which is the 1855 text. In relation to the "brawny" and "limber" English language, the poet plays supposedly "opposite" roles, "mother" and male, stabilizer and disseminator, alternately one and then the other:

> And I know I am solid and sound,
> To me the converging objects of the universe perpetually flow,
> All are written to me, and I must get what the writing
>   means.   (p. 26)

Here is the fundamental nexus of transformation in the first edition of *Leaves of Grass:* "converging objects" not only "cohere" to produce the poet, to give him a body and a material/maternal (first-phase) identity, they are also (as he takes them) a form of writing, or rather, "written to [him]," and in order to disseminate the "gotten" meanings of the object-writing which "perpetually flow[s]" toward the poet, he must make himself as fluid as this perpetual and infinite process of writing which he takes the universe to be. Whitman amplifies these issues considerably in the third (1860) edition of *Leaves of Grass,* as I shall discuss in Chapter 4. In shaping himself and allowing himself to be shaped by autoerotic and homoerotic forces, as he does here in the first edition, the poet has the purpose of empowering himself to exude writing as nature (the "objects of the universe") does.

WHITMAN repeatedly enfolds discourses of rebellion against racist oppression with others of the revisionary discourses of the 1855 *Leaves of Grass.* His recurrent use of the terms "master(s)" and "mastery" manifests a structural asymmetry analogous in kind to the one I have pointed out in his representations of women and men. (As I shall discuss in relation to the second edition of *Leaves of Grass*, these terms of "master" and "mastery" take on even more highly charged resonances as the national crisis over slavery intensifies in the years just before the outbreak of the Civil War.) In some of Whitman's uses of "master/y" in the 1855 *Leaves of Grass*, the word bears only positive connotations, as in the Preface, where he calls the great American poet "one of the *masters* of the artists of all nations and times" (p. viii, my emphasis), or when, on the same page, "something in the soul" is said to assert, "Rage on, Whirl on, I tread *master* here and everywhere, *Master* of the spasms of the sky and of the shatter of the sea, *Master* of nature and passion and death" (my emphases).

Elsewhere in the 1855 text, however, "mastery" is by no means an unequivocally positive or honorific quality; rather, implicit in its (ostensible) opposites "slave(s)" or "slavery," it denotes the social and political role of slavemaster—one which the text, written in the midst of the decade of most intense conflict between opponents and champions of the enslavement of blacks in the United States, represents as an oppressive one. In the most explicitly abolitionist or abolitionist-derived sections in the first *Leaves of Grass*, the passages on "[a] slave at auction" and "[a] woman at auction" (in "The bodies of men and women engirth me," pp. 80–81; later sections 7 and 8 of "I Sing the Body Electric"), antislavery discourse and a general antiracist discourse are enfolded with each other. "Gentlemen," the speaker says, "look on this curious creature, / Whatever the bids of the bidders they cannot be high enough for him." Although a reader might well assume that the "slave at auction" is black, Whitman "unfolds" abolitionist discourse midway through this passage to place persons of other colors in the slave-position: "Examine these limbs," he further addresses his imaginary slavebuyers (into whose position also the rhetorical structure of this passage repeatedly thrusts the reader), "red black or white."[18]

Exfoliating this "leaf of grass" one fold the more, Whitman enfolds the discourse of women's rights into this section, along with its general humanitarian discourse of the underlying identity of persons of different skin-colors and its abolitionist discourse of the impossibility of one person's holding property in another. The section beginning, "A woman at auction," like the one that precedes it, condemns the

81

enslavement of blacks (since it is they and not whites or Indians who are subject to public sale in some parts of the author's America) but does so without explicitly specifying the "woman's" race, but only her gender—she is "[a] *woman* at auction" (my emphasis); that is, any woman (not just other black women) might stand in her imaginary place in the text. This is not to suggest that this passage has the simple and absolutely determinate meaning, "*All* women are slaves," but rather something like, "No woman is entirely free in a society that allows some women to be bought and sold," and, further, "The oppression of blacks in this country is in some, if not all, ways related to the oppression of women."

These two and other figures of black Americans in the 1855 *Leaves of Grass* (for example, the "runaway slave" who is the subject of the ten lines immediately preceding "Twenty-eight young men bathe by the shore" in "I celebrate myself") are included in the text but effectively excluded from its "fluid" dynamics; like many of its female figures, they are represented as being disseminated not instantly (so to speak), through the central "fluid" and specular transactions carried out through the text, but only gradually, through their (potential) genealogical positions:

> This is not only one man....he is the father of those who shall
> be fathers in their turns,
> In him the start of populous states and rich republics,
> Of him countless immortal lives with countless embodiments
> and enjoyments. (p. 81)

And a few lines later:

> She [the "woman at auction"] too is not only herself....she is
> the teeming mother of mothers,
> She is the bearer of them that shall grow and be mates to the
> mothers.

What is exceptional about *Leaves of Grass* is not that it in some ways reproduces political commitments of the culture in which it was produced which were oppressive to nonwhites and women, but that it also provides the means for making a critique of these commitments. The 1855 *Leaves*, I believe, can be shown to exceed at many points the oppressive political tendencies in which it to some degree participates. For example, the famous second line of "I celebrate myself," "And what I assume you shall assume," can be read as being not simply a coercive disablement of the reader to resist the specific assumptions which impel the poetry (although it is that, too). It is at the same time an invitation to the reader to "assume" the totalizing stance of the speaker, to foreground his or her own self's needs and desires and to "celebrate" them as the poet does. "I know perfectly well my own egotism" (p. 47), Whitman writes; his use of the term "perfect" may cue the reader that "egotism," literal self-centeredness, is the fundamental quality the text ascribes to the (white) male, as "perfect motherhood" is the fundamental quality it ascribes to the (white) female. But this "allowance" Whitman makes for his "own egotism" as determinant of the contents and thrust of his "song" opens up a space in the text which allows for the possibility—although it does not itself enact it—of a woman's, or a black or Native American man's, voicing and/or writing such powerfully repudiatory words as, "I too am untranslatable" (p. 55)—which is to say, the terms of my selfhood (or what you may insist on calling my selfhood, despite my own refusal of the term) are irremediably different from yours.

When Whitman insists as he does near the conclusion of "I celebrate myself" on the translatability of selfhood (foregrounding especially the "fluent" translatability of male selves, owing to what he sees as their peculiar specularity and commutability), he is, I think, not (at least not only) attempting to obliterate differences between himself and others and to "cover up" the totalitarian coerciveness of his own position, as he has often been accused of doing. The text can serve to empower others—genuine others, that is, women and nonwhite men, not just homotypes of the (male) poet—to assert their own respective difference or "untranslatability."

NATIVE AMERICAN figures, male and female alike, bear a transitional significance in the race-and-gender system (re-)encoded in the first *Leaves of Grass*. In a major poetic episode in "I wander all night in my vision" (later "The Sleepers," section 6)—the most extensive representation of lesbian desire in *Leaves of Grass*—the speaker relates the story of his mother's strong emotional response as a young woman to an itinerant "red" woman:

Now I tell what my mother told me today as we sat at dinner
 together,
Of when she was a nearly grown girl living home with her
 parents on the old homestead.

A red squaw came one breakfasttime to the old homestead,
On her back she carried a bundle of rushes for rushbottoming
 chairs;
Her hair straight shiny coarse black and profuse
 halfenveloped her face,
Her step was free and elastic....her voice sounded exquisitely as
 she spoke.

My mother looked in delight and amazement at the stranger,
She looked at the beauty of her tallborne face and full and
 pliant limbs,
The more she looked upon her she loved her,
Never before had she seen such wonderful beauty and purity;
She made her sit on a bench by the jamb of the fireplace....she
 cooked food for her,
She had no work to give her but she gave her remembrance
 and fondness.

The red squaw staid all the forenoon, and toward the middle of
 the afternoon she went away;
O my mother was loth to have her go away,
All the week she thought of her....she watched for her many a
 month,
She remembered her many a winter and many a summer,
But the red squaw never came nor was heard of there again.

(p. 74)

This section bears an interesting relation to the patterns of homosociality and the "fluid" incorporation through the gaze of the desiring
subject into the scene of desire that I have described in "The Child's
Champion" and the "twenty-eight bathers" episode. Age and relative
autonomy in relation to her family are significant differential factors
here, as in the early tale. "A nearly grown girl living home with her
parents" here falls in love with an autonomous and presumably mature
woman. But in contrast to my other two examples, race is highly
significant in this one: this is an account of a white girl's loving response to "beauty and purity" of person which are represented in terms

of a specifically ethnic physical type, beginning with the woman's "hair straight shiny coarse black and profuse halfenvelop[ing] her face," and extending to her "free and elastic" step, her "exquisite[ ]" voice, and "the beauty of her . . . face and full and pliant limbs." Here, the various parts of the Native American woman's person, her hair, her face and body, "profuse," "halfenvelop[ing]," "free and elastic," themselves constitute the "fluid" scene of desire and object of the gaze—the position that the all-male drinking-and-dancing party in the tavern holds in the tale and the all-male swimming party holds in the "twenty-eight bathers" passage. "The more she looked upon her she loved her," is a line that occurs in the middle of this episode, and it is a line on which much of the episode's dynamic character can be made to turn. It is, I believe, a rare instance in *Leaves of Grass* of the representation of a moment of full specularity and "fluidity" being achieved by two women. As usual in such moments, the indeterminate "rollings over" on one another of the pronouns or "shifters" are crucial linguistic signs of the nonlinguistic aspects of this process. "The more she looked upon her she loved her": the reader may take both "she's" as denoting the girl-subject, but there is nothing in the syntax here to prevent one from allowing the "she . . . her . . . she" shifter-structure to keep rebounding between one "she"—the desiring subject (white girl)—and the other—the desired object of the gaze ("red" woman). Then the sentence takes on a mirror-structure of this type: "the more the girl looked upon her (the woman) the more she (the girl) loved her (the woman)"; but also, "the more the girl looked upon her (the woman) the more she (the woman) loved her (the girl)." An indeterminable relationship governs the alternative ways of assigning referents to the string of feminine pronouns, in much the same way that such a relationship governs the indeterminable meanings of the unimpeded gaze that at least momentarily binds the white girl and the Native American woman together.

". . . [T]oward the middle of the afternoon she [the woman] went away," ". . . [S]he [the girl] watched for her many a month, / She remembered her many a winter and many a summer, / But the red squaw never came nor was heard of there again." So this episode culminates, reversing as it does so the process of producing affectionate physical presence between persons in which "The Child's Champion" and the "twenty-eight bathers" passage culminate. Disseminated into their respective texts as present to each other (as they are in a sense to the author and his readers, too), the boy and his "champion" are ultimately united by "fluid" bonds, as are the "twenty-ninth bather" and his/her twenty-eight fellows. The white girl and the Native American woman in "The Sleepers" are disseminated through the text in absence from each other. Their relationship is not represented as being infinitely recursive ("But the red squaw never came nor was heard of there again"), as the other two relationships are. The parties who are here disseminated through the text in presence to each other are the (male) speaker and his mother ("Now I tell what my mother told me today as we sat at dinner together"). One might hypothesize that the chief scene of female-female "fluidity" in the 1855 *Leaves of Grass* must culminate in the absolute absence of the women to each other (except in the [male] speaker's memory of his mother's memory of their momentary presence to each other) in order to reinforce the absolute presence of the mother to her speaker-son (but not necessarily his to her). Such an analysis recalls the terms of the exclusion of the feminine, except in the metonymic form of the-voice-of-the mother-to-her-son ("Don't drink"), in "The Child's Champion." Rather than reducing the mother's account in "I wander all night in my vision" to a text that excludes the feminine with the near-thoroughness that the early tale does, I would argue that this episode is the most significant instance of something approaching what one might call genuine feminine utterance in *Leaves of Grass*. In it, the woman's voice exceeds the conventional narrative constraints (and the cultural constraints they reinscribe) which would confine her utterance to addressing the son about the son's own interests. Instead, she tells a story of her own about her love and loss of another woman of a different race— an inconceivable act for a figure like the mother in "The Child's Champion."

The Native American man represents quite a different set of possibilities in the 1855 edition from his female counterpart. "The friendly and flowing savage....Who is he? / Is he waiting for civilization or past it and mastering it?" ("I celebrate myself," p. 44, later the opening lines of "Song of Myself," section 39). That the "savage" is "friendly and flowing" would seem to qualify him as an emblematic embodiment (a "kosmos") of the highly privileged qualities in the first *Leaves of Grass* of specular, male-homosocial "fluidity," but one notices that he is not represented as standing in relation to any other person, male *or* female. His mode of relation is represented as being both solitary and grandiose; it is fundamentally not to other persons as such but to "civilization" as a whole, a state that he has always either not yet attained or already surpassed.

In a passage forty lines earlier, in a line which Whitman canceled after the third edition, one finds an obverse figure of a "savage" in which solitariness and grandiosity are raised to an even higher pitch. This figure is martyr and American Oedipus at once: "What the savage at the stump [said], his eye-sockets empty, his mouth spirting whoops and defiance" (p. 42). Represented not in a state of "fluid" immersion in another man or a group of other men but bound to a "stump," suffering torture and execution, this "savage" is the 1855 text's most explicitly violent figure for its revisionary aims ("his mouth spirting whoops and defiance"). Suppressed in later editions of the book, the figure of the "savage" author "def[ying]" his culture is a figure of the failure of his revisionary "attack": all the violence of the encounter is registered in his mutilated face, in his eye-sockets "empty" and "his mouth" full of "whoops and defiance." Blinded but still refusing to be silenced, "whoop[ing]" when rendered incapable of more articulate utterance, "the savage at the stump" is a figure of the demonic "down-side" of the happy consciousness that for much of the 1855 text insists on the immediate accessibility of "fluid" union to the author and his (male) readers. As I shall discuss in the next chapter, the meanings of this vision of the castrated "savage"-martyr for the *Leaves of Grass* project of revising Whitman's culture's conceptions of the proper limits of bodiliness—meanings only briefly glimpsed in the first edition and almost entirely suppressed in later ones—dominate the second (1856) edition with the disturbing force we have learned to associate with the return of the repressed.

3

Dividing the Text and Crossing the Gaze in the Second (1856) Edition of *Leaves of Grass*

From the First *Leaves of Grass* to the Second: The Oedipal Moment in the Text

As I have argued in the foregoing chapters, a "fluid" self—not one simply identical or continuous with that of the man or the author Walt Whitman, but rather a collective or composite self designed to accommodate the reader as well as the author, to bring them into affectionate contact with each other—is amply situated in the first (1855) edition of *Leaves of Grass*. The 1855 Preface and the long inaugural poem, "I celebrate myself" (later "Song of Myself"), are the principal sites where this "fluid" self is produced in the text. The first edition is in several senses a text undivided, not least in its peculiar (and at times confusing) eschewal of such conventional poetic means of demarcation as titles, headings, section breaks, or division into stanzas.

Even a cursory examination of the second (1856) edition of *Leaves of Grass* suggests that it was not designed to represent untroubled "fluidity"—either of selves or of texts—as the 1855 edition had been. The poems now have titles and other signs of authorially imposed division, and one may take these changes at least in part as signs of the author's increased willingness to fulfill readers' expectations in the wake of the first edition's general failure to find an audience. However, it is important in considering the revisionary history of the *Leaves of Grass* project to recognize that the new demarcations in the text of the second edition represent more than merely practical changes meant to allay readers' difficulties with the text; they can also be read as a sign of an intensified awareness on Whitman's part of the insuperable difficulty of simply overruling division and difference as he had attempted to do with his program of "fluidity" and specularity in the 1855 *Leaves of Grass*. The second edition is a text scored by division, as are the selves which it struggles to situate. It may well strike the reader as being the work of a newly divided self, a self split in ways that had not been manifest in the first edition. The "fluid" world in which the first edition locates itself, the "kosmos"-selves which seek and find each other endlessly reflected in the mirror of its text, are riven by difference in the second edition.

Once Whitman had delivered himself of the text it could no longer be considered to be simply continuous either with himself, his body, or the utopian "fluid" economy through which affectionate (male) physical presence could be endlessly disseminated. A crucial moment at which this separation of text from author is marked in the text of the second edition occurs in Whitman's revision of the famous concluding sentence of the 1855 Preface, "The proof of a poet is that his country absorbs him as affectionately as he has absorbed it." Incorporated along with a substantial amount of the rest of the Preface into the 1856 "Poem of Many In One" (later retitled "By Blue Ontario's Shores"), the sentence is altered to read, "The proof of a poet shall be sternly deferred till his country absorbs him as affectionately as he has absorbed it" (line 219).[1] The unproblematic process of mutual affectionate absorption that links poet and country, "proving" the poet, has been effectively disrupted in the interim: the prevailing mode of the second edition is quite different from the 1855 one of cheerful, unimpeded "interwetting" (to anticipate a term Whitman introduced in the 1860 "We Two, How Long We Were Fool'd": "We are seas mingling, we are two of those cheerful waves rolling over each other and interwetting each other," line 15). The aftermath of the publication of the 1855 *Leaves* represents the oedipal moment in Whitman's literary career, when the stream of largely undifferentiated ("fluid") transactions between self (selves) and specular homotypes becomes riven by difference, when the recognition is forced on the subject that the actual achievement and enjoyment of the imaginary satisfactions of the "fluid" realm have been and must be "sternly deferred": the publication of the "fluid" text turns out to be a very different thing from, and quite anterior to, the actual achievement of "fluidity" on a wide scale.

On publication, the text of *Leaves of Grass* became a product, an object, an artifact—a "solid," in short—with a definitiveness and distinctness that Whitman may not, perhaps could not, have entirely anticipated. The second edition embodies his attempts to come to terms with this profoundly disturbing "reversal" of his text, which, in being published, had become "different" not only from himself but from itself as well. The most compelling emblem for the second edition of *Leaves of Grass* as a whole is the broad-axe. Whitman proposed in a manuscript note of late 1855 or early 1856 that it should be made the principal emblem of the United States, in place of the long-established eagle, and he devotes one of the major new texts in the 1856 edition ("Broad-Axe Poem," later "Song of the Broad-Axe") to exploring its complex meanings.⁷

In this chapter I shall be considering what happens when Whitman turns from what he had called in the 1855 Preface "the mirror" of the text in search of a mode of writing and a mode of vision capable of representing difference in some more effective way than the first *Leaves of Grass* does. In order to accomplish this, in addition to dividing the text and otherwise privileging tropes of division and difference in it, he also crosses the "fluid" and specular gaze which characterizes the interactions of author and reader in the 1855 text with another kind of gaze which one might call the "long view." This is a mode of vision and perception extended and removed beyond the specular field of two persons which situates itself between a gazing subject and a distant object. This object is essentially threefold, and it includes the "vistas" of American history, geography, and the poet's posterity, his posthumous readership (as in his *Democratic Vistas* to come, of 1868–69). This "long view" is the characteristic mode and object of vision not only in "Broad-Axe Poem" but in the other most representative new poems of the 1856 edition as well, chief among them "Sun-Down Poem" (later "Crossing Brooklyn Ferry"), but also including the aforementioned "Poem of Many In One" and "Poem of Salutation" (later "Salut au Monde!").

There are, then, two primary kinds of gazing represented in the second edition. The first is face-to-face, specular gazing between two persons, which is primarily "inherited" by the second edition from the poetry of the first which reappears in it. The second is a kind of gazing that might be called "keep[ing] vista" (in the words of the 1856 "Poem

of Many In One," line 119); it involves taking a "long view," directing a gaze at remote objects (the American past, the future, the landscape and the people who inhabit it) which do not immediately return
it, its return being "sternly deferred" in keeping with the new constitutive constraints of this edition. These two kinds of gazing conflict with
each other at a fundamental level. The 1856 *Leaves of Grass* tends to
represent these conflicts as a series of gender differences between men
and women, fathers and mothers, and mothers and sons. Furthermore,
it tries to align the objects of its "long views" of American history,
geography, and posterity with a highly oedipalized version of these
gender differences, that is, it represents these differences as arising in
catastrophic scenes of castration and "lack" in which fathers have
violently and bloodily prevailed over mothers and children who have
been thoroughly subjected to the fathers. Finally, as I shall discuss in
relation first to "Broad-Axe Poem" and then to "Sun-Down Poem,"
the 1856 edition also frequently critiques and revises the oedipal system from which it derives much of its representational program.

The 1856 *Leaves of Grass* opens as the 1855 one does, with the
long poem which was eventually entitled "Song of Myself," here called
"Poem of Walt Whitman, an American." This is immediately followed
in the second edition by the 1856 "Poem of Women" (later "Unfolded
Out of the Folds"). It is significant that "Poem of Women," of the
eighteen new poems in the second edition, is set in first place. I take
its position of priority as another indication of the primary significance
the question of sexual difference has in the 1856 *Leaves*. The poem
represents the female body as being a capacious, voluminous, involuted
matrix, the indispensable source—in the senses of both site-of-origin
and stuff where and out of which everything which human beings
create is made. Production is, however, figured as being a male pre-
rogative here, one which proceeds by a kind of process of exfoliation
(*Leaves*-making) from female (or feminine) "material": male bodies,
"the poems of man" (which in the 1856 "Bunch Poem" are said simply
to be penises), men's brains (and by extension their minds and ideas)
are all imaged as entities that are produced by turning women's "folds,"
the insides of their bodies, "poems," and brains, "inside out."

The word *mater* is a significant lexical element of the "materialism"
Whitman expounds here as elsewhere in the early editions of *Leaves
of Grass*. Whitman's tendency to "maternalize" feminine sexuality and

subjectivity in *Leaves of Grass* has often been remarked.[3] What has largely escaped comment, though, are the quite different sexual-political valencies that Whitman's constructions of femininity as maternity take on at different phases in the formation of *Leaves of Grass*. Excluded from the "fluid" male-homoerotic transactions of 1855, the figure of the mother reemerges as a central one in the pervasively oedipal 1856 text (the figure will play quite another role in the dramas of birth, death, and rebirth of the Civil War poetry of the fourth [1867] edition).

The crucial text in the 1856 edition in which to consider these matters is "Broad-Axe Poem," the third of the poems first published in the 1856 edition. This text begins with one of the most curious passages in *Leaves of Grass*:

> Broad-axe, shapely, naked, wan!
> Head from the mother's bowels drawn!
> Wooded flesh and metal bone! limb only one and lip only one!
> Gray-blue leaf by red-heat grown! helve produced from a little seed sown!
> Resting the grass amid and upon,
> To be leaned, and to lean on.

Commentators have frequently pointed out that these lines represent a significant, albeit brief, "regression" in the development of Whitman's poetic technique, insofar as they are not "free" verse, but conventionally metrical and rhymed.[4] Several critics have further pointed out that one rationale for the poet's employing traditional poetic devices here is that this passage is cast in the traditional, even archaic (Anglo-Saxon) literary form of a verse riddle.[5] I wish to argue that the reason Whitman sees fit to imitate a traditional poetic form, specifically the "riddle," at this point in the development of the *Leaves of Grass* text is that this represents a point of such stress in the text that it must to some degree be "occulted," that is, it must be brought (or perhaps "smuggled") into the poem "in disguise"—in this case, in the "disguise" of a readily recognizable and familiar, even archaic, verse form, unlike any other in the *Leaves of Grass* text in any of its versions. What the reader is being "protected" from seeing (or prevented from seeing too quickly) is that what is being openly and even "nakedly" introduced into the text at this point is a fetish, a sign of the maternal phallus, the talisman "drawn" "from the mother's bowels" which is supposed to protect its invoker from castration or castration anxiety.

The representation of the simultaneous recognition and denial of sexual difference which is a hallmark of the 1856 *Leaves* finds a fit emblem in the "broad-axe," which is ostensibly feminine and specifically maternal in origin but which the poem celebrates for accomplishing the putatively masculine "executive deeds" (as they are called in line 92 of the poem) of both founding cities (by clearing forests and building) and destroying (by beheading) the politically fallen. The common confusion in infantile fantasy of "baby" with feces and of childbirth with the act of excretion also takes its place among the indeterminate range of meanings of the emergence of the "head" of the broad-axe "from the mother's bowels."[6] An entry in the same notebook in which Whitman seems to have first experimented with the kind of free-verse line and the practice of writing poetry of cultural and political critique and mediation which would first culminate in the 1855 *Leaves of Grass* ("I am the poet of slaves and of the masters of slaves. . . . I am the poet of the body and I am the poet of the soul") provides a significant analogue to the fusion of anality and childbirth effected in the opening lines of "Broad-Axe Poem." In this notebook entry Whitman writes,

> Among murderers and cannibals and traders in slaves
> Stepped my spirit with light feet, and pried among their heads
>   and made fissures to look through
> And there saw folded foetuses of twins like the foetuses of twins
>   in the womb,
> Mute with bent necks, waiting to be born.[7]

Whitman originally wrote "foeses" (feces?) in the third line, then deleted it and wrote "foetuses." In the opening lines of "Broad-Axe Poem" the titular object of the poem represents (among other things) not only the fetish or maternal phallus but also the kind of fusion of "foeses" with "foetuses" which appears in the form of a parapraxis in Whitman's notebook entry. It is present in what would seem to be a less unwitting form in "Broad-Axe Poem" in the figure of the extraction of the "head" of the broad-axe "from the mother's bowels."

In addition to the "foeses/foetuses" notebook passage, it may be

useful to consider briefly one other early Whitman text which is potentially pertinent to my discussion of the particular way in which the
"magic-dirt complex" that Freud first recognized and theorized is con-
figured in Whitman's writing.[8] This complex takes its name from its
"magical" infantile-fantasy transformation of "dirt" (feces) into precious substances (jewels, money)—even into precious living substances (babies). According to Freudian theory, the series circulates
the following phantasmatic equations: phallus = feces = baby =
gift = "dirty"/"precious" gem/metal/money.

The early Whitman text in question is a recently discovered 1840
letter of his to a male friend. Its opening paragraph reads:

> Dearly beloved Moved by the bowels of compassion,
> and pushed onward by the sharp prickings of conscience, I
> send you another epistolary gem.— For compassion whispers
> in mine ear that you must by this time have become accus-
> tomed to the semi-weekly receipt of these invaluable morsels;
> and therefore to deprive you of the usual gift, would be
> somewhat similar to sending a hungry man to bed without
> his supper.— Besides, conscience spurs me to a full confes-
> sion; which generally operates on me like a good dose of
> calomel on one who has been stuffing immoderately, making
> a clear stomach and comfortable feelings to take the place
> of overburdened paunch and rumbling intestines.— Excuse
> the naturality of my metaphor.—[9]

Arthur Golden, who edited this and a small group of companion letters
to the same correspondent for publication, notes that the salutation
here plays on the wording of the opening of the marriage ceremony in
the Book of Common Prayer, but goes on to argue that the letters in
no way represent "an early expression of the 'Calamus' sentiment on
Whitman's part."[10] While Golden is right to treat Whitman's use
of the ceremonial phrase "Dearly beloved" as a salutation as a point
that raises questions about the relation of this writing to male homoeroticism, he is imperceptive (and/or homophobic) to ignore the
phallo-anal language Whitman uses to describe the impulses which
motivate the letter he is writing: "Moved by the bowels of compassion,
and pushed onward by the sharp prickings of conscience," Whitman
writes, that is, under the double stimulus of two kinds of (symbolic)

pressure on his anus, he produces for his friend another (symbolic) "gem"; the text is explicitly presented to its "dearly beloved" recipient not only as a jewel but also as a "gift," one in a series of "invaluable morsels." Whitman excuses the "naturality" of his metaphor by claiming that it may be related to the excessive "naturality" of the country folk of rural Woodbury, Long Island, among whom he was boarding and schoolmastering at the time:

> Speaking of "naturality" reminds me of the peculiarities that distinguish the inhabitants, young and old, of this well-bred and highly romantick village.— For instance, I was well entertained the other day at dinner, with a very interesting account by the "head of the family" . . . . of his sufferings from an attack of the gripes; how he had to take ipecachuana, and antimonial wine; the operation of those substances on his stomach; the colour and consistency of the fluids and solids ejected from the said stomach; how long it was before epsom salts could be persuaded to take pity on his bowels; with many and singular concomitant matters, which, you may well imagine, contributed to a high degree to the improvement of my appetite.— I frequently have the felicity of taking my meals surrounded by specimens of the rising generation.— I mean little young ones getting out of bed; and as "to the pure all things are pure," the scene of course is in a high degree edifying to my taste and comfort.[11]

Except for a comment on the weather and a query about how their political party is faring back home, the two paragraphs quoted above constitute the entire document in question. The joke of its alimentary production, along with the more outrageous joke that the writer's "dearly beloved" correspondent depends on these "invaluable morsels" for food (as the writer himself has recently been subjected by his host to a discourse of diarrhea along with his dinner), is the "message" of the letter, insofar as it may be said to have one. If one notices that this text as a whole takes as its subject the matter of the interplay of "fluids and solids"—albeit here in grotesque fecal form ("the fluids and solids ejected from the said stomach")—its relation to much of the rest of Whitman's early writing, from "The Child's Champion" of the following year to the early editions of *Leaves of Grass*, becomes evident.

No term of the transformative "magic-dirt" series is missing from this 1840 letter of Whitman's, but one notices that in the form the symbolic chain takes in this text, the babies, the "specimens of the rising generation," are represented as being disjunct from the other elements in the sequence; they are other people's offspring, rather than being more directly the products of the bowels-moving/pricking/ writing process which the letter describes and of which it is itself said to be a product. It may be helpful in trying to dispose some of the terms of this series into some order of relative significance to each other in relation to the text of "Broad-Axe Poem" if we consider that the form of childbirth represented in its opening lines produces not an ordinary baby but rather a fetish, in the form of the "head" of an axe. A comment of Naomi Schor's on what she calls the "conspicuous absence" of a baby at a comparable point in a nineteenth-century French literary text is pertinent in this connection: "The lack of the compensatory baby," Schor writes, may be said to "reduplicate . . . the initial lack [that is, the mother's "lack" of a phallus]"; this "redundancy" of putative "lacks," Schor goes on to say, "insures the reader's perception" that the text is situated along "the line . . . [which] Barthes has termed 'the axis of castration.'" [12]

As the opening lines of "Broad-Axe Poem" make clear, the text is located simultaneously on the axis of the "magic-dirt complex" and on what Barthes calls the "axis of castration." Chief among the meanings of the broad-axe and of the way it is shown being brought into the text are that it is simultaneously fetish or talisman-against-castration and instrument-of-castration. It is an object that can be used simultaneously to cover and to uncover, to recognize and to deny, sexual difference. Most important, it is a complex sign that is highly compatible with the reinscription of sexual difference in the tendentious form in which it is cast in oedipal fantasy: as universal feminine castration. What Schor calls the "redundancy" of "lacks" imputed to women, far from being a notion that needs to be imported from psychoanalytic theory into the discourse of the second edition of *Leaves of Grass*, is a redundancy that Whitman multiplies throughout the text of the second edition, as in the opening lines of the 1856 "Poem of Procreation" (retitled "A Woman Waits for Me" in 1867), where the putative "lack" of the woman is repeatedly invoked:

> A woman waits for me—she contains all, nothing is lacking,
> Yet all were lacking, if sex were lacking, or if the moisture of
> the right man were lacking.   (*Variorum*, p. 238)

These lines epitomize the generative contradiction in the second edition: "woman . . . contains all," *yet* "lacks" everything as long as she
"lacks" "the moisture of the right man." These lines' assertion that
both "nothing" and everything "is [simultaneously] lacking" in
"woman" locates the text directly in the oedipal realm—on "the axis
of castration."

The axe's "head" which emerges at the opening of "Broad-Axe
Poem" may be taken as a way of figuring liminally the "cutting" or
castrative potential of this emblem of the second edition. It is not
analogous to the human body but only to detached parts of the body,
possessing as it does "limb only one and lip only one," respectively a
quarter and a half of the normal human complement. Lest the reader
should think my choice of the broad-axe as emblem of the 1856
Leaves capricious or arbitrary, I would point out before proceeding
further that the "Broad-Axe Poem" itself represents it (in lines 4 and
5) as a revised type of a "leaf" of "grass": the axe's "head," we should
notice, is a "leaf" (line 4), and the axe is depicted as "[r]esting [on]
the grass." But this is a "leaf of grass" unlike any represented in the
1855 version of the text. Rather than signifying a state of unproblematic nondifferentiation like the emblematic leaves of grass which compose "a uniform hieroglyphic" in the first edition (p. 16), the broad-
axe is a leaf of "grass" that is both an instrument and a product of
division and difference, and consequently of lack and castration. In
this same passage in the 1855 "I celebrate myself" (later "Song of
Myself," section 6), "the grass" is explicitly said to be "itself a
child....the produced babe of the vegetation," growing (perhaps) "from
the offspring taken soon out of their mothers' laps." Finally, the grass
is said to be itself "the mothers' laps." The birth process represented
in the 1855 text is conspicuously nonviolent and unruptured in comparison with the process represented in the opening of "Broad-Axe
Poem." For example, "offspring" are "taken . . . out of their mothers'
laps" (my emphasis) in 1855, but from the mother's "*bowels*" in 1856.
The "young men," "old people," "women," and "offspring" who are

the material sources of the "curling grass" of 1855 are all represented as being dead, buried, and, apparently, decomposed, but they are depicted, in the text's term, "[t]enderly," whereas the scene of birth which inaugurates "Broad-Axe" is violent (even if much of the violence is suppressed until the bloody sections I shall discuss farther on), "axed" by the axis of castration.

Another significant quality of the broad-axe to be noted from the opening lines of the poem is that, unlike ordinarily "produced babes" (1855, p. 16), which are born powerless and must be supported by others (the mother or her surrogate), the broad-axe is a fully phallic "offspring"—"born standing," one might say—not only "to be leaned" as ordinary babies are, but also "to lean on." The broad-axe is no ordinary infant but an "offspring" which is represented as being from the moment of its appearance capable of supporting the hyperphallic figure of the father, whose marked absence haunts the text until he fully emerges in lines 166 and following of "Broad-Axe Poem":

> I see the European headsman,
> He stands masked, clothed in red, with huge legs, and strong
>   naked arms,
> And leans on a ponderous axe.

Here is the "rest" of the figure of the (axe's) "head" which emerges in the opening lines of the poem, "clothed in red" like both a tumescent penis and a bloody newborn. With his "huge legs and strong naked arms," he is himself, these terms suggest, a giant infant of a sort and the long-delayed product of the "unnatural" birth process depicted in the poem's opening lines. In "lean[ing] on a ponderous axe" the figure of the "headsman" recapitulates the relation represented between the axe and its users at the opening of the poem, where it is said to exist "[t]o be leaned, and to lean on."

It is significant in the context of this edition's emphasis on oedipality that the figure of the violent and omnipotent father is introduced in the 1856 text explicitly as an object of the speaker-subject's vision ("I see . . ."), rather like a figure in a *tableau vivant*, "stand[ing] masked" and "clothed," "lean[ing] on a ponderous axe," as if posing as the figure of the Strong Man/Castrator—the grisly "lead" in the oedipal "drama" in all its overdeterminedly static quality and in all its exorbitant theatricality (the would-be observer/spectator always having arrived after the "piece" has ended).

A series of looks represented as being mere rapid and "passing" glances projected by a male observer/speaker at phallic object(s) of desire are the medium through which most of the rest of the text is transacted. The "masculine trades" of line 7 of the text are not only the various kinds of labor in which a series of eroticized male figures are represented as being engaged in the poem, they are also the sexual exchanges between males which these activities metonymically (and consequently only partially) "cover." "The beauty of wood-boys and wood-men with their clear, untrimmed faces," "The limber motion of brawny young arms and hips in easy costumes": lines like these manifest the close (metonymic) connection between human figures like the beautiful "wood-boys" and their tool the axe, which is itself an eroticized "wood-boy" ("wooded flesh"). The sexual exchanges or "masculine trades" which impel this text are largely concealed not only because they are homosexual but because they are so along the most tension-ridden lines that male-homoerotic relations take in our culture: those between father and son. The text (mis)represents and (dis)figures the son's erotic desire toward his father or toward parts of his father's body as "work," as (in the text's terms) the masculine imposition of "shape" on a field of inchoate natural objects by means of tools. That the "Broad-Axe Poem" takes as its ostensible subject the pseudo-epic exploits of the broad-axe and its "beautiful" male wielders ("The butcher in the slaughter-house," "Lumbermen," "The housebuilder," "The city firemen") provides the text with its rationale for hectically overvaluating the phallic. The unmistakable signs of this overvaluation are the covert allusion to the fasces (the bundle of axes and stakes representing the irresistible power of the state) which are borne in by the "Roman lictors" of line 80, and the "screams of women" as they are raped by "brigands" during "[t]he sack of the old city" at line 89. Although the men who bear the fasces into the text are explicitly said to be ancient Romans, that is, denizens of the "old world," as are the rapist-"brigands" farther on in the passage—an old world against which (according to the text) America has defined itself in opposition—there are some signs in the text that the state violence and misogynist aggression attributed to the "old world" (most notably in the figure of the "European headsman") are equally characteristic of the "new," since all such violations, past and present, are said to attest to, and supposedly be justified by, "[t]he power of personality just or unjust" (line 93). "Muscle and pluck forever," as the line following reads, is the keynote of the poem's central sections; the "great city stands" (new "Rome" as well as old), the text keeps asserting, where there stands "the brawniest breed of orators and bards," "Where . . . the healthiest fathers stand," and the "best-bodied mothers" (lines 115, 132, 133).

All members of the symbolic family repeatedly inscribed in this text in the terms just quoted partake of a specific set of characteristics— "Muscle," "brawn," "health"—which supposedly distinguishes them from other, less "fit," peoples and races. The contradiction in representing the text's ideal family in such hyperphallic terms immediately asserts itself: it is difficult to distinguish among the "brawny" members of such a family, for boundaries of gender and generation disappear in their shared "muscularity." The "solution" to this "problem" is a catastrophic one: even in this otherwise indistinguishable family, gender and generational differences forcibly reassert themselves in moments of oedipal violence, such as those represented in the following lines:

> I see the clear sun-sets of martyrs,
> I see from the scaffolds the descending ghosts,
> Ghosts of dead princes, uncrowned ladies, impeached ministers,
>   rejected kings,
> Rivals, traitors, poisoners, disgraced chieftains, and the rest.
>
> (lines 171–174)

Given a "family" whose members can be recognized only under conditions of oedipal violence, it is impossible to keep the "old world" against which the "new" is supposedly defining itself sufficiently remote from the scene of the poem; the murderous "old world" appears reborn in the new at the very moments in the 1856 text where oedipal family relations reassert themselves in all their phantasmatic violence, as when the speaker of the poem claims to see not only the gigantic "European headsman" resting from his bloody work but also the "Ghosts of dead princes, [and] uncrowned ladies"—that is, the "headsman's" "victims" sited along the axis of castration, his castrated sons and wives (Whitman revised "princes" to the more sym-

metrical, less obviously oedipal "lords" in all editions after the 1856
one).

The bloody and violent hierarchies which are supposed to characterize European history *in ostensible contrast* with American history,
past and future—lines of power which manifest themselves in the
appearance and behavior of a figure like the "European headsman"—
cannot be kept sufficiently remote from the text's representations of
the appearance and behavior of American wielders-of-the-axe; rather,
images of the violence of state power and the violent repression of
women (like the parading of the fasces and the "screams of women in
the gripe of brigands" in line 89) repeatedly contaminate the "cleaned-
up" representations that the poet would make of American history ("I
see the blood washed entirely away from the axe, / Both blade and
helve are clean"). The "long view" which Whitman texts like "Broad-
Axe Poem" invite the reader to take cannot effectively serve as a
means of absolving American culture of the state violence and misog-
ynism which these texts attempt to project outward and backward
onto "the old world," because American history, as a text like "Broad-
Axe Poem" represents it, forms an unbroken line with European history. This "old-world" history never deviates from the axis of castration
which splits the culture into two mutually exclusive "master"
categories, the phallic and the castrated.

"Broad-Axe Poem" is a disturbing text because it at least partially
recognizes and enthusiastically celebrates a fundamental assumption
which is only implicit in most of the rest of Whitman's early work:
the necessity of maintaining and extending the prevailing conditions
under which symbolic castration in a multitude of forms is a prerequi-
site to one's assuming any social role whatsoever in the culture. The
poem culminates in a long dithyramb organized around the recurring
exclamation, "The shapes arise!" The conditions under which these
repeatedly heralded shapes are said to arise are these:

> The axe leaps!
> The solid forest gives fluid utterances,
> They tumble forth, they rise and form . . . .   (lines 186ff.)

As I have argued at length in the previous chapter, "solid" and "fluid"
stand in significantly less invidious relation to each other in the 1855
edition, in which "solids" are represented as being "liquidated" in a

relatively nonviolent fashion. Here the process of transformation, rather than being carried out as it has been in the 1855 text by means which are as unproblematic as they are unspecific, is explicitly represented as being castration: "The axe leaps," and the "fluid utterances" which produce the human world pour forth, imparting to that world the material objects which fill it and the culture which sustains it and imbues these objects with meaning:

> Hut, tent, landing, survey,
> Flail, plough, pick, crowbar, spade,
> Shingle, rail, prop, wainscot, jamb, lath, panel, gable,
> Citadel, ceiling, saloon, academy, organ, exhibition-house, library,
> Cornice, trellis, pilaster, balcony, window, shutter, turret, porch,
> Hoe, rake, pitch-fork, pencil, wagon, staff, saw, jackplane, mallet, wedge, rounce,
> Chair, tub, hoop, table, wicket, vane, sash, floor,
> Work-box, chest, string'd instrument, boat, frame, and what not.   (lines 189–196)

This inventory of material-cultural constructions, part of the "[l]ong varied train of an emblem [the broad-axe]" projected in the poem's eighth line, culminates in the figure of a door, the one of these "constructions" which marks the liminal point on which Whitman's texts so frequently turn. The door here marks the liminal point in the career of an oedipal son:

> The door whence the son left home, confident and puffed up,
> The door he entered again from a long and scandalous absence,
> diseased, broken down, without innocence, without means.
>   (lines 237–238)

Here the text proffers a "scandalous absence" (the son's, and the ostensibly "scandalous absence" of the phallus which is attendant on his castration, which has been executed offstage, as it were) in order to cover up what one might call the "scandalous presences/absences" which impel the text but which the text attempts to disguise and downplay. Chief among these is the text's representation of the paternal phallus(es): the "multiple penises of the father" (in Richard Klein's phrase),[13] one (some) of the most intensely desired objects of unconscious early-childhood fantasy, are explicitly proffered to the reader in a five-line passage excised from the text in all editions of *Leaves of Grass* after the 1856 one:

> Their shapes arise, the shapes of full-sized men!
> Men taciturn yet loving, used to the open air, and the manners
>   of the open air,
> Saying their ardor in native forms, saying the old response,
> Take what I have then, (saying fain,) take the pay you
>   approached for,
> Take the white tears of my blood, if that is what you are
>   after.   (*Variorum*, I, 188n.)

"Whose is that blood upon you so wet and sticky?" the speaker asks the European headsman, rendering him indistinguishable from his "ponderous axe" and what the poet elsewhere calls its "executive deeds" (line 92). The possibility that the five excluded lines quoted above raises is the "scandalous" one that the "wet and sticky" blood the text repeatedly represents as being the red blood shed by the castrated son is replaced at some moments in the text with the "white . . . blood" of semen exuded by the multiple paternal phallus(es) of unconscious fantasy.

The broad-axe as fetish, as the paternal phallus(es) which the mother (in pre-oedipal fantasy) retains in her body after sexual intercourse and eventually expels in the form of babies (rather in the same fashion as the trees of the "solid forest" emit "fluid utterances" under the axe, "utterances" which in turn "tumble forth, . . . rise and form" the shapes which are coextensive with the material culture), is, as I have argued earlier, explicitly figured as the maternal phallus in the opening lines of the text.[14] The emergence of the fetish, "the mighty and friendly emblem of the power of my own race" (line 183), "from the mother's bowels" has ambiguous consequences for the ensuing representations of the mother and her body in this text. It is in relation to her that the limitations of pressing pre-oedipal fantasy into service as a form of non-oedipal or anti-oedipal discourse, as Whitman seems to be doing at some points in "Broad-Axe," become most clearly apparent, for the oedipal phase and the kinds of perceptions it fosters replace pre-oedipal fantasies so forcibly and in a sense catastrophically in our culture that it is nearly impossible to "think" the pre-oedipal phase in any other terms than oedipal ones. The mother of the opening lines of the text is only liminally phallic, the axe drawn "from [her] bowels" a sign of both her phallic potential (in pre-oedipal fantasy) and of her defining lack "along the axis of castration" imposed by the oedipalization of subjects in our culture.

When the figure of the mother reappears in what became the penultimate section of the poem (p. 11), she is represented as being phallic only insofar as she is (paradoxically) virginal, impervious to "contamination" by oedipal sexuality—which is to say, sexuality which has been formed in and by verbal utterance (the "fluid utterances" which the "solid forest" emits when "[t]he axe leaps"):

> The gross and soiled she moves among do not make her gross
> and soiled . . .
> Oaths, quarrels, hiccupped songs, smutty expressions, are idle
> to her as she passes.   (lines 241, 245)

The "masculine trades" (in the sense of "exchanges") which impel this poem, such as the "pay[ment]" of "white tears" which the "taciturn yet loving" men of this text offer to the reader, may take place under the aegis of the broad-axe as maternal phallus, but the mother herself may be located securely in the text only insofar as she is represented as willingly accepting her exclusion from the circuits of language and sexuality:

> She is silent, she is possessed of herself, they do not offend her,
> She receives them as the laws of nature receive them, she is
> strong,
> She too is a law of nature, there is no law greater than she is.
> (lines 246–248)

Here the woman's eloquent silence, her "receptiveness" which does not open her to contamination, the ability which is attributed to her of moving through the midst of the phallicized realms and discourses of oedipal sexuality ("hiccupped songs, smutty expressions") while appearing to remain (paradoxically) both inside and outside of it—these are the contradictions imputed to femininity in this particular text and in the broader culture it reinscribes, where the oedipal is insistently put forward as the highest "law of nature."

Must the imperviousness of the figure of the mother be made to depend on her exclusion from the circuits of language and desire as these are constructed along oedipal lines, and as these are represented (at least in relation to femininity) in "Broad-Axe Poem"? Can desire be disengaged from the oppressive circuits of oedipality which are constitutive of it? These are questions central to Whitman's culturally revisionary enterprise in general and to the exploration of oedipal conditions peculiar to the second edition of *Leaves of Grass* which I want now to consider in relation to the best known of the 1856 poems.

ALONG WITH "Out of the Cradle Endlessly Rocking" and "When Lilacs Last in the Dooryard Bloom'd," "Sun-Down Poem" ("Crossing Brooklyn Ferry") has generally been regarded by formalist critics as Whitman's most successful poem. Of the three, "Sun-Down Poem" is the earliest and has received more critical attention than any of the other 1856 texts. It has been widely interpreted as a "triumphal" statement of the poet's successful transcendence of the limitations of material existence, and as an ecstatic affirmation of his ability to bridge the chasms which separate him from his readers, present and future.[15] The editors of the standard (Comprehensive Reader's) edition of *Leaves of Grass* not only categorically proclaim in a note to the poem that it is "the most distinguished of the new poems of 1856" but also provide a brief critical commentary on it which sounds more like Wordsworth's prose than Whitman's, and indeed would probably be more appropriate to some of Wordsworth's poems than to Whitman's:

> With exalted and sustained inspiration the poet presents a transcendent reality unlimited by the tyranny of time or person or space, a poetic demonstration of the power of appearances . . . to affirm the soul.
> Philosophical in theme, the poem is yet profoundly personal—his own daily experience made illustrious—and its strength lies in its aesthetic vision.[16]

A comparable statement by James E. Miller, Jr., is similarly heady in tone: "'Crossing Brooklyn Ferry' achieves, in triumphing over space and time, an imaginative fusion of the poet and the reader."[17]

More recently, a number of Whitman's critics have argued that the mode of transcendence the poem affirms is less complete, enduring, or satisfactory for author and reader than critics had previously suggested, or that the act of affirmation the poem makes is more qualified and less buoyant and triumphal than had been generally recognized.[18] Two of the text's most recent readers, David Cavitch and M. Wynn Thomas, have directed their respective readers' attention to what they both see as a fundamental division in the poem between nature and society, with the former of these two factors privileged far over the latter. Both critics locate what they see as this invidious division in the contrasting kinds of structures of address to be found in the poem's opening lines, between the direct greeting of nature made in the first two lines and the "rather wary and circumspect" acknowledgment of other persons made in the following three:[19]

> Flood-tide of the river, flow on! I watch you, face to face,
> Clouds of the west! sun half an hour high! I see you also face
>   to face.
> Crowds of men and women attired in the usual costumes, how
>   curious you are to me!
> On the ferry-boats the hundred and hundreds that cross are
>   more curious to me than you suppose,
> And you that shall cross from shore to shore years hence, are
>   more to me, and more in my meditations, than you might
>   suppose.

Like Cavitch and Thomas, I think that the unmediated way in which the sunset and the reflection of the face in the water are saluted and "faced" in these lines, in contrast with the indirection and indistinctness with which the poet's fellow ferry passengers are represented ("Crowds of . . . the usual costumes"), is highly significant. I wish to argue, though, that the particular significance of the contrasting views these lines afford is not that they express or reveal an antisocial orientation on Whitman's part but that they locate the reader at the very opening of the poem in a position of crossed gazing. He or she is invited to assume a vantage point which lacks all middle range: only two objects of vision are offered, the sight of one's own face in the water as one leans over the rail of the boat, or the vast and remote spectacle of the sunset.

Rather than reading the elision of the faces of the "crowds" in the opening lines of the poems as a sign of some personal moral failing or social deficiency on Whitman's part, I would interpret the faceless crowds as a sign that the opening of "Sun-Down Poem" is located at a moment of sunset martyrdom like the one elaborated in lines 166–183 of "Broad-Axe Poem," where once again two objects of vision (like the face reflected in the water and the distant sunset in the opening lines of "Sun-Down Poem"), the sunset itself and the ghosts of political martyrs, are represented as obliterating other possible objects ("I see the clear sun-sets of the martyrs, / I see from the scaffolds the descending ghosts," and so forth; see "Broad-Axe Poem," lines 171ff.)

These lines from "Broad-Axe Poem" depict the oedipal scene of "martyrdom" at the same time that they register the radical political disaffection manifest at a number of points in the 1856 edition, insofar as Whitman's representations of new-world realities cannot be kept uncontaminated by the state violence which is supposed to characterize only old-world conditions. To relate the opening sunset vision which impels the entire text of "Sun-Down Poem" to scenes of political martyrdom like this one in "Broad-Axe Poem" or the one in "Poem of Salutation" not only calls into question readings of "Sun-Down Poem" which profess to find its supposedly transcendent affirmations untroubled but also challenges some more recent readings of this text which take it as a sign of Whitman's alleged narcissism or fundamentally antisocial nature.

Rather than taking the speaker's desire to face and greet the distant sunset and his own reflection in the water while omitting to "face" his fellow passengers as a sign of an abiding sense of "detachment" from other persons on Whitman's part, as critics such as Anderson, Cavitch, and Thomas do, I prefer to take the speaker's omission to "face" his fellows directly in these lines as a sign of the intensity of Whitman's attention to exploring certain difficult questions of desire, especially the dynamics of oedipalized desire. What manifests itself in the text's avoidance of "facing" the crowds on the ferry is the "strain" of attempting to conceive desire otherwise than oedipally, here and elsewhere in the 1856 text. It may be appropriate in considering the meaning of the speaker's not "facing" the ferryboat crowd to recall the words of Jacques Lacan, another searching student of the channels of desire in culture, who once wrote, "It is not, after all, for nothing that analysis is not carried out face to face."

The particular kind of "analysis" that the text of "Sun-Down Poem" carries on is an exploration of the question of whether the extended gaze, the "long view," spatial and/or temporal, can serve as an effective vehicle of desire. The poem begins and ends with what look like affirmations that the gaze of the "long view" can serve as an effective vehicle of desire despite the perils to which it is susceptible, but these affirmations are at least partially self-canceling. For example, the first line which ostensibly affirms the power of the poet's desire to transcend the limits which might frustrate or diminish it, "It avails not, neither time or place—distance avails not" (line 20), casts this "affirmation" in the intensely negative form of asserting that "time," "place," and "distance" are all in a sense "[un]avail[ing]," that is, unavailable or unusable as pathways for desire. Nothing "avails" but the sheer rhetor ical force of the poet's assertions that his experience of desire and its frustrations are identical with his readers' experiences of them:

> I too lived,
> . . . .
> I too felt the curious abrupt questionings stir within me,
> . . . .
> I too had been struck from the float forever held in solution,
> I too had received identity by my body . . . .
>
> (lines 57, 59, 62–63)

According to this poem, the temporal distance between the poet and his readers may increase, but this will not diminish the capacity of the text for recreating the poet's position of uncanny nearness to future readers: "Who knows but I am as good as looking at you now, for all you cannot see me?" (line 91). The text arises from the poet's overlooking (so to speak) the persons around him to gaze at the sunset and at his reflection in the water, in order to generate what one might call a mode of vision which permits him, or at least his texts, to peer over the shoulders of his readers in perpetuity. Here, as elsewhere in the second edition of *Leaves of Grass*, this gazing has the double effect of disseminating the poet's affectionate presence among his readers *and* ·unsettling readers into a state of particular susceptibility to this affec- tionate presence with the uncanny capacity of his texts for accomplish- ing this dissemination on its own peculiar terms.

The paradox which generates this uncanny "overseeing" on the poet's part toward sunset, flowing waters, the reflection of his own face, his "unfaced" contemporaries, and his uncannily "faced" or at least "gazed on" posterity is contained in one of the phrases he uses to negotiate the passage from his contemporaries to his future readers: "Others the same":

> The men and women I saw were all near to me,
> Others the same—others who look back on me, because I
>   looked forward to them.   (lines 51–52)

The men and women of the future "who look back on" him (that is, who read his poetry) are the same as his men and women contemporaries—except that the text foresees them becoming sufficiently "other" from the poet and from his contemporaries that they (posterity) can complete the circuit of desirous gazing which his contemporaries cannot, or at least do not. Posterity can do so because by the time they come to his text he will be dead, and, consequently, his identity will be at least partially precipitated into it, leaving only its traces in the form of representations of the range of subject-positions from which he (and, he asserts, everyone else in his culture) has experienced desire. In ordinary experience, the circuit of the loving gaze can never be successfully completed or resolved: "When, in love, I solicit a look, what is profoundly unsatisfying and always missing is that—*You never look at me from the place from which I see you.*"[20] What ultimately "avails" in "Sun-Down Poem" is that it locates just such an uncanny place where the reader can "look at" the poet from the precise textual "spot" where the poet once "looked at" the reader.

Once the location of this "spot" in the text is recognized, it is important to note that it cannot be stabilized or fixed: it is "there," but only liminally so; the text ultimately produces not a "place" on which the reader can fix but a "crossing" of that place—indeed, a crossing of that "crossing." The text "avails" itself of one crossing—a ferry passage—to launch a secondary, uncanny crossing, between poet and reader, past and present, on which these respective positions cross and recross each other's paths without being permitted by the text to "settle" at any of the terminal points of these paths. Most critics have tended to misread "Sun-Down Poem," even those who recognize and acknowledge its "dark" side—the unsatisfactoriness or impermanence of the affirmations it supposedly proposes—because they have exaggerated the degree to which the text serves to "bridge" the remote objects and realms through which it moves. "Sun-Down Poem" does not construct a bridge between the points it represents; rather, it circulates the reader back and forth between the points of desirously gazing and of being gazed at desirously, exploring as it does so the contradictions of the cultural conditions that make one long to be looked at by the beloved from the place where one looks at the beloved—even as one knows one never can be, except under certain peculiar conditions available (a crucial term in "Sun-Down Poem") in writing. Time, place, distance "avail not"; writing avails—not in the totalistic fashion in which one may dream of something "availing" with regard to one's desire, but in its own peculiar, partial, liminal, uncanny terms.

WHAT *IS* "faced" in "Sun-Down Poem" is the prevailing cultural condition that desire cannot simply be transported back to some point anterior to the formation of the axis of castration along which it moves. If desire must always be "crossed," divided from/against itself in order to constitute desire in oedipal culture, then it is an error to imagine, as the 1855 *Leaves of Grass* does, that desire can circulate in uncrossed, undifferentiated, unproblematically "fluid" form. Rather than imagining himself simply immersed with his specular doubles in the "Floodtide" he "watch[es]," as he might have in the 1855 *Leaves of Grass*, Whitman "sternly deferred" the assumption of a "fluid" state of sociality in "Sun-Down Poem" in the manner characteristic of the 1856 edition. Complete "fluid" passage "from shore to shore," effortlessly achieved at numerous points in the 1855 edition (for example, in the Preface, where "the long Atlantic coast stretches longer and the Pacific coast stretches longer" and the "bard" "easily stretches with them," p. iv), is similarly deferred. Even when the speaker of "Sun-Down Poem" has been commonly taken by readers to be claiming to engage in direct reciprocal gazing with another person who is immediately present to him, a close look at the lines reveals that a more complicated, highly mediated kind of interaction is being represented:

> What is more subtle than this which ties me to the woman or
>   man that looks in my face?
> Which fuses me into you now, and pours my meaning into you.
>   (lines 96–97)

The speaker may engage in direct gazing with other persons "outside" the space of the poem, but he does not do it here or elsewhere *in* the poem. In these lines he only gestures toward the "subtle" bond that a mutual gaze may engender between persons physically present to each other, claiming as he does so that the dynamics of this bond are acting on the reader as he or she reads these lines, "fus[ing]" the poet into the reader, "and pour[ing] [his] meaning into" the reader. The gaze "exchanged" across these lines between present author (as he writes them) and absent reader, or absent author and present reader (as he or she reads them), is as close as the poet of the second edition seems to be willing to come to claiming that his writing is capable of producing "fluidity" ("fus[ing] and "pour[ing]") between himself and his reader(s).

Rather than merely reproducing the untroubled gaze that the subject might have exchanged with a specular double in the poetry of the first edition, "Sun-Down Poem" provides a useful locus for exploring the ways in which the text represents the "crossing" of these gazes:

> [I too] looked toward the lower bay to notice the arriving
>   ships,
> Saw their approach, saw aboard those that were near me,
> Saw the white sails of schooners and sloops, saw the ships at
>   anchor,
> The sailors at work in the rigging or out astride the spars,
> The round masts, the swinging motion of the hulls, the slender
>   serpentine pennants,
> The large and small steamers in motion, the pilots in their
>   pilot-houses,
> The white wake left by the passage, the quick tremulous whirl
>   of the wheels,
> The flags of all nations, the falling of them at sun-set,
> The scallop-edged waves in the twilight, the ladled cups, the
>   frolicsome crests and glistening,
> The stretch afar growing dimmer and dimmer, the gray walls of
>   the granite store-houses by the docks,
> On the river the shadowy group, the big steam-tug closely
>   flanked on each side by the barges—the hay-boat, the
>   belated lighter,
> On the neighboring shore the fires from the foundry chimneys
>   burning high and glaringly into the night,

> Casting their flicker of black, contrasted with wild red and
> yellow light, over the tops of houses, and down into the
> clefts of the streets.   (lines 36–48)

This passage has often been treated as a virtuosic set piece in its
own right, a luminist word-painting to challenge comparison not only
with contemporaneous literary practice but with the work of visual
artists like Fitz Hugh Lane and John F. Kensett.[21] What I want to
emphasize about the passage is not its merits as a discrete lyric but, on
the contrary, the thoroughgoing continuity with which it participates
in the figurations of various aspects of the oedipal conflict common to
the rest of the 1856 edition. This passage begins (at lines 27–28) by
inviting the reader to assume the subject-position of the primal scene,
"watch[ing]" an indeterminate number of "oscillating . . . bodies"
"floating" before the viewer. Rather than being drawn into participation in the scene as the reader might have been in the 1855 edition,
the observing subject/spectator remains an observer/voyeur in this representative 1856 passage. Here as elsewhere in the 1856 edition,
what is represented as being striking about this vision is the prominence of some body parts and the obscurity of others ("I saw how the
glistening yellow lit up parts of their bodies, and left the rest in strong
shadow," line 29).

Characteristically, with the looming into sight of a group of workingmen ("sailors at work in the rigging") midway through the passage,
the vision represented to this point in the text becomes transformed
into another spectacle of phallicized shapes in a state of frenetic and
"fluid" motion:

> The round masts, the swinging motion of the hulls, the slender
> serpentine pennants,
> The large and small steamers in motion, the pilots in their
> pilot-houses,
> The white wake left by the passage, the quick tremulous whirl
> of the wheels,
> The flags of all nations, the falling of them at sun-set,
> The scallop-edged waves in the twilight, the ladled cups, the
> frolicsome crests and glistening . . . .

Here we see restaged once again the frolics of "the greatest poet" of
the 1855 Preface with the (male) bodies of waters who are his "fluid"

reflections. What is different about this version from the representation of the "fluid" revels of the 1855 Preface is not only that the speaker/subject remains outside the "fluid" circle but also that this later one is represented as coming to an end, under the aegis of "falling" political standards: "The flags of all nations," which are significantly said to "fall[ ] . . . at sun-set," the time assigned to political martyrdoms and oedipal ghost-sightings in the 1856 text. In the following section I discuss a way of representing the landscape which modifies the intense and rigid oedipality of scenes like this one in "Sun-Down Poem."

IN THE second edition of *Leaves of Grass*, "keep[ing] vista" means habitually taking the panoramic overview, of time, space, or persons. This activity takes the crucial place in the textual dynamic of this edition which specularity played in the 1855 *Leaves*. Critical attention to the propensity of the major 1856 poems for taking "long views" has tended to take the form of critiquing this propensity as a significant aspect of Whitman's "catalog" technique. In my discussion of these common critical attitudes, I want to interrogate the formalist bias in some of his most influential critics' notions of what Whitman is about when he "strings together" poetic "lists" of occupations and localities supposedly occurring across the breadth of the United States. These critics have divided down the middle, as it were, as to whether Whitman is making a general political point (for "democracy" or "democratic inclusiveness")—Henry Nash Smith being perhaps the most influential proponent of this view—or whether he is indulging a psychological foible of his own, in the form of a desire to attribute only enough formal distinctness to "phenomena" to make them readily assimilable to his inappeasable self. Quentin Anderson, the leading proponent of this view, goes so far as to call Whitman's relationship to his world "psychotic."[22]

Critics following Henry Nash Smith's example have interpreted Whitman's catalogs as one of his chief ways of extending his program of making his writing more "inclusive" or "democratic," as it (according to these critics) celebrates without reservation the burgeoning of the population of the country and its massive and supposedly irresistible movement westward—a movement which had in 1850 been given the magniloquent name "Manifest Destiny" by Whitman's former editor from his tale-writing days of the 1840s, James L. O'Sullivan of the *Democratic Review*. In his chapter on Whitman in his 1950 study *Virgin Land: The American West as Symbol and Myth*, Smith placed Whitman's work directly in a "tradition" of American writing in justification of the country's relentless westward expansion; in the opening words of the chapter, Smith characterizes him as "the poet who gave final imaginative expression to the theme of manifest destiny," and, in the closing words of the chapter, he salutes him—in a burst of post–World War II patriotic fervor—for maintaining that "intrepid idealism that so triumphantly enabled [him] to see in the march of the pioneer army a prelude to peace and the brotherhood of nations."[23]

Anderson's "psychological" theory that the catalogs are Whitman's means of momentarily constituting in language and then quickly "dissolving" and absorbing the external or objective world into his "self" does not provide a genuine alternative to Smith's imperialistic one. In fact, taken together, the "ideal" (that is, unquestioningly imperialistic) politics that Smith attributes to Whitman and the pathological personal psychology with which Anderson endows him constitute a smoothly functioning "critical" rationale for the practice of taking Whitman's work as an untroubled celebration and justification of the history of American "expansion" while dismissing the poet himself as having been a deficient or inadequate person. In considering Whitman's use of catalogs in "Broad-Axe" and other 1856 poems, I am attempting to break down the false dichotomy that Whitman criticism has tended to maintain between "political" and "psychological" categories of explanation. Rather than interpreting Whitman's catalogs either as untroubled celebrations of American expansionism (as Smith and others have done) or as symptoms of a "pathological" need on Whitman's part to use his writing to drain the social world of any significance that does not contribute to his allegedly grandiose sense of "self," I hope to demonstrate that the representations Whitman makes of the various bodies (men's, women's, the American landscape) and their respective parts effectively repudiate the notion that the political and the psychological constitute discrete categories in his writing. In considering both the strong disaffection from prevailing political conditions which the 1856 poems register, and the complex responses to various bodies and their respective parts which the same poems no less frequently and powerfully register, I am relating these representations to their grounds, which I believe in both cases are to be found in particular configurations of the landscape as an undecidably gendered body.

Rather than interpreting Whitman's landscape vista according to the intensely oedipal (and imperialistic) model found in work like Smith's, as being simply a phantasmatic female virgin inviting and accepting (white-) male possession and domination, or according to the masturbatory model advanced by Anderson and others, in which the landscape (like other aspects of the "external world") is called up only in order to be mentally annihilated in moments of private self-indulgence and self-aggrandizement, I read the kinds of representations of landscapes which are foregrounded in the second edition as attempts to figure the body of the American landscape as one of undecidable gender. Such moments in the second edition tend to counter those other parts of the text where hyperphallic masculinity is represented as dominating a virginal femininity excluded from the circuits of desire. Critics like Smith take such intensely oedipal moments for the whole text, no doubt because making such a tendentious reading of a politically and sexually adversary writer like Whitman is the only way of recuperating his work for the disciplinary discourses of American militarism—a politics that *Leaves of Grass* powerfully opposes. It is in such moments of gender rendered indeterminate (not "androgynous" or "hermaphroditic," but genuinely undecidable, *either* male or female) that the 1856 text exceeds both the thoroughly oedipalizing perspective to which critics like Smith would restrict its meanings *and* the equally oedipalizing perspective which causes Anderson to reduce its complex representations of the relations between sexualities and power to masturbation fantasies.

Whitman's practice in the 1856 edition with respect to the gender of the body of the landscape represents a significant departure from his 1855 practice, where the vistas he describes are determinately and explicitly "Landscapes projected masculine full-sized and golden" ("I celebrate myself," p. 33). Although there are catalogs both of persons and of material objects in the 1855 *Leaves*, there are no catalogs of the American countryside or landscape of the kind of which there are a number in the second edition (for example, the landscape of "[s]uch gliding wonders" that opens "Poem of Salutation"/"Salut au Monde!";

the passage from "Poem of Many In One"/"By Blue Ontario's Shore"
that I shall discuss below)—except for a few in the 1855 Preface.
There, as in the poetry of that edition, the landscape is explicitly
figured as male; when the poet interacts with it, and when he is even
said to "incarnate" it (p. iv), these interactions are represented as
being the frolics of "the greatest poet" with his specular homotypes in
the "fluid" medium of the text:

> His spirit responds to his country's spirit....he incarnates its
> geography and natural life and rivers and lakes. Mississippi
> with annual freshets and changing chutes, Missouri and
> Columbia and Ohio and Saint Lawrence with the falls and
> the beautiful masculine Hudson, do not embouchure where
> they spend themselves more than they embouchure into
> him. . . . When the long Atlantic coast stretches longer and
> the Pacific coast stretches longer he easily stretches with
> them north or south.   (p. iv)

In the 1856 "Poem of Many In One," into which much of the 1855
Preface was intercalated when Whitman dropped it from *Leaves of
Grass* in its original form, there is a partial reversal of this way of
representing poet and landscape as both male. In addition to the
various examples of figures of masculine camaraderie between poet and
nature I have previously adduced (and to which I shall momentarily
return), there is in the 1855 Preface a striking example of a figure
whose gender at a crucial point in the text is "veered away from,"
rather than rendered genuinely indeterminate. This is the figure of the
"land" whom the poet is said to "attract . . . body and soul to himself
and hang on its neck with incomparable love and plunge his semitic
muscle into its merits and demerits" (p. xi). This is the moment in
the 1855 text when the contradiction between the poet-subject's
infantile status ("hang on its neck") and his phallic status ("plunge his
semitic muscle into it[ ]") reaches its tensest and most evident point.
It veers away into bathos ("into its merits and demerits") at the moment in the 1855 text when the gender of the body of the poet's
"land" is about to be, but never is, specified—as it would be by the
identification of the site and mode of penetration to which the poet
supposedly subjects the body of the "land."

This becomes a pivotal moment in the 1856 text's figuration of the

undecidable gender of the "land's" body. Here these lines are incorporated into a passage in "Poem of Many In One" where they are combined with a pair of other key passages from the 1855 Preface (those
which concern the poet's interactions with the land's bodies of waters,
and its coastlines, quoted above). I take this 1856 revision as a representative example of the rendering undecidable of the gender of
the body of the "land" and its parts that partially reinflects the sexual-
political program of the *Leaves of Grass* project:

> Attracting it body and soul to himself, hanging on its neck
>   with incomparable love,
> Plunging his semitic muscle into its merits and demerits,
> Making its geography, cities, beginnings, events, glories,
>   defections, diversities, vocal in him,
> Making its rivers, lakes, bays, embouchure in him,
> Mississippi with yearly freshets and changing chutes, Missouri,
>   Columbia, Ohio, St. Lawrence, Hudson, spending
>   themselves lovingly in him,
> . . . .
> If the Atlantic coast stretch, or the Pacific coast stretch, he
>   stretching with them north or south,
> Spanning between them east and west, and touching whatever
>   is between them . . . .   (lines 72–78)

Two kinds of actions which are kept pages apart in the 1855 Preface
are brought together in this 1856 revision of those passages: the poet's
penetration of the body of the land, and, in reverse sexual action, the
penetration of the poet's body by the land's bodies of water.

Corresponding with this making the "land's" gender undecidable in
these lines is a self-censoring gesture that further destabilizes the determinate gendering of poet and landscape in the 1855 edition. This
gesture occurs in Whitman's revision of the description of the waters
"spending themselves lovingly in" the body of the poet: the Hudson
River has in 1856 been shorn of the explicitly male-homoerotic 1855
adjectives "beautiful masculine" (perhaps we witness the return of this
particular "repressed" in the 1856 text in the figure of "the beautiful
nocturnal son," Bacchus, in "Poem of Salutation"), and in the "beauty
of [the] wood-boys and wood-men" in "Broad-Axe Poem"). I take this
as yet another instance of the marked tendency of the second edition

to render indeterminate the gender of the "land-bodies" it represents in order to explore nonoedipal modes of conjunction between them and the bodies of the author and the reader(s), modes of relation other than those of patriarchal domination. The seductive component of Whitman's rhetoric in *Leaves of Grass* has been much remarked in recent years, often unfavorably. Even if one thinks that in his seductive appeals to the reader Whitman assumes a posture of patriarchal dominance, which I do not, one should not fail to see that the poet-speaker of *Leaves of Grass* assumes not just one but a whole variety of sexual attitudes toward the text and toward the reader. The de-gendering of the American landscape that he initiates in the second edition provides an important example of the ways in which Whitman complicates his characteristically sexualized metaphors for his relationship both to "the land"—the physical landscape *and* the nation—and to the reader, his fellow inhabitant of the land. Given the complex mediation of corporeality in the second edition and afterwards through such ambiguously gendered figures as that of the body of the landscape, it is highly reductive to interpret the poet-speaker's role in *Leaves of Grass* as simply that of a sexually importunate male.

The strategic advantages for Whitman of keeping the gender of the body of the landscape undecidable are considerable. The principal one is that it obviates the need for the text to specify perhaps the principal thing it is prohibited from specifying: that the desire it represents includes the desire of one male (body) for another. A less obvious but (I think) no less significant advantage of this body's being of undecidable gender is that such a condition opens up the possibility of relations beyond those of oedipalized male homosexuality, the only form in which male-male desire can officially be conceived, according to the oedipal code prevailing in Whitman's culture. Male-homoerotic desire and behavior in the United States in the second half of the nineteenth century were made to conform with the culture's violent oedipalizations of other forms of sexual desire and behavior. In the case of desire between males, rape was the model: conceptions of male-male sexual behavior as necessarily taking the form of painful, punitive, and humiliating forms of sexuality were the only conceptions the culture publicly recognized. The notion that one man's (or a group of men's) forcing sex on another to demonstrate the inferiority of the "passive" man and to punish or humiliate him is the ordinary, even the inevitable, form male-homosexual behavior takes is a fundamental one impelling the elaborate disciplinary discourses of male-male relations which pervade Whitman's culture. The impulse to "think otherwise," and to think not only homoerotic desire but other kinds of desire otherwise than in the rigid forms into which they have been cast, otherwise than in forms compatible with the workings of its oedipal law, informs Whitman's representations of the undecidably gendered bodies of "the land" in the second edition. Thinking otherwise in the context of this edition amounts to a partial return to the previous edition's ideals of fusion, this time cast in another, highly unspecified register, rather than in the form of "fluidity."

I want to insist in this connection that revisionary gestures in the second edition such as Whitman's cancellation of the words "beautiful masculine" in this passage are not simply acts of self-censorship, that is, they do not only serve the purpose of concealing or at least obscuring to some degree the male-homoerotic meanings of his writing. An adjectival phrase like "beautiful masculine," after all, carries relatively little erotic weight in comparison with the imaginary orgiastic exchanges that constitute the passage: the "[a]ttracting" of the body of the "land" to the poet, his "hanging on its neck" and "[p]lunging his semitic muscle into it[ ]," his "[m]aking its rivers . . . embouchure in him," the five rivers named "spending themselves lovingly in him," and so forth. Passages like this one remain redolently male-homoerotic for the reader who does not refuse to perceive such meanings, but with the excision of superfluous signs that all the figures involved are "masculine," such passages extend throughout the text the broadening of its erotic and sexual-political scope which Whitman began in that unique moment in the 1855 text when he incorporated the bodies of the woman-observer and the male speaker-observer into the composite and indeterminately gendered figure of "the twenty-ninth bather."

The high price (so to speak) of producing this figure of an erotically active agent of undecidable gender in the text of the first edition is the rendering of the figure—"the twenty-ninth bather "—invisible. In revisions like the one he makes for the second edition of what had been in the 1855 Preface simply an imaginary all-male swimming-hole idyll, Whitman continues the project of making male-homosexual desire at least liminally visible while bringing other kinds—including feminine desire—into visibility in his writing.

There are, finally, two ways of reading Whitman's ideas in the second edition of *Leaves of Grass* about the inevitability of desire's taking oedipalized forms. A text like "Sun-Down Poem" powerfully suggests that there is a "long view" to be taken of desire and connection between persons which is capable of escaping oedipalization. Whitman's revisions of parts of the 1855 Preface in the 1856 "Poem of Many In One" suggest a somewhat different conclusion: that as a desire approaches the limit of escaping oedipalization, it and its object rapidly recede from visibility. It is to this range of vanishing points that the most characteristic poetry of the second edition keeps returning us, inviting its readers to try to imagine something of which it can give no stable or clear description: desire detached from the culture's dominant modes of structuring it that does not cease to be desire.

From the Second (1856) Edition to the Third (1860)

The irruption of the oedipal—the pervasive and oppressive canalization of desire which structures the fundamental forms in which our culture and its major antecedent cultures have conceived difference, self-difference, and sexual difference—is most marked in the second edition of *Leaves of Grass* in the recurring scenes of the martyrdom of the son in the 1856 poems. These are explicit in the "sunset-scaffold-martyrs" passage of "Broad-Axe Poem," and powerfully implicit (or so I have argued) in the sunset setting of "Sun-Down Poem." The third and final one of these 1856 scenes I want to consider occurs in "Poem of Salutation," at a point when the poet pauses in the transit of celebration he is making around the globe to consider a group of temples and the martyrdoms that inaugurated the respective cults of a series of what one might call "dead-god bodies" ("I see the temples of the deaths of the bodies of gods," line 96):

> I see Christ once more eating the bread of his last supper in the
>   midst of youths and old persons,
> I see where the strong divine young man, the Hercules toil'd
>   faithfully and long and then died,
> I see the place of the innocent rich life and hapless fate of the
>   beautiful nocturnal son, the full-limbed Bacchus,
> I see Kneph, blooming, dressed in blue, with the crown of
>   feathers on his head . . . .   (lines 97–100)

Here the text emphasizes the pathos and glamour of the son-martyr, ranging in order to do so from the familiar (the Last Supper) to the exotic and more explicitly male-homoerotic ("the beautiful nocturnal son, the full-limbed Bacchus"; blue-robed, "blooming," feather-crowned Kneph). The culminating fifth line of this passage eschews the exoticism and descriptive superabundance of the lines which immediately precede it, rendering the dying speech of one of these martyr-figures in a run-on verse-paragraph of strikingly simple, predominantly monosyllabic, language:

> I see Hermes, unsuspected, dying, well-beloved, saying to the people, Do not weep for me, this is not my true country, I have lived banished from my true country, I now go back there, I return to the celestial sphere where every one goes in his turn.   (line 101)

Only the relatively elaborate phrase "celestial sphere" links the diction and tone of this long line with the lines preceding it. Whitman was fully capable of describing representations of intense emotion in the face of death in highly melodramatic and physically violent terms, as when he wrote in 1851 of the Italian tenor Bettini's performance in Donizetti's *La Favorita:* "The strains of death, too, come plaintively from his lips. Never before did you hear such a wonderful gushing sorrow, poured forth like ebbing blood, from a murdered heart."[24] The statement the martyred young "god-body" Hermes makes to "the people" is not a "performance" of martyrdom like Bettini's, words and blood "gushing" out together. It is not a "religious" message at all, but a counsel of complete political apostasy. Rather than supporting the notion that texts like "Poem of Salutation" are untroubled in both their "patriotism" and their "philanthropic" internationalism/ imperialism, writing of Whitman's like the dying speech of "Hermes" to "the people" points the reader to places in those Whitman texts where the "land," the nation, cannot be recuperated in the figure of a body of undecidable gender, and the poet can imagine no fate for himself and for others like himself except that of a martyred Oedipus.

Besides being highly congruent with the oedipal thematics of the second edition, the representation of scenes of martyrdom of young male gods (Christ, Hercules, Bacchus, Kneph, Hermes) in "Poem of

Salutation" and other representative texts of the 1856 *Leaves of Grass* leads directly into the quite different although by no means unrelated thematics of the third (1860) edition, in which Whitman's ambitions to "inaugurate a Religion" ("Proto-Leaf," 1860 ed., p. 11) and to make *Leaves of Grass* its scripture come to the fore.

4

The Politics of Nature and the Decomposition of God: "The Great Construction of the New Bible" in the Third (1860) Edition of *Leaves of Grass*

> All you are doing and saying is to America
>   dangled mirages,
> You have not learned of Nature—of the politics of
>   Nature. . . .
>
>   —Whitman, "To a President" (1860)

"The New Bible"

Soon after the publication of the second edition of *Leaves of Grass*, Whitman began to record what appear to have been new ideas about the nature of the book he was gradually producing. In a manuscript note dated June 1857 in his own hand, he writes: "The Great Construction of the New Bible. Not to be diverted from the principal object—the main life work—the Three Hundred and Sixty-five.—It ought to be ready in 1859."[1] In the same month, Whitman wrote a letter to Sarah Tyndale—a Philadelphia abolitionist who had accompanied Thoreau and Bronson Alcott on their famous visit to him in the summer of 1856—in which he says: "I wish now to bring out a third edition—I have now *a hundred* poems ready (the last edition had thirty-two)—and shall endeavor to make an arrangement with some publisher here to take the plates from F. & W. [Fowler & Wells] and make the additions needed, and so bring out the third edition."[2]

Taken together, these two passages suggest that by June 1857, around the time he might reasonably have been expected to be publishing a third edition (the first two had appeared in July 1855 and September 1856), Whitman began to think of his *Leaves of Grass* project in two quite different ways. On the one hand, he planned simply to expand the second edition with a third annual edition containing the approximately sixty-eight new poems he apparently had written in the second half of 1856 and the first half of 1857. On the other, he had another plan that interfered with this short-term plan: the gradual elaboration of the poems he was producing into a "New Bible," a collection of *Leaves* that would within a few years amount to the great annular number of 365. Annularity, the making of a great ring or cycle of poems that would have the status of scriptural texts, replaced annuality as Whitman's ideal mode of production for his project around the time of the appearance of the second edition (1856). As 1858 and 1859 passed, Whitman did not fulfill his extremely ambitious plan of continuing to produce new work in each of those years at the extraordinary rate he had achieved in 1857, when he wrote approximately a hundred new poems. When the third *Leaves* did appear in 1860, it contained about a hundred and fifty poems, less than half the number Whitman had envisioned for the "New Bible" he was constructing. Nevertheless, the scriptural ambitions he had first articulated for his project in 1857 account for some of the most significant differences between the 1860 *Leaves* and its two predecessor-editions. [3]

In an anonymous article published in the *Saturday Press*, a New York literary journal, a few months before the appearance of the third edition, Whitman wrote, "We are able to declare that there will . . . soon crop out the true 'Leaves of Grass,' the fuller-grown work of which the former two issues were the inchoates." He goes on to say:

> Those former issues, published by the author himself in little pittance-editions, on trial, have just dropped the book enough to ripple the inner first-circles of literary agitation, in immediate contact with it. The outer, vast, extending, and ever-wider-extending circles of the general supply, perusal, and discussion of such a work, have still to come. The market needs to-day to be supplied—the great West especially—with copious thousands of copies.
> Indeed, "Leaves of Grass" has not yet been really published at all. [4]

The highly invidious terms in which Whitman here contrasts the forthcoming third edition with its two predecessors ("inchoates," "little pittance-editions," "not . . . really published") I take as an indication of a desire on his part to claim a kind of primacy for the third edition which he now wants to deny to the two previous editions, by belatedly deciding that the earlier editions were more tentative ("published . . . on trial") and "inchoate[ ]" projects than they actually had been.

Whitman straightforwardly announces in the new introductory poem of the 1860 edition that he is claiming a scriptural authority for the third *Leaves* which he has not claimed for the previous editions, or which he has at least not hitherto articulated explicitly: "I too . . . inaugurate a Religion" ("Proto-Leaf," 1860 ed., p. 11).[5] What kind of scripture this text is and what kind of religion it inscribes are the chief questions I want to consider in this chapter. I intend to explore the way in which the third edition attempts to conciliate the extremes of the first two by means of Whitman's appropriation and thoroughgoing revision of Christian and stoic doctrines of reality and corporeality. I will illustrate the change with an analysis of the 1860 poem "Leaves of Grass. 1" (later retitled "As I Ebb'd with the Ocean of Life") and then offer a psychoanalytic framework for understanding the change. Finally, I will consider the consequences of this change for the "Calamus" poems, the most significant new texts in the third edition besides the three "Paumanok" poems: "Proto-Leaf" (later "Starting from Paumanok"), "Leaves of Grass. 1," and "A Word Out of the Sea" (later "Out of the Cradle Endlessly Rocking").

Substantiating Corpo/reality: Typologies of the Body in the Third *Leaves of Grass*

In his revision of Christian tradition in the "New Bible" of the third edition, Whitman appropriates the term "type" and redefines the practice of typology in order to reconceive the idea of the self as "fluid," without either overvaluing the idea of "fluidity," as he had in the first edition, or making it seem inextricable from oedipalization, as he had in the second. The subject represented in "Leaves of Grass. 1"/"As I Ebb'd" speaks of "wend[ing] the shores" of Long Island "seeking types," thinking "the old thought of likenesses" or correspondences between natural objects and their ostensible spiritual meanings (p. 196).[6] Besides the typological meaning of "type," two other senses of the term are significantly in play in the "Paumanok" poems of the 1860 edition. The first of these is the sense the word had in mid-nineteenth-century evolutionary theory, "a biological species or genus"; after Lyall's extremely influential *Geology* of 1830, the term in this sense was most widely disseminated in discourses of how various biological "types" had been and remained subject to extinction as part of the evolutionary process.[7] The other significant sense in which "type" occurs in the 1860 *Leaves* is to mean printer's type. Whitman takes "type" as printer's type to provide the primary model in this edition for the ways in which what he calls the "real body" possesses "substance"; he announces this in a crucial passage in the text's introductory poem, the first of the "Paumanok" poems, "Proto-Leaf" ("Starting from Paumanok"). "Type" in the senses of both "natural object embodying spiritual meaning" and "biological class or genus subject to extinction" is foregrounded in the second of the "Paumanok" poems, "Leaves of Grass. 1"/"As I Ebb'd with the Ocean of Life." Bringing these disparate senses of the term into play in these key passages of the third edition, Whitman redefines typological practice in a way that ceases to privilege a transcendent, divine, spiritual realm of alleged fulfillment and plenitude ("substance") over against an immanent, human, material or corporeal realm which is mere promissory "shadow." Rather, he puts forward "type" in the sense of "print" or "text" as a model for what he in this edition calls "indifference," which is not a refusal to recognize difference (as in the "fluidity" of the first edition), but a commitment to recognizing difference without overestimating its insurmountability (as the second edition had).

"Shadow" and "substance" have been the most frequently employed pair of terms in typological tradition to denote type—"shadow," the foreshadowing or promissory person or event—and antitype—"substance," the person or event which fulfills the type's promise.[8] The "politics of nature" and the new "Religion" based on it which Whitman promulgates in the third edition are designed to give *Leaves of Grass* more substance than the self-gratifying fantasy of limitless self-dissemination which unsympathetic readers—apparently including, in some moods, the poet himself—had felt was informing the poetry of 1855 and 1856. Without wishing to claim primacy for the third edition, as Whitman did at the time of its appearance and as a number of critics—Roy Harvey Pearce, most influentially—have done since,

I do wish to argue that the 1860 *Leaves* is substantially different in some ways from the two earlier editions. Indeed, it is the version of the text in which the question of "substance" (a key term in the 1860 volume) is most intensively explored and thematized.[9] Whitman attempts in the third edition to substantiate the claims of the *Leaves of Grass* project about the necessity of the dominant culture's revising upward its generally low valuation of the corporeal and natural realms, especially as these converge on the condition of human bodiliness, by launching a more comprehensive critique of prevailing notions of body-soul relations than he has previously done. The 1860 *Leaves* continually foregrounds questions of how bodies can and cannot be said to be natural phenomena, and, similarly, in what senses they can and cannot be said to be integral phenomena. How can the body be divided or penetrated, and what can be separated from it, without radically altering its nature or its place(s) in nature? The imaginary specular unity of the (male) body that informs the 1855 edition and the oedipalized notion of irremediable sexual difference that informs the 1856 edition are put to the test in the 1860 one, which ceases to privilege notions of physical integrity over competing notions of physical disintegration and decomposition, but which at the same time declines to figure conditions of bodily disintegration simply as castration.

Whitman appropriates one of his primary means for carrying out his reconceptualization of the body in the third edition from the Christian hermeneutical tradition of typology. He does so in order to redefine in what senses the self and the body from which it proceeds are "real"—rather than simply in what senses they are "fluid," as he had represented them as being (at least for males) in the first edition; or in what senses they are not "fluid," as he had tried to work out in the second edition. As I mentioned earlier, the term "type" itself is crucial in this process, for Whitman uses it to denote both printer's type and the "types" of typological tradition—an important prior way of simultaneously reading out of "both God's books," the scriptures and Nature, or interpreting "natural" phenomena as signs of spiritual realities, especially as this had been practiced in the New World by Jonathan Edwards and subsequent typologists.[10]

Following long-standing practice, Samuel Mather, in his *Figures and Types of the Old Testament* (1683), the most widely disseminated of

American Puritan typology manuals, contrasts shadowy *"Mosaical Ceremonies"* with *"Christ* the Body and Substance."[11] Christian tradition associates both "Body" *and* "Substance" with the Godhead, intensively so with the Second Person of the Trinity. It is this that Whitman appropriates for the human self in his "New Bible" of 1860. In it, the three new "Paumanok" poems as well as the new "Calamus" section focus their inquiry about the naturalness, integrity, and reality of human bodiliness around the central question of what is *substantial* about the body and its experiences of desire and death, its own and others'. Christian doctrine had traditionally elaborated a conception of the human body (in contrast with the divine, conjoint "Body and Substance" of the Godhead) which emphasized the "fallen" materiality of the human body at the same time that it relegated the body and its desires to an ontological status of relative insubstantiality in comparison with the "true" substantiality or spirituality of the human soul. In other words, "true" substance is spiritual, and consequently intrinsic to the soul but only extrinsic to the body.

In addition to Christian typological tradition, Whitman drew heavily on a second philosophical system in his attempt in the third edition to construct a conception of the "real body" which would repudiate and replace Christian devaluations of the human body in favor of the soul—namely, a set of classical, specifically stoic and epicurean, doctrines of reality and corporeality. Although critical attention to the relation of *Leaves of Grass* to stoic discourse has been largely nugatory—studies have been limited almost entirely to anecdotal accounts of Whitman's fondness for reading a few of the Stoics (Epictetus and Marcus Aurelius) and to scattered examples of the "influence" on Whitman's writing of the stray line from these authors—the body of basic stoic doctrine is deeply consonant with the aims of the *Leaves of Grass* project in general and especially of the "New Bible" of the third edition because of the double impulse they share toward, on the one hand, naturalist and, on the other, religious or post-religious categories of explanation of reality and corporeality.[12] Stoicism and, as Whitman might call it, its "younger brother," epicureanism, base their respective critiques of dominant social morality on a renovated physics or theory of nature which is essentially atomistic and radically corporealist—that is, insistent that soul is at most equal, not superior, to body; that souls no less than bodies are corporeal entities; that everything real, with a few significant exceptions (for example, the void) is corporeal; and that the atomic composition of bodily materiality is what fundamentally links all bodies (including the "bodies of souls") to each other and to the rest of nature. This radical corporealism is the conceptual basis of much stoic and stoic-influenced philosophy. "No idea is more deeply ingrained in Stoic philosophy than the conviction that everything real is corporeal," begins one historical account of stoic thought. "According to the Stoics, the only things that really exist are material bodies."[13] The Stoics extend the idea of corporeality far beyond ordinary bounds: for them, virtues, vices, qualities in general, and even the soul itself are all corporeal entities. The early Stoic Chrysippus's influential philosophical proof of the corporeality of the soul is representative of much subsequent stoic discourse in its concern with the possibilities of conjunction and separability between bodies: "Death is the separation of soul from body. Nothing incorporeal is separated from the corporeal, for nothing incorporeal is conjoined with the corporeal. The soul is joined to and is separated from the body. Therefore the soul is corporeal."[14] The terms and categories of this and many similar stoic and epicurean discourses of corporeal conjunctions and disjunctions are thoroughly compatible with Whitman's concern, in the foreground of the third edition, with the status of bodies as natural, integral, "substantial" phenomena.

Whitman inscribes his new scripture and his revisionary notions of the relations of body, nature, and materiality in general to soul and to "substance" in a series of crucial passages in the 1860 text. The following lines from "Proto-Leaf" provide a good example of the new disposition of such matters as body, soul, "substance," and "type" in the writing new to this edition:

> Was somebody asking to see the Soul?
> See! your own shape and countenance—persons, substances,
>   beasts, the trees, the running rivers, the rocks and sands.
>
> All hold spiritual joys, and afterward loosen them,
> How can the real body ever die, and be buried?
>
> Of your real body, and any man's or woman's real body, item
>   for item, it will elude the hands of the corpse-cleaners, and
>   pass to fitting spheres, carrying what has accrued to it from
>   the moment of birth to the moment of death.

> Not the types set up by the printer return their impression, the
> meaning, the main concern, any more than a man's
> substance and life, or a woman's substance and life, return in
> the body and the Soul, indifferently before death and after
> death.   (1860 ed., p. 16)

It is an index of the radical character of Whitman's revision of religious
tradition in the 1860 edition that in a passage like this one he attributes spiritual prestige to printing technology—not to the "types" of
Christian typological tradition but to sheer modern typography, "the
types set up by the printer" (by himself, among many others, as a boy
and youth). He takes printer's type as his model for the nontranscendent kind of "substance" he attributes to the "real body." For him, the
"real body" is the substantial component of all material entities ("persons, . . . beasts, the trees," and so on), the part which "hold[s] . . .
and afterward loosen[s]" "spiritual joys." It is not simply identical with
the "material" body, but neither is it simply identical with the "soul,"
the traditional repository of all "spiritual joys," according to Christian
theology, and the superior, immortal spiritual entity that for a time
animates the inferior, mortal, material "clay" of the body. But, as this
passage from "Proto-Leaf" goes on to say, "the body includes and is
the meaning, the main concern—and includes and is the Soul" (p.
17) in a way that the soul cannot be said to "include" the body. Rather
than simply and literally being "alive" for some time and then definitively "dead" in the way the "material" body may be said to be, this
"real body" is not delimited by literal death but participates in an
open-ended process of "hold[ing]" and "loosen[ing]," embodying and
dispersing, "substance" of an indeterminate variety of kinds.

In his redefinitions of "real body" and "substance" in the third edition Whitman could not simply revive stoic and epicurean attitudes
and beliefs as "pagan values" over against Christian ones, as some of
his critics have maintained he did, because owing to the extensive
assimilation of stoic and epicurean techniques of self-examination and
self-discipline into the practice of the early church, these overlap with
Christian moral doctrine at many points, rather than providing a clear-
cut alternative to Christian tradition.[15] Anyone who refuses, as Whitman did, to minimize the significance of historical and political factors
in determining the meaning of writing is keenly aware that the physics

or philosophy of a remote period and place cannot simply be "revived," but have to be thoroughly reinscribed in relation to new circumstances. Hence Whitman's statement in the 1860 edition that it is the role of "These States" not simply to revive but also to "justify"— to place in new right relations with religion and politics—"the antique." These terms occur in "Proto-Leaf": "In the name of These States, shall I scorn the antique? / Why These are the children of the antique, to justify it" (1860 ed., p. 9).

Although it may not be possible to say exactly what the "real body" as Whitman redefines it in the 1860 edition is, or how it performs its function of mediating the realms of materiality and immateriality, that text gives us significant terms for understanding what it means. The conception of the "real body" in the passage quoted above from "Proto-Leaf" as elsewhere in the poetry of 1860 bridges a group of disjunctive, dualistic categories—body/soul, life/afterlife, matter/spirit, shape/substance—but more through assertion than demonstration. "Real body" is the text's name for the power the person holds in his or her body to override the culture's systematic and categorical devaluations of bodiliness, devaluations which Whitman attempts to recuperate in this edition in the context of a new politics and religion of nature. The text is designed to impel readers to rediscover and reclaim their own "real bodies," first in the text and then in themselves, and thereby to undo to some degree the culture's devaluations of bodiliness.

Although Whitman leaves much unsaid about the function of the "real body," in the last line of the passage quoted above he provides a rich figure for the process the "real body" carries out: "the types set up by the printer [which] return their impression, the meaning, the main concern . . . indifferently." One significant thing this tells us about the power of the "real body" is that it is recursive in the way printer's type is, capable of "return[ing] [its] impression . . . indifferently"—that is, without being impeded by the kinds of terminal horizons to which human bodies are subject, for example, illness or death. There is a significant revision in these lines of the way the analogy between the human body and print is figured from Whitman texts in which the author's passing through print in order to be disseminated to the reader is characterized as a "chill[ing]" and "poor[ ]" experience compared with that of contact with the reader ("I was chilled with the cold types and cylinder and wet paper between us. / I pass so poorly with papers and types....I must pass with the contact of bodies and souls" ["Come closer to me"]). In the 1860 text the printing process, rather than being used to figure a debilitating but unavoidable form of mediating authorial presence, becomes instead a primary figure for the recursive powers of (to compress Whitman's terms into a single phrase) "returning impressions indifferently" that distinguish the "real body" from sheer material corporeality or its converse.

In discovering the shared powers latent in the "real body," nature, democracy, and writing, the 1860 text discovers the categorical imperatives of the *Leaves of Grass* project. Whitman succinctly restates this discovery about politics, nature, the human body, and writing in a brief passage in the late (1881) essay, "Poetry To-Day in America—Shakspere—The Future":

> Not only is the human and artificial world we have establish'd in the West a radical departure from anything hitherto known—not only men and politics, and all that goes with them—but Nature itself, in the main sense, its construction, is different. The same old font of type, of course, but set up to a text never composed or issued before.[16]

The 1860 *Leaves of Grass* enacts and invites its readers to enact the radical perception that "real bodies," politics, nature, and written and printed texts are all *alike* insofar as they are all "construction[s]" which have been fundamentally revised in the New World and are still highly susceptible to revision, and, at the same time, all *different*—from each other, and, insofar as they are all "radical departure[s] from anything hitherto known," from themselves, from what they have traditionally been or been considered to be. To be sure, the material components of all these entities have not substantially changed— "[t]he same old font of type, of course"—but the respective "construction[s]" of "real bodies," New World politics, "Nature," and so on, are unprecedented—"set up to a text never composed or issued before."

In passages like the one from "Proto-Leaf" under discussion, Whitman strives to produce a set of terms for what he sees as certain unprecedented conditions for the existence of human bodies, nature, and "the real." In such passages, the third edition of *Leaves of Grass* becomes one of the first American texts to register the political interests in the mid-nineteenth-century United States attaching to practices which (to put this in a somewhat different way from my previous discussions of "fluid" versus "solid" corporeality) tended either to reify the body in the ways the predominant culture was then tending to do or to resist such reifications of the body. As Whitman had discovered, his initial notion of a (male) body capable of "fluidly" resisting being reified in the ways fostered by the culture's new disciplinary discourses of "purified" sexuality, of strenuous individualism, "self-reliance," and familial domesticity, had itself not been immune to reification—had, in fact, been reified to a considerable degree in the 1855 edition. His attempts to de-reify this "fluid," specular (male) body in the second edition by working it back through the oedipal system of division and difference predominant in his culture, though perhaps necessary from his point of view, had carried the process of representing bodies as standing in relations of irremediable difference to each other to an undesirable extreme. The body-politics of the 1860 *Leaves* falls neither entirely on one side nor on the other of the reification/de-reification processes; it explores the implications of both and finds ways of mediating them. Whitman's principal models for representing these processes are the phenomena of textuality and textual production as he sees them emerging from the intersection of familiar materiality in the form of printer's type ("same old font of type") with originary textual practice ("a text never composed or issued before").

The terms of this latter phrase are strikingly similar to Whitman's terms for *Leaves of Grass* ("not yet . . . *really* published at all"; my emphasis) on the eve of the appearance of the third edition, in his anonymous *Saturday Press* article about the status of the *Leaves of Grass* project in early 1860. According to Whitman, the publication of *Leaves of Grass* had not "really" happened until the third edition because it was only in producing that text that he first succeeded in elaborating his critique of the reification of the body in his culture by means of applying to prevailing conceptions of the body, and of its nature and "reality," the de-reifying powers of textuality of "returning impressions indifferently."

Taken together, the three terms of this phrase compose an epitome of sorts of the textual dynamics of the third edition. The powers which are attributed to the "real body" and to print constitute the third edition's primary strategy for mediating the "fluid" unity between (male) bodies posited in the first edition and the irremediable differences between bodies posited in the second. Identity and difference had been at base mutually exclusive possibilities in the first two editions; the third discovers ways of figuring identity and difference in dynamic contact with each other: the "impressions" which are "return[ed] . . . indifferently" in the poetry of the 1860 text are at different moments "impressions" of bodily identity, of difference, of identities within differences, and of differences within identities. Rather than simply meaning "no difference," "indifference" functions in this text as a power of transgressing the predominant boundaries of the culture while preserving those boundaries as a (negative) value for critique—instead of imaginarily eliding them out of existence, as the first edition tends to do, or overvaluating them as the "hard" or permanent foundations of culture, as the second edition does. I want now to consider the significance of the discovery of the power of "returning impression[s] indifferently" for one of the three new "Paumanok" poems, "Leaves of Grass. 1"/"As I Ebb'd with the Ocean of Life."

ON THE BEACH

The poem to which Whitman gave the title "As I Ebb'd with the Ocean of Life" in the 1881–82 edition of Leaves of Grass bore a series of different titles on earlier publications: "Bardic Symbols" in the April 1860 Atlantic Monthly, "Leaves of Grass. 1" in the (May) 1860 edition of Leaves, and "Elemental Drifts" in the 1867 edition. This last title derives from two lines which open the poem in all its appearances from 1860 to 1876, but which were canceled thereafter:

> Elemental drifts!
> O I wish I could impress others as you and the waves have just
>   been impressing me.   (1860 ed., p. 195)

In its 1860 version, then, the poem begins by taking up the analogy posited in the passage from "Proto-Leaf" discussed earlier, between the recursive powers of "the body and the Soul" to "return their impression . . . indifferently before death and after death" and the poet-speaker's powers of similarly "return[ing] impression[s] . . . before death and after" through writing, and specifically through the recursive medium of print or type.

The poem figures the speaker's powers of "returning impressions" as being at a low ebb in comparison with the unimpaired powers of nature of which he expresses his envy in the opening lines. What "the waves have just been impressing" the poet with, the poem goes on to show, is not merely their "fluidity," as the reader of the 1855 edition might expect, but rather their capacity for serving as a medium for regularly alternating processes of composition (including among its meanings writing) and decomposition (including among its meanings organic decay). The ceaseless and "impress[ive]" "drifts" or "waves" of the ocean are the poem's model for the similar ways in which texts and selves are, ideally speaking, endlessly subject to being composed and decomposed, divided and reunited within themselves, divided from and reunited with others.

These processes have been disrupted at the beginning of the poem. In its first half, the speaker acts out (so to speak) his fears that the "flow" of composition and the conditions that permit it have receded from him, perhaps never to return. He is figured as being literally stranded on the margin of the sea between fluid and solid realms (gendered as "mother" and "father," respectively, here), from both of which he has strayed into the position of loss/being lost through which he is wandering at the beginning of the poem:

> As I ebbed with an ebb of the ocean of life,
> As I wended the shores I know,
> As I walk where the sea-ripples wash you, Paumanok,
> Where they rustle up, hoarse and sibilant,
> Where the fierce old mother endlessly cries for her castaways,
> I, musing, late in the autumn day, gazing off southward,
> Alone, held by the eternal self of me that threatens to get the
>   better of me, and stifle me,
> Was seized by the spirit that trails in the lines underfoot,
> In the rim, the sediment, that stands for all the water and all
>   the land of the globe.   (1860 ed., p. 195)

In the second half, he regains access to the "flow," not as one might expect by immersing himself in the water (the ocean, "the fierce old mother")—for reasons that will become clear later, the events of this poem all take place at some distance from this (female) body of water—but by means of a dual action of (re)discovering a set of "types" capable of "stand[ing] for all" that the poet would incorporate into his writing, and of recuperating a previously ruptured relation to what the poem's speaker later calls the "tangible land," his "father," "Paumanok" (the Long Island shore). Before looking more closely at the inter-actions between the figures in the first half of the poem, I want to discuss briefly how representations of composition/decomposition in "As I Ebb'd" and in the third edition overall differ from representations of the same processes in the two previous editions of *Leaves of Grass*.

COMPOSING *LEAVES*/DECOMPOSING BODIES

The connection between the process of composing *Leaves of Grass* and the process of decomposition to which the human body, along with the rest of the organic realm, is subject, is of course not new to "Leaves of Grass. 1"/"As I Ebb'd" or to the 1860 edition as a whole. It had entered the *Leaves of Grass* project near its inception, in the passage early in "I celebrate myself" that begins, "A child said, What is the grass?" (later section 6, lines I have previously discussed in relation to the redefinition of "leaf of grass" in the opening lines of the 1856 "Broad-Axe Poem"). One set of responses that the 1855 poet-speaker makes to the child's question is that the grass is what "transpire[s]" from the bodies or body-parts of the dead buried in the ground: "from the breasts of young men," "from old people and from women, and from offspring taken soon out of their mothers' laps." Physical decay or decomposition per se is not emphasized in this 1855 passage; it represents the transmutation of parts of dead bodies into grass as simply a change of color:

> This grass is very dark to be from the white heads of old
>   mothers,
> Darker than the colorless beards of old men,
> Dark to come from under the faint red roofs of mouths.

It is precisely physical decay and decomposition that are brought to the fore when Whitman takes up the question of the relation between (re)composition and decomposition a second time in the 1856 "Poem of Wonder at The Resurrection of The Wheat." In this poem, physical decomposition after death is treated not as simply a "natural" process of organic breakdown but as a pathological one which is potentially threatening to living persons, death here being the continuation of disease "by other means" rather than the end of it. The speaker marvels "[t]hat when I recline on the grass I do not catch any disease," despite the fact that "probably every spear of grass rises out of what was once a catching disease!" The difference between "grass" and dead bodies, which are more alike than different in the 1855 text, is grotesquely intensified in the 1856 one: here, "grass" is represented as being fresh, lovely, and nourishing, while dead bodies are sick and sickening, "foul liquid and meat."

In the 1856 poem, both objects are turned into kinds of food—one sweet and delicious fruit and the other noisome flesh—while *neither* had been presented as food in the earlier text. The reconception of both "leaves of grass" and dead bodies in relation to oral consumption is a sign of the 1856 text's infantilization of this question, an appropriate conversionary tactic given that text's foregrounding of oedipal conflict in general. This infantilizing tendency of the poem is also evident in the way the speaker maintains a stance of childlike naiveté throughout "Poem of Wonder at The Resurrection of The Wheat." The poem has clear rhetorical affinities with the kinds of questions small children raise as they experiment with integrating one strand of newly acquired knowledge with another by arranging them in possible causal narrative sequences. If people get sick, die, and are buried in the earth, and we eat the fruits of the earth, aren't we eating sickness and death? Why are grass and grain not infected with the diseases of the dead who lie in the ground?

In "Poem of Wonder" these relations are mediated by a simple process of organic renewal: the reason the earth and its inhabitants have not become totally diseased is that the grass or fruit absorbs the nutrients but not the infectants from "this compost" (the poem's title beginning with the fourth [1867] edition). Largely unmediated in the 1855 passage, and mediated solely by a simple, "wholesome," "natural" process of organic purification in the 1856 one, all these kinds of relations are mediated in the 1860 "As I Ebb'd" through a complex figuration of texts and selves as figuring in an endless process of composition and decomposition. The self that utters "Poem of Wonder" remains "safe[ly]" (line 34) outside the decompositional process about which it "wonders" (speculates and marvels). The self that utters "As I Ebb'd" is in that text centrally subject to the powerful compositional/decompositional process that poem represents.

Finally, in "Poem of Wonder," it is as if the universal purifying and reintegrating process it represents were being carried out in order to make possible (and "safe") the only relationship in the poem that is represented as exceeding the simple process of the mediation of decay by organic renewal that otherwise governs relations between bodies in it. This is the direct, even "amorous," contact into which the speaker is permitted to enter with the sea's "tongues" without fear of "infectio[n]," thanks to the "chemistry" that purifies earth and sea of the countless corpses consigned to them:

> What chemistry!
> That the winds are really not infectious!
> That this is no cheat, this transparent greenwash of the sea,
>   which is amorous after me!
> That it is safe to allow it to lick my naked body all over with
>   its tongues!

The ultimate effect of the more complex kinds of mediation at work in "Leaves of Grass. 1"/"As I Ebb'd"—between the "decomposing"/ disintegrating events of the first half and the "(re)composing" ones of the second—is to incorporate (to the limited degree that it is possible to do so) figures of the mother, the father, and death and decomposition into the scene of the vivifying erotic exchange between a "fluid" body and a human (usually male) body or bodies which remains Whitman's primary figure for the program of disseminating affectionate physical presence through *Leaves of Grass*. The by now familiar scene of "fluid" exchange between poet-speaker and other males in Whitman's texts itself "suffers a sea change" in "As I Ebb'd," as its specular, male-homosocial symmetries of gender and identity are disrupted and violated by the introduction of a set of figures that are only partially assimilable to it.

CREATURES OF THE MARGINS

The events of the first half of "As I Ebb'd" bring the speaker into a series of encounters with several demonic figures: his "eternal self" that "h[o]ld[s]" him and "threatens to get the better of [him]," a "spirit that trails in the lines underfoot" and "seize[s]" him, and "the real ME" that "withdraw[s]" from and "mock[s]" and "strik[es]" the speaker. Many critical readings of "As I Ebb'd" have tended toward reductiveness insofar as they have been based on various kinds of doomed attempts to stabilize the identities of the main figures in the poem and their relations to the poet-speaker. It may not be possible to say exactly what such entities as the "eternal self," "the spirit . . . underfoot," or "the real ME" in this poem *are*, in the same way that it may not be possible to say exactly what the "real body" that figures in "Proto-Leaf" is—although I do think one would be right to conclude that the "real ME" in this poem is different from the "real body," the basic distinction between the two being that the "real ME" reasserts itself at points of crisis between the parts of the self, while the "real body" manifests itself at points of transition between different states of the self, most notably between life and death.

The third edition represents such figures as "eternal self" and "real ME" as powerful ones, but it also represents their powers as being more relational and functional than absolute and inherent; that is, these figures are designed to serve as *names* for certain kinds of constraints over the compositional powers of author and reader rather than as stable embodiments of these constraints in imaginary identities—and it is in this latter form that critics have frequently tried to interpret them. The relationship of a figure like "the eternal self," for example, to a possibly comparable figure in another powerfully revisionary challenge to traditional Christian belief such as Emerson's transcendental oversoul, or of the "real ME" to comparable figures in Thoreau's writing where a part of the self mocks the rest, is a complex one. Whitman had certainly read Emerson ardently, and had quite probably read some of Thoreau's work, before 1860. Without wishing to deny that significant connections may well exist among comparable figures in the writings of all three writers, I wish to limit severely the potential interpretive value of such connections for the account I am making here of figures like "the eternal self" in "As I Ebb'd," because I am analyzing the poem and its dominant figures in the specific context of what one might call the internal dynamics of Whitman's own writing.

Possibly more pertinent to understanding a figure like the "spirit . . . underfoot" than a comparable one from Emerson's writing is a highly figural passage Whitman wrote about the man whom he had hailed as his "Master" in the 1856 edition but toward whom he subsequently expressed more ambivalent feelings. Three years after Emerson failed to persuade Whitman to de-emphasize the representation of sexuality in the third edition, Whitman wrote of him, in terms that echo the passage from "As I Ebb'd" in which the "spirit . . . trails in the lines underfoot": "The most exquisite taste and caution are in him, always saving his feet from passing beyond the limits, for he is transcendental of limits, and you see underneath the rest a secret proclivity, American maybe, to dare and violate and make escapades."[17] The poet represented in "As I Ebb'd," in contrast, has made no "secret" of his "proclivity . . . to dare and violate" American limits—the "proclivity" being, in his belatedly American-revolutionary view of his own project, as "American" as "the limits" are. Rather than having "his feet" "sav[ed]" by the "exquisite taste and caution" that reside in a writer like Emerson, Whitman's poet is subject to brutal treatment, "threat[s]," "stifl[ings]," "seiz[ures]," and beatings. Unlike Emerson, his peculiar gifts do not keep his "proclivity . . . to dare and violate" safely "secret" and "underneath the rest" (of himself). The poet in "As I Ebb'd" is not represented as being "exquisite[ly]" and securely ensconced above the subversive impulses that impel his writing. He is figured as getting literally tripped up in the limits, in "the lines underfoot"—a phrase which surely includes in its referents the "lines" of poetry in trailing metrical "feet" in which his utterance is fashioned—and as becoming painfully trapped in the metonymic margins of his own writing.

Shifts (or "drifts") of power and identity, within the poet-speaker or among parts of himself in the first half of the poem, and then between himself and others in the second, keep occurring in the poem. The first of these comes as the poet finds himself "[a]lone, held by the eternal self of me that threatens to get the better of me, and stifle me," and "seized by the spirit that trails in the lines underfoot." It may initially seem curious that the poet introduces the figure of his "eternal self" by speaking in the same line of being simultaneously "[a]lone" and "held" by this figure. The "eternal self," apparently, is both intrinsic and extrinsic to the speaker; that is, it and he partake of what Kenneth Burke has called the "paradox of substance," what one might call the double position in which the "substance" of any entity stands in relation to that entity, insofar as it is both in one sense "within" it and in another "underneath" or "underlying" it.[18] Similarly, the "spirit" that is said to "seize[ ]" the speaker also bears a "substantial" relationship to him, "underfoot" and therefore in one sense extrinsic, but in another at least momentarily a part of his self (in the sense of being "his" spirit) and consequently intrinsic.

Despite the grip these figures have on him, the poet-speaker soon demonstrates that he, too, is "transcendental of limits," in his own very arduous way—a way programmatically opposed to the habitual "exquisite taste and caution" that Whitman saw guiding and "saving" Emerson in his writing. Although he does not fully recover the means of "returning" the "impressions" that are overwhelming him at the poem's beginning until its second half, he *begins* to recover them even while he remains in the grip of "eternal self" and "spirit." "[H]eld" fast as he is by "eternal self," and "seized by the spirit . . . underfoot," the speaker stands "[f]ascinated," and he begins to move his eyes, perhaps the only part of his body not restrained by the double grasp of "eternal self" and "spirit," a grasp that is constricting and discomfiting in some ways but is now revealed as also being constitutive of his vision:

> Fascinated, my eyes, reverting from the south, dropped, to
>   follow those slender winrows,
> Chaff, straw, splinters of wood, weeds, and the sea-gluten,
> Scum, scales from shining rocks, leaves of salt-lettuce, left by
>   the tide;
> Miles walking, the sound of breaking waves the other side of
>   me,
> Paumanok, there and then, as I thought the old thought of
>   likenesses,
> These you presented to me, you fish-shaped island,
> As I wended the shores I know,
> As I walked with that eternal self of me, seeking types.

Looking not upward, the conventional direction for the gaze that aspires to be "transcendental of limits," but downward, at the decaying detritus that "trails" underfoot, the speaker contemplates the bits of matter that he will later in the poem embrace as the very "types" he, in company with his "eternal self," is "seeking" at its beginning. They are not of the transcendent kind that linked historical figures and events with an overarching providential schema—the traditional way of thinking "the old thought of likenesses" through "types"—but an array of small natural phenomena that are fragmentary and aleatory to the point of ostensible worthlessness and meaninglessness, "[c]haff," "splinters," "weeds," "scum."

It is at this point that the poem's thematic of decomposition first engages with the processes of composing and decomposing texts, not only at the literal level of writing them but also of setting, printing, and striking (that is, de-composing) them as actual lines of type.[19] Although the term "type" in the sense of printer's type does not explicitly figure in this poem, as it does in "Proto-Leaf," I would argue that the poem's primary concern with the loss and recovery of the power of "returning" powerful "impressions" through writing and publishing ("impress[ing] others") justifies the reader's taking the debris, the little fragments or drift washed up on the shore to which the speaker likens himself ("I, too, but signify, at the utmost, a little washed-up drift," line 25), as representing (among other things) bits of type—especially since the speaker asserts that "[t]hese little shreds shall, indeed, *stand for all*" (line 42; my emphasis)—as material signifiers, meaningless in themselves, but potentially highly meaningful "in composition."

Negotiating the Cultural Terrain of Paranoia

"As I Ebb'd" is impelled by anxieties of at least three different, although not unrelated, kinds. The broadest of these anxieties are those about the possibility of human extinction at the species level—fears that had been widely felt by Whitman's contemporaries since the discovery of fossil evidence that suggested the extinction of entire species or "types" (one of the poem's key words) in the 1830s.[20] The setting of the poem on the beach, the scene of much early evolutionary research and the primary "frontier" between early and later forms of organic life, along with its privileging of "natural" cycles of decay and renewal, links the thematics of the poem to early evolutionary theory in several significant ways.

A second impelling set of anxieties for this poem concerns the prospect of personal extinction, of the individual body's death and decomposition into its constituent elements. But perhaps the strongest anxieties attendant on this text—and those most closely related to the splits in the self that it represents—are those arising from the threaten-

ing possibility to the self of being temporarily or permanently overwhelmed by the powers of "unduly powerful impressions" that Freud,
in his case study of Daniel Paul Schreber's *Memoirs*, argued it is the
function of paranoia in its decompositional phase to control.[21]

In the fifth verse-paragraph of the poem (later the middle paragraph
of section 2), the speaker approaches the nadir of the two-part cycle
the poem represents. After having become reduced to "a little washed-
up drift" ("I, too, but signify, at the utmost, a little washed-up drift")
and having professed complete despair of his project (*Leaves of Grass*
becomes "dead leaves"), the speaker is "baffled, balked, / Bent to the
very earth." "[T]he real ME" of the speaker then emerges, "mocking"
and "[s]triking" him "till [he] fall[s] helpless upon the sand" (p. 197;
this last phrase quoted here appears only in those versions of the text
published during 1860).

In the three following brief and climactic verse-paragraphs (subsequently condensed to the last three lines of section 2 and the first
three of section 3) the speaker first sees even Nature itself transformed
into a hostile and vengeful figure:

> I perceive Nature here, in sight of the sea, is taking advantage
>   of me, to dart upon me, and sting me,
> Because I was assuming so much,
> And because I have dared to open my mouth to sing at all.
>
> (p. 197)

Having been beaten onto the sand by his "real" self, and then "dart[ed]
upon" and "st[u]ng" by Nature, the beleaguered speaker "submits" to
the imaginary gang of personified nature-figures surrounding him:

> You oceans both! You tangible land! Nature!
> Be not too rough with me—I submit—I close with you,
> These little shreds shall, indeed, stand for all.

The poet here figures his relationships to these nature-figures as
something like being assaulted, even gang-raped—his "submi[ssion]"
to these figures follows upon his having been "bent to the very earth,"
and then "struck," "tak[en] advantage of," "dart[ed] upon," and
"st[ung]." It is as if the specular "fluid"-male figures into which he had
personified nature in passages like that in the 1855 Preface when he
claimed to "incarnate[ ] [his country's] geography and natural life and

rivers and lakes" had turned on the poet with a vengeance—or (to cast back even further for analogies in Whitman's writing) as if Lankton had not rescued the boy Charles from the drunken sailor's assault.

The text represents this act of submission as enabling the poet to recover the "fluid" powers of composition which he had formerly exhibited in untroubled fashion in the 1855 *Leaves,* but which had become highly problematic in the interim. He here regains access to a specific form of "fluidity," namely, "composition"—the mediating powers of print, language, and writing to "return" (that is, to keep producing and sending back) powerful "impressions," to keep powerful "impressions" generated by other bodies from permanently overwhelming the self. Here, he does this by means of himself seizing on the metonymic bits of seashore trash that lie "underfoot."

A standard reading of "As I Ebb'd" such as R. W. B. Lewis's, referred to earlier, orders the poem as a series of antinomies of the conventional order of, for example, temporality in the first half versus timelessness in the second. Lewis treats these antinomies as readily reconcilable ones; he interprets the poem—as have many of its other readers—as "a triumph over its own content," insofar as

> [a]nyone who could construct an image of the higher power—the one he aspires toward—standing far off and mocking him with little satiric bows and gestures, comparing and consigning his verses to the sandy debris under his feet: such a person has already conquered his sense of sterility, mastered his fear of spiritual and artistic death, rediscovered his genius, and returned to the fullest poetic authority.
>
> (p. 457)

Yet the entire poem, and not just its explicitly disintegrative phases, contradicts the triumphalist-imperialist rhetoric—conquest, mastery, discovery, superlative plenitude and untroubled authority—that Lewis would impose on it. I would argue that the poem in its entirety represents no such magical "rags-to-riches" transformation of a sense of anguished constraint into masterful authority as some critics have thought it does. To the contrary, what strikes me about the way it represents the poet's conflict or crisis and the means by which it is resolved (to the degree that it is) is the close congruence of both conflict and resolution with Lacan's account of the oedipal crisis from the point of view of the male subject. The partitioning of the self Whitman carries out in "As I Ebb'd" leads to a scene of persecution of the poem's speaking subject which Whitman elaborates in oedipal terms. Having ultimately failed to critique the oedipal and to imagine an alternative system of desire in the second edition of *Leaves of Grass*, Whitman returns anew to exploring the possible means of subverting the oedipal in the third edition. It is at such points in the 1860 text as the one under discussion that the relevance of the Lacanian model becomes clear. According to it, the (male) child, beset with threats of castration perceived as proceeding from the figure of the father, renounces the hitherto "fluid" identity he has shared with the figure of the mother and, in "the Name of the Father," renounces his "fluid" identity and accepts an oedipalized "male" one (for which the mother and other males are prohibited objects) and takes his place in the oedipally ordered fields of language and culture. "I take what is under-foot," the speaker of "As I Ebb'd" announces as he asserts the adequacy of the smallest bits of refuge to "stand for all": "What is yours is mine, my father." (This is a direct reversal of sorts of the inaugural assertion of *Leaves of Grass*, "what I assume you shall assume." Does the "as-sumption" of the father's role on the speaking subject's part in such texts as "As I Ebb'd" empower the famous exhortative assumption in the second line of "Song of Myself"? Not entirely, or not without considerable mediation, I would argue.) Far from representing a "triumph," the speaker's accession to the oedipalized male position at this point in "As I Ebb'd" places him in a relationship to the figure of the father and the father's body which can ultimately be resolved in the poem only by the decomposition of both.

There are two different dynamics simultaneously at work throughout the poem. The first of these is the dual one of ebbing and flowing, which is represented as being a "natural" and endless process, one from which the speaker has become temporarily estranged but into which he is reintegrated in the course of the poem. The second is the triple one of more complicated and more highly mediated kinds of inter-actions between the poet-speaker and various split-off parts of himself, and between himself and others, specifically the figure of the father. This second dynamic is represented as being a psychological and cul-tural process, that is, as taking place between parts of the self and between figures in related gender roles (father and son). These two dynamics are not entirely compatible with each other, although the text is designed to make them appear so: one strong tendency of the text is to cover up the perception that there is nothing "natural" about oedipalization, and to conceal to some degree the related perception that the gender-roles of "father" and "son" represent a complex and in many ways oppressive cultural formation, rather than a complementary, two-phase "natural" phenomenon of the order of the flow and ebb of energies in nature.

It is precisely this text's ways of making the exchanges between the speaker and the other male figures in the poem appear to be "natural," and the volatile and in some ways deadly relations that prevail among them "inevitable"—when they are in fact neither—that I want to interrogate. Does "As I Ebb'd" merely reinscribe the exclusion of the feminine and the violent subjection of all males to patriarchal formations that it may at this point in my discussion seem to? In the following section I shall argue that it does not, as I consider its means for critiquing these formations.

CULTIVATED DISINTEGRATIONS

How is one to think of the speaker's being persecuted for having been so presumptuous as to write (for "hav[ing] dared to open [his] mouth")? "As I Ebb'd," like some of the other most powerful poems in the 1860 edition, explores the disintegration of stable selves in response to the kinds of divisions—death, madness, the extreme depression or sense of "loss of self" that can follow on an experience of rejection in love or of failure at an ambitious project—which strongly resist or are not susceptible to "unifying fluidity." Julia Kristeva has theorized the connection between profoundly conflicting perceptions of unity and division in the formation of the subject and has linked the subject's need to unify the schizoid perceptions of infancy to the manifestation of a paranoia which she asserts is a fundamental precondition of the formation of the subject:

> The subject is a paranoid subject constituted by the impulse of Desire that sublimates and unifies the schizoid rupture. Not only is paranoia therefore the precondition of every subject—one

becomes a subject only by accepting, if only temporarily, the paranoid unity that supersedes the heterogeneous other—but paranoia also lies close to the fragmenting that can be called schizoid, camouflaging its secret even while drawing on its energy. Although the "fluidity of differences" constitutes the unity of self-consciousness, it is also a threat to that unity, for in this fluidity alone there is no place for any unity . . . on the contrary, what determines this division is death, rupture and differentiation with no unifying fluidity.[22]

Kristeva's notion of paranoia as a precondition of subjectivity rather than as personal pathology, and of subjectivity itself as a condition in which the subject is always liable to oscillating between schizoid division or fragmentation on the one hand and the paranoid unity imposed on this division on the other, provides a useful model for understanding the significance of what one might call the stance of cultivated paranoia which is the particular subject-position informing the new writing of the 1860 edition. I prefer to think of the "paranoia" that a text such as "As I Ebb'd" manifests as a means of exploring and critiquing Whitman's culture's dominant modes of constructing identity and sexuality rather than simply as ostensible evidence of Whitman's personal "instability" at this point in his life. The paranoid posture the poet-speaker assumes in "As I Ebb'd" serves as a highly effective strategy for critiquing his culture's dominant modes of configuring bodily desire in relation to writing and print as well as to nature and God.

The speaker begins situating himself with respect to "father" Paumanok by extending his identification with this "father" and his body and properties ("What is yours is mine, my father"):

> I, too, Paumanok,
> I too have bubbled up, floated the measureless float, and been washed on your shores;
> I too am but a trail of drift and debris,
> I too leave little wrecks upon you, you fish-shaped island.
>
> (pp. 197–198)

"I too have . . . floated the measureless float" sounds somewhat like the characteristic 1855 line, "I fly the flight of the fluid and swallowing soul." Here, though, it is not the fluid "flight" (or "float") in itself that is being emphasized as much as it is the assertion of identity between the speaker and the figure of the father in the recurrent phrase "I too," as if the alleged commonality of the experience were more important in this context than the experience itself. "[F]loating the measureless float" also echoes a significant line from the 1856 "Sun-Down Poem" ("Crossing Brooklyn Ferry"): "I too had been struck from the float forever held in solution"; that is, the speaker (like everyone else in his culture) had been differentiated by birth and again by oedipalization from the "float" of undifferentiated nature "forever held in solution." In the 1856 poem, there has been no disruption of the ceaseless regularity of the process of "the pouring-in of the flood-tide, the falling-back to the sea of the ebb-tide" (the last line of "Crossing Brooklyn Ferry," section 2) as there has been at the beginning of "As I Ebb'd."

The instauration of the paternal phallus is an imaginary event one might expect to take place at the point in the poem where its speaking subject invokes the name of the father. That one of the significances of the twice-invoked "fish-shaped island," the "tangible land" dividing the two oceans ("You oceans both!") lying on either side of it, should be the paternal phallus will be unsurprising to readers familiar with the much more elaborate evocation of the paternal phallus (as well as a phantasmatic maternal phallus) in the 1856 "Broad-Axe Poem." Here, though, the subject's relation to it is quite different from that of the awed and envious oedipalized subject of 1856. In this text he "leave[s] little wrecks," "a trail of drift and debris," "dab[s] of liquid and soil" across the body and phallus of the father; that is, he figuratively enacts the infantile fantasy of urinating and defecating on them. Incongruous as this interpretation may at first seem, it conforms to the unconscious logic underlying both halves of the text, insofar as the father ("Paumanok") has been represented as being among the phantasmatic males the subject has imagined "tak[ing] advantage" of him.

Instead of assuming a fuller identification with the paternal phallus as we might expect him to do at this point, the poet-speaker commences his task of "gather[ing]" or recomposing the "fragments" at his feet. Rather than accepting the paternal phallus as chief signifier, the poet-speaker rejects such a monolithic hierarchy of signification in favor of a disintegrated font of "shreds," "splinters," and bits of "scum," an alternative model of language and writing which foregrounds their metonymic and recursive potential. The process of "seeking [new kinds of] types" that is carried out in the poem culminates in the speaker's declaration that "[t]hese little shreds shall, indeed, stand for all": in this line, minimal scraps, of debris, of printer's type, are pronounced adequate to signifying the new meanings of a nature conceived of as having been (and being) constructed rather than either divinely created and ordained "once and for all" or eternally subject to patriarchal domination.

The subject directly challenges the figure of the father not by attacking him hostilely but by "throw[ing] [him]self" upon the father's breast and refusing to "unloose" him until the father answers his question. "Kiss me, my father," the speaker says, "Breathe to me, while I hold you close, the secret of the wondrous murmuring I envy, / For fear I shall become crazed, if I cannot emulate it, and utter myself as well as it" (p. 198). To "utter" himself "as well as" (and at the same time that) he utters the murmur of the ocean would be for the subject to achieve in his writing the ideal of unfragmented "fluidity" which first impelled it but which can no longer serve it in its pure, undifferentiated form. Difference unmistakably asserts itself at this point in the text: rather than serving as an unfailingly responsive, perfectly specular double of the speaking subject, the father neither returns the subject's kiss nor tells him "the secret" he desperately entreats of him.

The melancholiac character of many of the utterances of this text combined with the manic behavior of the subject toward the father's body ("I throw myself upon you[ ]," "I cling to you," "I hold you so firm," "Kiss me," "Touch me," "Breathe to me, while I hold you close") suggest that one of the things being represented at this point in the poem is the return of powerful unconscious impulses, both sexual and aggressive, toward the father's body—impulses of a more intense kind, it might seem, than one is likely to feel toward the father after early childhood, except as part of the mourning process. The poem counters the "return" of overwhelming unconscious "impressions" of feelings of love, terror, and envy toward the father and his body in the aftermath of his death—literal or not, for the father in this text is undecidably either or both dead in the way an actual father might be and in the imaginary way God might be said to be dead.

Representations and figurative reenactments of the death(s) of the father(s) had been a staple in America since the death of Washington, whose cult was still flourishing in Whitman's childhood. Death itself is reconstructed literally along different lines in this poem, as it is at other points in this edition. Rather than being a one-time passage for the individual self from immanence to transcendence, death is instead a recurrent phase in the flowings and ebbings of a generally reconstructed nature. The latter part of this poem suggests that the "death" which is the object of so much anxiety in Whitman's culture is not simply the actual physical event as such; it is the symbolic use to which death has been put by the culture, as its chief model of the imaginary effects of the threat of castration that is used to channel subjects into the oedipal system. One reason "As I Ebb'd" is such a difficult text is that it registers a number of fundamental contradictions Whitman uncovers in his own and other men's engagement with their culture, including the victimization of the (male) subject by oedipalization as well as the possibility—if also the extreme difficulty—of resisting and subverting this process.

Death-Effects: Oozing from Dead Lips

Central among the signs of the dominant culture that 1860s texts such as "As I Ebb'd" revise is that of God as transcendent father-figure. This figure is naturalized by a process of decomposition in the new religion and politics of nature promulgated in "As I Ebb'd," in which decomposition is not only decay *and* de-composition, the unwriting of writing generally, but the unwriting of the culture's dominant writing or scripture, the "old" (that is, Christian) Bible. The result of this dual process of disassembling "type(s)"—not only printed type but also traditional scriptural types—carried out in this text is not death as Whitman's readers are probably used to thinking of it—as the universal fate of the natural realm including its human inhabitants, as part of the punishment imposed by God on fallen mankind (as Judeo-Christian tradition would have it)—but merely a death-effect or a range of such effects, one which includes God in its range.[23]

"Leaves of Grass. 1"/"As I Ebb'd" revises the sentimental cult of the death of the father by scandalously combining it with the idea of the death of God. The poem engages with these matters most directly in the notorious pair of lines which James Russell Lowell censored from the poem when he published it (apparently grudgingly, as a favor to Emerson) in the *Atlantic*.[24] These lines turn the poem back around into its decompositional mode and refocus its religious concerns with death and possible forms of the afterlife; in them, decaying God, dead or dying father, and de-composing poet speak with one voice:

(See! from my dead lips the ooze exuding at last!
See—the prismatic colors, glistening and rolling!)

This utterance emerges from between parentheses, themselves bits of "type" which form a typographical figure or "impression" of the "dead lips" which enclose as they disclose what is said, encrypting the poet's voice far within the text and, indeed, launching its utterance from a posthumous position, from "beyond" the space of ordinary human utterance which the reader presumably still occupies and from which the first two editions of *Leaves of Grass* were written. Having kissed "dead lips," the subject now speaks from between them, as he literally and materially does to the reader from between the parentheses on the page. What the "dead lips" say is the secret the subject earlier begged the father to tell: in order to "utter" oneself at the same time that one utters the undifferentiated murmuring of the ocean, one must make the utterance through "dead lips." Only "dead lips" can tell ("utter") the difference between self and ocean at the same time they utter them together, because "dead lips" are decomposing; they not only speak but at the same time drool an "ooze" in which one can see "the prismatic colors, glistening and rolling"—a "return" on "dead lips" of a very different but still not unrecognizable "impression" of "those cheerful waves, rolling over each other" (in the words of the 1860 "Enfans d'Adam. 7," later retitled, "We Two, How Long We Were Fool'd").

The term "exuding" may call to mind its use in a passage of the 1855 Preface in which, as in "Leaves of Grass. 1"/"As I Ebb'd," Whitman's writing at times seems very close to Christian theological language: "If there shall be love and content between the father and the son and if the greatness of the son is the exuding of the greatness of the father there shall be love between the poet and the man of demonstrable science" (1855 ed., p. vii). The language Whitman applies here to "father and . . . son," rather than being familial or domestic according to nineteenth-century American conventions, is strikingly close to the traditional Christian Trinitarian vocabulary for describing relations ("love and content," "the exuding of the greatness of the father") between the divine Father and Son. The Son is more usually spoken of as "reflecting" the Father's glory (thereby maintaining the perfect male specularity which characterizes what Irigaray has called the fundamental "hom(m)osexual economy" of God desiring his Son [and vice versa]).[25] It is the father's "glory" that the son is said to "exude" in the 1855 Preface; it is a stream of drool from "dead lips" that God, father, and poet jointly "exude[ ]" in "Leaves of Grass. 1." Whitman's new religion requires the vocabulary and techniques of scientific-materialist analysis rather than Trinitarian tradition to locate and to name the modified, thoroughly naturalized kind of "glory" which inheres in the "ooze" of "impressions" "returned" in the third edition: a band of "prismatic colors," a tiny rainbow which may recall the promissory rainbow of the "old" Bible, but which appears in this context in much diminished form, in keeping with this text's representations about the perils and powers of disintegration and decomposition.

The poet-speaker finally speaks of the detritus in relation to which he has reconstructed his identity as having been "[b]uoyed hither, from many moods, one contradicting another." These seem to be his last words on the conflicts that generate the poem: he finally places what had been represented as being warring parts of himself in simple paratactic relation to one another, "many moods, one contradicting another." In the poem's last pair of lines the referents of its two primary linguistic "shifters" (pronouns) are conclusively reassigned:

> We, capricious, brought hither, we know not whence, spread
>   out before You, up there, walking or sitting,
> Whoever you are—we too lie in drifts at your feet.

Here, the "I" that is partially and painfully separated from its constituent parts in the first part of the poem and partially reunited with "father" and "mother" in the second part shifts to being a "We"—a "We" that denotes neither the (re)union of speaker and the parts of himself nor he and his "parents" (the ocean and the shore) but rather the reunion of the speaker and the bits of flotsam with which he has identified the powers of his self and his writing to "return" powerful "impressions." In the figure of the "You, up there, walking or sitting," the position of the transcendent God, which this text downgrades by reconstructing as the demonic, nontranscendent "phantom" looking down on the speaker, is recuperated by being transformed into the position of the reader "looking down" at the page and at the figure of the poet-speaker—or rather at the bits of type on the page which are the only sign of his metonymic presence. The conflicts that impel the poem dissipate themselves in what it represents as being an author-reader relation restored on a new basis from which oppressive authority, figured as dying God, dying "father," and "hoarse and angry" mother, have been exorcised through having been encountered and faced down in the fullness of their threat to the willfully "paranoid" subject (that is, the poet-speaker, "stand-in" or metonym for both author and reader).

To describe "As I Ebb'd" in this way may be to make it sound as if it provides some kind of model of a completely successful therapeutic recuperation of a self or selves previously riven by culturally dominant kinds of division, as if its exorcism of warring parts of the self, of dying father and angry mother, represents the kind of unequivocally positive achievement that many of Whitman's critics have taken it to be. As may have been evident from my earlier remarks about the transitional interactions in the middle of the poem which take the form of a rape-beating of the poem's speaking subject, I have considerable reservations about the kinds of exchanges and substitutions through which the changes represented in the course of this text are effected. "As I Ebb'd" does not just begin as a disturbingly conflicted text but remains one because of the homophobic assumptions it takes over from the broader culture, which manifest themselves chiefly in what seems to have been Whitman's felt need at the crucial transitional midpoint in this text not only to represent the exchanges by which the divided parts of the speaker's self are reintegrated with(in) him as erotic ones, but also to make this figure's recuperation of his powers seem to be in some way specifically the consequence of his having been sexually violated by other men. The ultimate effect of the poem is to displace the violence associated with its substitution of mere print for "sacred" type onto the person of its poet-speaker protagonist and "stand-in" for both author and reader. I take the way in which the scapegoating of this figure is both allowed and (to some degree) covered over at the poem's midpoint as a significant lapse in Whitman's program of "thinking otherwise" about the politics of identity and sexuality in his culture, and as an index of the costs for both author and reader for challenging his (and, with regard to its constructions of sexuality, to some degree our) culture on one of its most treacherous terrains.

In order for Whitman to carry out this project of "justify[ing]" "antique" moral philosophy in relation to his new politics and religion of nature, it was necessary for him to engage Christian tradition more fully than he had done in the first two editions, as I have shown him doing as he revises the doctrine of "types" in "As I Ebb'd with the Ocean of Life." Whitman had hitherto sidestepped the question of whether *Leaves of Grass* carried a critique of Christianity and the Christian God: "Be not curious about God," he writes near the end of "I celebrate myself," "For I who am curious about each am not curious about God" (1855, p. 54); similarly, another passage in "I celebrate myself" reads:

> I find letters from God dropped in the street, and every one is
> signed by God's name,
> And I leave them where they are, for I know that others will
> punctually come forever and ever.

Such distancing gestures are characteristic of the general exclusion of God from the first two editions of *Leaves*: "letters from God" may be lying in the street, but the poet is content to leave them there, unread. In the third edition, however, Whitman neither merely ignores God nor advises the reader to do so; he directly challenges in his writing the transcendent position God has been supposed to occupy. In order to launch his challenge against this God-position, the subjects who speak in the poetry of the third edition frequently traverse and temporarily occupy cultural terrain which psychoanalytic theory has taught us to recognize as that of paranoia, a range of psychic states characterized by anxieties about being threatened, overwhelmed, and persecuted by figures who are perceived by the subject as being hostile and alien. Freud's basic theoretical contributions to the understanding of male paranoia were two: his perception of how paranoia frequently serves as an unconscious defense against homoerotic impulses ("I, a man, do *not* love another man; after all, he *hates* me—i.e., persecutes me"); and his working out of the roles of religious and megalomaniac fantasies in the unconscious construction of paranoid delusions.[26] In these delusions, the malevolent motives and intentions which the subject imagines are being directed toward him by figures of patriarchal authority (God, father, employer, mentor, or a beloved male whom the subject perceives as being older, more powerful, more highly favored, rejecting of the subject, and so forth) take on boundary-shattering significance in the mind of the subject. In the extremes of paranoia, he is thrown into conflict simultaneously with a whole phantasmatic array of imaginary representatives of the patriarchal order, one which extends upward in the traditional hierarchy to include the deity.

As I have pointed out in the context of "As I Ebb'd," the primary sign of God in the third edition is in the often grotesque processes of blockage and decomposition that figure in it. Besides being present in images of decay ("rotten excrement of maggots," 1860 ed., p. 409; "bowels clogged with abomination" and "Blood circulating dark and poisonous streams," p. 415), God is also manifest in the "mocking" voice which repeatedly resounds through the 1860 text, not only in the projected hostile self which is said to "mock[ ] [the poet] with mock-congratulatory signs and bows" (p. 197) but also in the "mocking-bird" of which the poet claims to be "Aware" at the end of the first verse-paragraph of "Proto-Leaf" and in the "mocking-bird[ ]" who sings the "reckless, despairing carols" and the great "aria" of death and loss in "A Word Out of the Sea" (pp. 269, 273, 275). Both persecuted subject and persecuting other in turn, the "mocking-bird" announces a destiny of ultimate destruction, rejection, and even "damnation" for the subject, appropriating the traditional language of Christian soteriology for *Leaves of Grass* as it does so.

One may wonder what relation there can be between the kind of thoroughly domesticated encounter between the poet and God glimpsed in "I celebrate myself" ("As God comes a loving bedfellow and sleeps at my side all night and close on the peep of the day, / And leaves for me baskets covered with white towels bulging the house with their plenty," 1855 ed., p. 15) and the impassable voids and wastes in which God is figured in the third edition. Bearing in mind my identification of the religious and persecutory fantasies that figure so frequently in the third edition as elements of a paranoid vision cultivated in the text, the psychoanalytically informed reader may well be reminded by Whitman's alternately domestic and decompositional modes of representing God of the similarly alternating versions of God that figure in the writing of the canonical Freudian male paranoid, Daniel Paul Schreber.[27]

The third edition of Leaves of Grass takes as its chief concern the de-compositional powers of rewriting and revising its culture's boundaries around bodies, God, and the real, and draws much of its power from representing the kinds of "unduly powerful impressions" that Freud argued it is the function of paranoia to control. Alice Jardine has theorized that, fundamentally, male paranoia involves a fear of boundaries becoming too painfully constrictive or a fear of the loss of boundaries altogether.[28] Both of these extremes figure importantly in what I have called the cultivated paranoia of the third Leaves. By means of representing this process as a potentially empowering one, the poetry of the third edition produces particularly compelling terms for its invitation to readers to recognize the pain of the oppressive cultural constraints under which they are laboring and the exhilarating—but also perilous—pleasure of attempting to redraw these boundaries along other lines. The desire to lose and the fear of losing the boundary lines in force around self-definition and sexual definition are both strongly impelled by the third edition, in which Whitman aspires to extend the scope of his revisions of culture to include his readers' notions of their relation to such basal elements of mid-nineteenth-century American culture as nature and religion.

Throughout the poetry of the 1860 edition Whitman has a special term, "indifference," for both what is most intensely to be desired (an awareness of difference that stops short of reifying it, and an awareness that body and soul, life and death are not really contrary and stably hypostatized states) and to be feared (rejection by a beloved object). In one sense, it is another Whitmanian term for the "fluid," to call it by its chief name in the first edition, and for what he began calling "adhesiveness" or "manly love" in the second edition ("adhesiveness," which only occurs once in the 1856 text, appears over and over again in 1860, most often in the "Calamus" cluster but in other new texts, too). "O to be relieved of distinctions!" the poet cries near the end of "Proto-Leaf": "O to level occupations and the sexes! O to bring all to common ground! O adhesiveness!" (1860 ed., p. 22). "To think the difference will still continue to others, yet we lie beyond the difference" (p. 443) is a notion which Whitman treats as a utopian prospect in this edition (significantly, in a poem subsequently entitled "To think of time," first published in the 1855 edition, which is entitled "Burial" in the 1860 text). In other contexts, "indifference" is made to stand for what the 1860 text represents as being the most painfully constrictive of boundaries: the experience of loss of self in rejection in love—a state that is particularly cultivated in the "Calamus" poems: "the sick, sick dread lest the one he loved might secretly be indifferent to him" ("Calamus" no. 10, p. 356).

In using the term "cultivated" in the preceding sentence to describe the status of "indifference" in its negative sense in the 1860 edition (rejection by the beloved), I mean to suggest that Whitman partially reverses his culture's negation of the experience of rejection in order to explore its implications thoroughly. Just as the "real body" is said to be capable of "returning impressions *indifferently*," that is, without being impeded by the kinds of limits to which the human body in itself is subject, for example, illness or death, the "love poet" of the "Calamus" section empowers himself to do what no rejected lover can do at the moment of rejection: to begin treating the other's "indifference" indifferently, by making a full exploration of the meanings of this painful but potentially empowering experience. Whitman keeps returning in "Calamus" to what he represents as being the deeply painful experience of "indifference" or rejection by the beloved because it is his most powerful means both of exposing his culture's rigid homophobia—self-aware male homosexuality in his culture is by definition "paranoid" homosexuality—and of gaining access to the psychic and emotional realities underlying his culture's fierce repression of homosexuality. By "constantly return[ing] to rejection," Kristeva writes, the subject attempts to recover "what lies beneath the paranoid homosexuality laid bare by signifying production: the schizoid moment of scission. Mallarmé's suffering body, and, later, the shattered and mummified body of Artaud attest to this loss of unity."[29] Kristeva might have also adduced the Whitman of the third *Leaves of Grass* as a model of the attempt—and of the consequences for writing of the attempt—to recover the schizoid moment of scission which can only be reached by de-composing the paranoid unity which "sublimates and unifies the schizoid rupture" that precedes it. The fierce energy with which Whitman keeps representing himself and his body in the 1860 text as dead, wounded, burnt, pulverized, buried, turned to "excrement[ ]" (pp. 266, 398) and "voided" (p. 266) is indicative of the intensity of his engagement in 1860 with attempting to redefine the bodily and the sexual in relation to the natural and the real, no matter how far it carried him and his readers onto the disturbing terrain of paranoia.

The Politics of Nature and the Scene of Disencryptment in "Calamus"

The third edition brings its representations of nature and reality into sharpest relief in its last quarter, in the poems of the "Calamus" cluster, where, among the poems new to the 1860 *Leaves*, the powers of "indifference" and decomposition are most clearly focused—especially since these function as supports for the representation in nonhomophobic terms of male homoeroticism, a "real" which is being relegated by the culture to a state of unrepresentability, or restricted to representation only in the homophobic terms of the emergent medicoforensic discourses of the alleged perversion, corruption, or "decadence" of erotic relations between males.

The "Calamus" section insists on the inalienable reality of such relations. The 1860 text's explorations around the anxious query from "Proto-Leaf" which impels this edition, "How can the real body ever die, and be buried?" (p. 16), culminate in the exhaustive investigation carried out in the "Calamus" poems of "the real something" (p. 353) which might serve as "the real ground" (p. 358) for the "real[ ] me" (p. 376), in order for the subject to arrive, ultimately, at "the last athletic reality" (p. 375), even, hypersemantically, at "real reality" (p. 344). The "politics of nature" that informs the third edition amounts to the application to the condition of human bodiliness of the fundamental tenet of stoic physics and nature-theory that identity and difference between bodies of all kinds are primarily determined by their specific capacities for conjunction with or separability from other bodies. According to the 1860 text, human bodies are highly volatile and unstable in combination with or disjunction from other bodies; and erotic attraction and rejection, especially in the powerful but largely occluded forms these take between men in Whitman's culture, are among the most important factors in the construction of male identity in the culture and consequently in the perpetuation of the patriarchal formations in which it is constituted. In reaction against the elaboration of a gender-polarizing code of sexual practices which tends to privatize and domesticize sexuality, the third edition attempts to substantiate the primary claim of the *Leaves of Grass* project: that sexuality is fundamentally a political matter because it is never simply "sexual," that is, unrelated to other economies in the culture besides the erotic, such as the way one inhabits one's class- or gender-position, or one's relation to one's work and to language and writing. This project of substantiation involves a working out of the implications for Whitman's "politics of nature" of his relocation of "substance" from the abstract or spiritual realm to human bodies in particular and to nature and the material in general. The mostly quite brief, concentrated "Calamus" lyrics represent what one might call a series of rotations of subject-position around a small set of questions about the meanings of a few significant forms of conjunction and disjunction between male bodies, including the following: what are the real political consequences of fulfilled desire between males? of male-homo-erotic object-loss through the death of the beloved? of a man's being rejected by another, beloved male?

The "successful" escape from homophobic tyranny initially envisioned by Whitman in the simple utopian terms of the water frolics of the 1855 Preface and the "twenty-eight bathers" section of "I celebrate myself," far from being "consequence-free," as it may have looked at first to him or to some of his readers, turns out to be laden with consequences, some highly desirable and others not. At such points, as at many other points in the first several editions of *Leaves of Grass,* Whitman's writing registers in a complicated way both the exciting possibility for many that patriarchal formations are constructs and are therefore subject to revision, and the daunting degree to which such a far-reaching and revisionary politics is fraught with difficulties, including the always-present threat of persecution and reprisal exerted by the dominant culture. In the intentionally "paranoid" realm of many of the "Calamus" poems, Whitman explores what recognizing, fearing, and facing down such threats might "feel like."

One kind of potential political consequence that experiences of the "indifference" of another may have, according to "Calamus," is to release prohibited desires and thoughts from encryptment, to dislodge them from their place "deep within the individual," so to speak, where dominant forces in the culture would banish them and have them contained, and to restore them to full social and political status, in the open air, as it were, or "in the midst of things." Various of the "Calamus" poems carry out not only the repositioning of what the culture has rendered marginal ("Calamus" no. 1 opens with the lines, "In paths untrodden, / In the growth by margins of pond waters,") but also the recovery of what it has rendered interstitial—that is, only intermittently or fleetingly perceptible. Consider the significance of interstitiality in the representation of fulfilled male-homoerotic desire in "Calamus" no. 29. To quote the poem in its entirety:

> One flitting glimpse, caught through an interstice,
> Of a crowd of workmen and drivers in a bar-room, around the
> stove, late of a winter night—And I unremarked, seated in a
> corner;
> Of a youth who loves me, and whom I love, silently
> approaching, and seating himself near, that he may hold me
> by the hand;
> A long while, amid the noises of coming and going—of
> drinking and oath and smutty jest,
> There we two, content, happy in being together, speaking
> little, perhaps not a word.   (p. 371)

What is encrypted in the "One flitting glimpse" taken in the opening line here is an all-male tavern revel, essentially the same kind of scene represented in Whitman's 1841 story "The Child's Champion." But rather than locating the subject-position in a boy who is literally drawn into the scene through the window as that story does, this text inscribes a split subject-position, one divided between the passerby catching the "flitting glimpse" of a crowd of workingmen crowded around the stove in a bar late on a winter night on the one hand, and, on the other, the speaker of these lines, "unremarked" by the passerby's glance, "happy," "content," holding hands with a beloved "youth," "speaking little" or not at all with him. I have compared the translation of the boy through the window in "The Child's Champion" with the passage through the window of the young woman (or perhaps rather the male speaker who replaces her with himself) in the "twenty-eight bathers" section of "I celebrate myself," and have argued of those scenes that the figure of the desiring subject who becomes translated into the scene of his or her desire may serve as model of reading for the 1855 text, which is designed to serve as a "fluid" medium into which ostensibly any desire—and any desiring subject—can be projected.

In "One flitting glimpse," in contrast, the passing spectator and the desiring subject are different persons; indeed, the desiring subject does not even figure in the scene as observed by the spectator. Significantly, he is the specific figure who is mentioned as missing ("unremarked") from the glimpsed scene: the rest of the crowd, including the "youth," are present in it. Although his absence from the "glimpse" might be taken as a sign that he is in some sense impervious to the scene around him, like the woman in "Broad-Axe Poem" who is said to pass self-possessed and unoffended through a stream of men's "Oaths, quarrels, hicupped songs, proposals, smutty expressions" (1860 ed., p. 140), I would argue that the relation of these two figures to the respective scenes of "drinking and oath and smutty jest" they inhabit is asymmetrical: the woman hears and sees what is going on, but remains effectively closed to the scene, while the (male) speaker of "One flitting glimpse" feels perfectly at home in the atmosphere of charged male sexuality (drinking, swearing, and "smutty jest"), although (one might say) he and his lover inhabit this sexually charged atmosphere differently from the way their fellows do. Hence the split subjectivity of this text: what is disencrypted in this lyric is what is invisible to the fleeting passerby and even to the denizens of the tavern as they "com[e] and go[ ]": the strong current of erotic intersubjectivity shared by the male couple who sit quietly together for "a long while." The boy Charles and his "champion" Lankton in the early story are similarly said to have sat and "held communion" with each other; I have argued in my discussion of the story that Whitman's subsequent 1844 revision of this phrase to read that they merely "conversed" together is one of a number of signs in the text of defensive or self-protective self-consciousness about and self-censorship of the pronounced homoeroticism of the tale as he initially wrote it. The kind of erotic intersubjectivity that is literally encrypted—made cryptic—in the revised versions of "The Child's Champion" is recovered in the brief course of "One flitting glimpse," but it is significant that that is not the subject-position from where the poem is launched; that position (the "flitting glimpse[ ] caught" by a passerby) is represented as being simply disjunct from the double subject-position the poem celebrates.

Far from being uniformly "fluid," consciousness and desire in "One flitting glimpse" do not come flowing into the scene of the text through a window. The tavern window the boy is lifted through in "The Child's Champion" and "the blinds of the window" behind which the twenty-eight-bathers woman "hides" have narrowed to "an interstice" in "Calamus," but rather than occluding homoerotic intersubjectivity this narrowing focuses it.

"Calamus" no. 43 presents a similar, if even more compressed, scene of disencrypted intersubjectivity:

> O you whom I often and silently come where you are, that I
>   may be with you,
> As I walk by your side, or sit near, or remain in the same room
>   with you,
> Little you know the subtle electric fire that for your sake is
>   playing within me.   (p. 377)

This lyric too plays off a split subject-position against a dual, inter-subjective one, both bringing together and keeping apart the speaking subject who avows his desire ("subtle electric fire") and the erotic object who is largely unaware ("Little you know") of it. This time the doubling of the subject-position is not represented as being shared by two lovers in the text but between the speaking subject and the reader, whom this text invites to assume both positions: that of the speaker avowing his desire and that of the object of the desire which the text avows. This latter reading places this text within the series beginning with several in the 1855 *Leaves* in which the poet avows his desire for the reader; the former reading draws the desirous reader, object unspecified, into the intersubjective pleasure not of desire fulfilled, as in "One flitting glimpse," but simply of desire avowed. That this "sub-tle electric fire" is represented as "playing within" the speaking subject "for the sake of" the erotic object may be read as another example of the 1860 text's revisions of the "fluid"/solid dichotomy prevailing in the poetry of the first two editions: this "fire" (neither fluid nor solid) "play[s] within" the speaker; it does not eradicate the boundaries be-tween the speaker and the object of desire, as it would be expected to do in the first edition. Moreover, here the erotic object's "indifference" is not represented as arousing the kind of uninterrogated paranoid response that male indifference (reconstrued as hostility) to the subject repeatedly does in the second edition.

As I have argued of the third edition overall, the male-paranoid subject-position it recurrently represents is a cultivated one; it takes male paranoia as privileged psychic territory to be explored for what it reveals about the culture's occluding dispositions of desire among males. Many readers have responded to the "dark" (that is, paranoid) side of "Calamus" by assuming that some of these poems manifest paranoia simply because Whitman "was paranoid" at the time he wrote them, or because they represent his recollection of paranoia in tranquillity, as he wrote them after the end of a painful love affair with another man. In other words, they read the pronounced paranoid element in "Calamus" as having been determined by Whitman's own putatively personal psychic disturbances. Rather than accepting such a privatizing account of the sources and meaning of Whitman's relation to the neurotic deformations of desire systematized in his culture, including paranoid modes of relation, I wish to argue that Whitman locates a complex double position vis-à-vis paranoia in his writing. As I have pointed out in relation to his practice in other poems, it is characteristic of Whitman to represent subjectivity simultaneously *in the grip of* a deforming cultural formation (of which paranoia is one example) and *in the act of,* or perhaps more precisely, *in the act of imagining,* subverting the formation.

The sometimes paranoid subject-positions represented in "Calamus" claim to be most deeply threatened by the prospect of rejection in love; the short "Calamus" poems tend to oscillate between exploring this attitude and a complementary one, that what is most to be desired is unvarying attachment to another man. Death is sometimes presented as being in some ways less terrible than, and sometimes as the most appropriate figure for, the experience of falling in love and being rejected by the beloved. In other contexts, death more closely resembles the ostensibly most desirable condition of forming an inseparable attachment to another man. These complex interweavings of desirous fear, satisfied desire, and death in "Calamus" are haunted by another kind of web of fear and desire that is generally less explicitly articulated in these texts, but which is brought to the foreground in no. 20 ("I saw in Lousiana a live-oak growing"), which provides a good example of the oscillation of the subject-position between being overwhelmed by paranoia and overcoming paranoia.

This poem begins with the phrase (as it is set in the 1860 edition) "I SAW in Louisiana," which may incline a reader aware of the dense interplay in Whitman's poetry between the gaze, desire, and utterance to suspect that she or he is once again being invited for the moment to inhabit a scene of desirous gazing, akin to the ones adopted by the boy Charles near the beginning of "The Child's Champion," the lonely twenty-eight-year-old woman in the "twenty-eight-bathers" episode of "I celebrate myself," or the speaker of "Sun-Down Poem" ("Crossing Brooklyn Ferry") and his auditor. Of these, the "live-oak" is most closely related to the lonely woman. It is her inverse: it stands "[a]ll alone," as she does when she is introduced gazing through her window, but, unlike her, it "utter[s] joyous leaves" in splendid solitude, "[w]ith-out any companion," "without a friend, a lover near," and without any apparent desire for one.

The speaking subject of this poem oscillates between two different attitudes: on the one hand, recognizing and admiring the live-oak's power to flourish, grow, and sing ("uttering joyous leaves") without being nurtured by anyone or anything else's love, and being sure that he himself could not live without the love of others, and, on the other, becoming "fixated," so to speak, on the beautiful image he has seen of the tree's magnificent autonomy, an image in which he has caught sight of himself:

> I SAW in Louisiana a live-oak growing,
> All alone stood it, and the moss hung down from the branches,
> Without any companion it grew there, uttering joyous leaves of
>   dark green,
> And its look, rude, unbending, lusty, made me think of
>   myself . . . .

The tree's "look" in the last line quoted provides what I have called a characteristic "fold" in Whitman's language, especially when it is concerned with bodily contact and/or the gaze. Is the tree's "look" an effect of the speaking subject's looking at the tree, the tree's in some sense "looking at" the speaker, or their looking at each other—and, in this case, apparently noticing a resemblance? Partial specularity between subject and object reemerges in this poem: the speaker sees at least a semi-double in the figure of the tree "[u]ttering joyous leaves . . . without a friend, a lover , near." The speaker goes on to insist that his position is entirely different from the tree's:

> . . . though the live-oak glistens there in Louisiana, solitary, in
>   a wide flat space,

Uttering joyous leaves all its life, without a friend, a lover,
   near,
I know very well I could not.   (1860 ed., p. 365)

The impelling anxiety in this lyric is that the writer has done and may
continue to do precisely what the tree does: produce "joyous leaves"
in solitude. If this solitude is only the effect of the indifference of his
readers or potential readers, then the poet can disavow his sense of
writerly solitude as not being his fault (so to speak), since he claims
in this poem that without beloved persons "near," he could not write
at all—his very ability to write at all being a sign that his "leaves" are
the product of homoerotic intersubjectivity, fully dependent on his
having "friend" or "lover near." However, this claim is contradicted
by what one might call this text's fixation on the power of the live-oak
to produce "leaves" continuously, even "joyously," in isolation. "I saw
in Louisiana a live-oak growing" enacts a crucial aporia—one repeatedly emphasized in "Calamus"—between, on the one hand, sharing homoerotic desire and consciousness of such desire in ways not
directly mediated by language and, on the other, writing about them.
The "twig with a certain number of leaves upon it" that the poet
breaks off the tree and exhibits in his room "makes [him] think of
manly love," but it is also a sign of the disjunctions which prevail in
the 1860 *Leaves* between homoerotic experience and its representations in language. Desire, as Lacan writes in terms strikingly consonant
with this and others of the "Calamus" poems, "takes its heavy soul
from the hardy shoots of the wounded drive, and its subtle body from
the death actualized in the signifying sequence." In the aporia between
"heavy soul" and "subtle" body generated out of the subject's reading
of signs of death in the very signifying process itself (again according
to Lacan), "desire is affirmed as *the* absolute condition."[30]
   Lacan's notion of a "subtle body" which is ultimately the product
not of the literal death of the subject but of death as an effect of the
signifying process bears a significant resemblance to Whitman's notion
of a "real body" capable, like a font of type, of "returning impressions
indifferently." Particularly germane to an understanding of the
strengths of the "Calamus" poems is Lacan's botanical metaphor for
the sources of the "heavy soul" of desire: "the hardy shoots of the
wounded drive." In Lacan as in Whitman, such metaphors are intended to bridge the material (biological, corporeal) and the psychic

realms—indeed, to provide a powerful figure for the way in which the psychic is rooted in the material, which, in both authors, is paradoxically both "wounded" and "hardy."

Botanical figures of this kind abound in several key "Calamus" poems in addition to no. 20 ("I saw in Lousiana a live-oak growing"); the entire section, one should recall, is the only section of *Leaves of Grass* in any of its editions to bear a botanical name, that of what Whitman presents as the phallic reed of the calamus plant that grows in the "margins of pond-waters" ("Calamus" no. 1). "Calamus" no. 2, "Scented herbage of my breast," provides the most extensive exploration of such a set of figures in the 1860 *Leaves:* through its address to such figures as "Tomb-leaves, body-leaves" (line 3), "Perennial roots" (line 4), and "blossoms of my blood," "bitter," "burning and throbbing" (lines 7, 10, and 8), the text figures a body, its desires, and its writing as a bunch of "Leaves" that are corrosive rather than therapeutic in their effects: in fact, midway in the poem, the speaking subject in the text identifies them with Death ("Indeed, O Death, I think now these leaves mean precisely the same as you mean") and declares himself "indifferent" to life and death ("I am not sure but the high Soul of lovers welcomes death most"). Then, in the second half of the poem, the speaker repudiates his botanical symbols and their blistering effects ("Emblematic and capricious blades, I leave you—now you serve me not," line 23) in favor of making a direct appeal to "Death," or rather the "Love and Death" that "are folded together above all" in a kind of male-homoerotic oversoul ("the high Soul of lovers"). The poet calls his leaves "blades" here, one suspects, not only because they are sharp and potentially injurious like knife-blades ("Calamus" no. 15 [later "Trickle Drops"] elaborates the fantasy only hinted at here in "blades" in terms of literal self-wounding and bleeding on the pages of "Calamus"), but also in order to avoid the lexical redundancy of "Emblematic and capricious *leaves,* I *leave* you." The redundancy Whitman avoids by writing "blades" is worth pausing over: leaving *Leaves,* abandoning his writing project is one of the possibilities he explores in "Calamus," not only here but also in no. 8 ("I am indifferent to my own songs—I will go with him I love"), a text which Whitman excluded in its entirety from all subsequent editions of *Leaves,* along with its partner, no. 9, "Hours continuing long, sore and heavy-hearted."

Another kind of organic figure for the body and its desires other than the "Tomb-leaves, body-leaves" which "burn and sting" in "Calamus" no. 2 occurs in "Calamus" no. 25; here the figure is not merely "leaves" but specifically "leaves of grass":

> The prairie-grass dividing—its own odor breathing,
> I demand of it the spiritual corresponding,
> Demand the most copious and close companionship of men,
> Demand the blades to rise of words, acts, beings,
> Those of the open atmosphere, coarse, sunlit, fresh,
>   nutritious . . . . (p. 368)

This figure for Whitman's ideal community of male lovers is a complex one: men are represented as being both "dividing" or separate from one another (not simply "fluid"), breathing their own odor (they are self-aware, that is, conscious of themselves as subjects), yet nevertheless as "close" to each other as they are "copious," like grass. In the 1860 *Leaves*, significant differences have developed among various kinds of "leaves" and of botanical figures in general, depending on their relation to the text's strategic negation of the dominant culture's negation of death and male-homoerotic love. Gone is the kind of casual associations and equivalences made between figures like "crotch and vine" or "The sniff of green leaves and dry leaves" in the opening lines of the 1855 "I celebrate myself" (lines 14 and 16).

THE POETRY of the third edition continuously registers the perception that the kind of absolute affirmation of desire Lacan sees as arising from the aporia between "heavy soul" and "subtle body" may be politically problematic—to say the least. In order to return desire, especially of proscribed kinds, to a place somewhere within the orbit of the political "real," Whitman found it necessary to denigrate it to some degree from the absolute status it had been granted in the first edition, along with the imaginary powers of simply "fluidifying" all existing cultural boundaries which *Leaves of Grass* had initially imputed to it. An interesting parenthesis—one recalls that parentheses are "dead lips" throughout the 1860 edition—in "Calamus" no. 4 provides an economical representation of the dynamics of the partial denigration of desire in these poems:

(O here I last saw him that tenderly loves me—and returns
   again, never to separate from me,
And this, O this shall henceforth be the token of comrades—
   this calamus-root shall,
Interchange it, youths, with each other! Let none render it
   back!)   (p. 348)

The double sense of the word "last" in the first line of this passage
locates a notable ambiguity in "Calamus" overall: the word suggests
both that the speaker has seen the man "that tenderly loves [him]" for
the last time *ever* (that is, he is dead or otherwise entirely lost to the
subject), and that the speaker has seen the man merely for the "last"
(most recent) time before he departed for a while, and that the speaker
is now anticipating their reunion, "never to separate" again. There is
a contradiction in these lines between the comrade-lover who is said
to be expected to return and never to leave the speaker again, and the
token of this love, the calamus-root, which is supposed to continue
circulating more and more widely, always in the same direction—that
is, without ever being returned. At such a point we come upon yet
another example of the aporia these poems keep discovering between
sharing desire and circulating signs of that desire. Between the range
of intense male-homoerotic feelings that the "Calamus" poems are
designed to celebrate and any signs that can be made of this range of
feelings in writing—any "tokens" of it that can be disseminated
through writing—there may well be, according to this text, a rupture
that can only be figured as the death, burial, and decay of, in some
cases, the desiring subject and, in others, its object.

Calamus no. 27 represents a liminal moment in the processes of
disencryptment enacted in the poems, a moment in which both the
subject's past encryptments and his present disencrypted state powerfully interact:

O love!
O dying—always dying!
O the burials of me, past and present!
O me, while I stride ahead, material, visible, imperious as ever!
O me, what I was for years, now dead, (I lament not—I am
   content;)
O to disengage myself from those corpses of me, which I turn
   and look at, where I cast them!

To pass on, (O living! always living!) and leave the corpses
  behind! (pp. 369–370)

Like "One flitting glimpse" and "O you whom I often and silently
come where you are," this text manifests a split subject-position. Here,
the split is located in the same "self," one who refuses to "lament" his
many past "burials" but who at the same time is still struggling "to
disengage" himself from "those corpses of [himself]" which survive in
the wake of his own disencryptment. This poem insists that to pro-
nounce "now dead" one's past selves and their encrypted desires does
not automatically dispose of them or "disengage" oneself from them or
disencrypt those desires; one is still engaged with these even when one
can self-dividedly "turn and look at [them], where [one] cast them!"
In its republications subsequent to 1860, Whitman suppressed the
erotic focus of this text by canceling its opening line ("O love!") and
thereby obliterating his intentionally "morbid" linking of "love" with
perpetual death: "O love! / O dying—always dying!" Relocated in
1867 in the much more conventionally "morbid," "melancholy," or
"funereal" section, "Whispers of Heavenly Death," the text was neatly
rewritten as a variation on the literary commonplace that one is always
in the midst of death in life; it was retitled "O Living Always, Always
Dying," and the representation of the aporia between life and proscribed desire that makes the latter closely resemble the state of being
encrypted dropped out of the text.
    Calamus no. 17, "Of him I love day and night, I dreamed I heard
he was dead," was also subsequently removed by Whitman from
"Calamus" and relocated in "Whispers of Heavenly Death." This poem
begins:

Of him I love day and night, I dreamed I heard he was dead,
And I dreamed I went where they had buried him I love—but
  he was not in that place,
And I dreamed I wandered, searching among burial-places to
  find him,
And I found that every place was a burial-place. (p. 362)

In such lines Whitman unburies desires that have perforce been
encrypted, utterable (to borrow terms from "As I Ebb'd") only by
"dead lips," in parentheses, as it were. He relocates these desires in a
less delimited series of spaces, until this enormously enlarged scene

becomes the entire city ("The houses . . . / The streets, the shipping, the places of amusement") and finally the entire country ("Chicago, Boston, Philadelphia, the Mannahatta"). The speaker imagines the country becoming a vast necropolis, "fuller, O vastly fuller, of the dead than of the living." Reassigning this poem to "Whispers of Heavenly Death" has probably tended to make readers interpret it as a representation of a subject-position distorted by extreme morbidity, one which in its subjective excesses of melancholia would turn the whole world into an enormous graveyard to satisfy itself. Rereading this poem in its initial context in the 1860's edition's religion and politics of nature, grounded in the power of "real bod[ies]" to "return . . . impression[s] . . . indifferently," and in the specific context of the "Calamus" section's critique of the culture's increasingly harsh repression of homoerotic desire as death-dealing, as indeed actually being "death" in a sense that sheer bodily death is not, one can recover the significance of the speaker's imagining "the memorials of the dead [being] put up indifferently everywhere," for that phrase "indifferently everywhere" is a precise indication of the enlarged scope of the third edition's critique. The phrase links up this poem with the whole range of revisionary themes and modes of perception that are peculiar to the third edition, including most notably its appropriation and subversion of the enormous (over)investment of mid-nineteenth-century American culture in its own constructions of death as ultimate negative value. The *Leaves of Grass* project, like the culture with which it is so thoroughly engaged and which it so rigorously critiques, seems at the moment represented by the third edition to be in some ways piteously unaware of and in others to be consciously awaiting and prepared for the historical shock of the Civil War and the unprecedented degree to which "every place" in the United States was about to be turned into "a burial-place."

5

"The Blood of the World": Gender, Bloodshed, and the Uncanny in the Fourth (1867) Edition of *Leaves of Grass*

> My limbs, my veins dilate;
> The blood of the world has fill'd me full—my
>   theme is clear at last . . . .
>   —"Song of the Banner at Day-Break"

The Two Rhetorics of "Drum-Taps" and Their Consequences

In late 1860 Thayer and Eldridge, publishers of the third edition of *Leaves of Grass*, began advertising "a new volume of poems by Walt Whitman" to be entitled "Banner at Daybreak." The firm went bankrupt shortly thereafter, and five years passed before a doubtless much altered version of the projected volume appeared in the form of *Drum-Taps*. This volume is commonly spoken of as containing "Whitman's Civil War poems," but although its elegies for slain soldiers and vignettes of armies in arrested motion are among his most widely known poems, scholars such as Roger Asselineau have argued persuasively that a substantial number of the poems that appeared in *Drum-Taps* were quite probably written before the war started, or in its first few months.[1] On inspection, between a third and half of the poems that appeared in *Drum-Taps*—twenty-two of fifty-three—turn out to have as their respective subjects not scenes or events of the war itself but the political attitudes that led up to it.

This distinction is crucial to an understanding of the pre–Civil War poems in *Drum-Taps*, as it is to the following analysis of one of the chief of them, "Song of the Banner at Day-Break." These poems were written circa 1861–1862, during the period before Whitman himself became involved in the war through nursing ill and wounded soldiers. Their characteristic tone is one of hectic anticipation in which the coming war is idealized and almost embraced, despite the terrible cost it will no doubt exact, because it promises to bring to a seismic crisis, if not to an end, what Whitman sees as the national stasis that has characterized the 1850s in the United States. As is clear from writing of his like the pamphlet "The Eighteenth Presidency!" (unpublished during his lifetime), written toward the end of Buchanan's tenure in office and before the election of Lincoln, Whitman's disgust with the greed of the American economic establishment and its increasingly oppressive treatment of the labor force was even stronger than his opposition to slavery.[2] Consequently, in these poems, dread of war's destructiveness is leavened with excitement and joy at the prospect of the political and social ferment the conflict will inevitably cause.

Reading these poems of the idealization and anticipation of war alongside the subsequent poems which treat the actual experience of it, one may suspect that some of the grieving tone of the latter poems derives not only from the losses they mourn but also from the poet's painful and belated sense of the gross inadequacy of his initially enthusiastic response to the coming of war. Whitman never made any attempt to separate these two kinds of poems in "Drum-Taps" or to indicate that they are of two quite different kinds, either in the volume of poems entitled *Drum-Taps* that was published in New York in 1865 or in the "Drum-Taps" section he first added to the fourth (1867) edition of *Leaves of Grass*. In both places the earlier martial poems are dispersed throughout the text, with lines like "Thunder on! stride on . . . strike with vengeful stroke!" ("Rise O Days from your fathomless depths") and the proto-Kiplingesque "It's O for a manly life in the camp!" ("Drum-Taps") side by side with the famous elegies and memorial poems ("A Sight in camp in the day-break grey and dim," "The Wound Dresser," "Pensive on her dead gazing, I heard the mother of all," among others).

Given the avowals of candor and openness on which his project was posited, Whitman may well have thought that it would be inappropriate to suppress what may later have come to sound to him (as it has to some other readers) like mere saber-rattling. He left both kinds of poems to stand in paratactic relation to each other in the "Drum-Taps" section of *Leaves of Grass*, without any apparent suggestion of what the relation between them might be. Later in his career, Whitman would fashion what one might call a textual or discursive "hinge" designed to present some terms for linking the war-rhetoric of "Drum-Taps" with its elegy-rhetoric; in 1881 he incorporated in its entirety the 1871 poem "Aroused and Angry" in a parenthesis which he inserted after the first three lines of the "Wound-Dresser":

> . . . (Arous'd and angry, I'd thought to beat the alarum, and
> urge relentless war,
> But soon my fingers fail'd me, my face droop'd, and I resign'd
> myself,
> To sit by the wounded and soothe them, or silently watch the
> dead;) . . . .

But no such transitional statement appears in the Civil War poetry in its initial 1865 form, as a separate volume, or in its 1867 form, as part of the fourth edition of *Leaves of Grass*. As a result, there are frequently striking, even jarring, shifts in rhetoric and tone between one poem and another—probably to a higher degree than in any other section of *Leaves of Grass*. These two discordant rhetorics are the most marked quality of "Drum-Taps."

Rather than interpret this discord as simply an aesthetic failing, I propose to analyze it in this chapter as a sign of the intensification in the poetry of Whitman's program of revising contemporary conceptions of the range and meaning of bodily experience. Even more so than in the 1860 "Calamus" poems of male-homoerotic love and community, the "Drum-Taps" poems (both the "enthusiastic" ones and the elegiac ones) foreground human bodiliness to a high degree. They are written "closer to the body," so to speak, than perhaps any other group of poems in *Leaves of Grass*, designed as they are either to excite a sensational response of kinetic excitement, as a military parade might (for example, the poem with the repeated line, "Beat! beat! drums!—Blow! bugles! blow!"), or to memorialize the sufferings of the injured and dead of the war. The proximity of the writing to the kinds of bodies which it tries to incorporate—some of them strong and victorious, but most of them wounded, diseased, dismembered, or dead—has two main consequences: it intensifies the sexuality and gender-characteristics of the bodies represented, and it frequently renders the relations of these bodies to each other and to the reader uncanny.

Matters of gender and sexuality in this text are extremely highly charged, arising as they do in relation to the desire(s) of or for bodies that are no longer capable of being perceived as whole, "healthy," and labile. Whitman undertakes his most radical exploration of the construction of sexuality and gender roles in relation to the beloved bodies of the soldiers and of the imaginary mothers (of the dying soldiers; "of all," that is, of the Union) which also figure significantly in this poetry. Consequently the phallus, under patriarchy the primary sign not only of sexual power but of all power, is a central concern of this writing. Despite—or, paradoxically, because of—its primacy as sign in patriarchal culture, the unrepresentability of the phallus on the literal level is one of the culture's constitutive prohibitions. It is the double effect of the patriarchal regime of the unrepresentability of the phallus that its primacy should commonly be presented as being entirely "natural," and therefore not susceptible to change, as well as being thoroughly mystified, and therefore not susceptible to analysis or even simply to understanding.

In "Song of the Banner" Whitman explores some of the ways in which differences of political attitude among different groups with regard to the coming of the war correspond to their differences of position in relation to the paternal phallus. Maintaining the status quo, and thereby retaining the phallus, is the Father's wish, while the Child is represented as becoming intoxicated at the prospect of the eruption of chaos at the outbreak of the war, and the consequent possibility of the phallus's becoming unmoored from the paternal position and circulating through the filial and/or maternal positions. What "Song of the Banner" does not critique that some others of Whitman's poems do are the oedipal and infantile character of the fantasy that impels this text of appropriating the paternal phallus, chief sign and marker of the oedipal system, for the maternal and filial positions. The phallus "circulates" through the positions of the restricted family, rather than inhering in the paternal position, only in infantile fantasies of the appropriation and retention of the phallus from the father's body by the mother for her body, whence it issues in the form of "babies." The process of ceasing to be a "baby" and, for the male, becoming a "man"—a "father"—in oedipal culture involves negotiating a hazardous passage from having in a phantasmatic sense *been* the phallus or at least *a* phallus to *possessing* the phallus.

To the objection that it is unnecessary to "literalize" Whitman's

representations of the shifts in power among various persons and political communities in this poetry as transfers or exchanges of the *phallus*,
I would reply that it is an indispensable feature of Whitman's project
to expose his culture's occlusion of its fundamental practice of sym-
bolizing power in terms of male sexual domination, and that he does
this in his own practice mainly by exposing the culture's appropriation
of sexual exchange—which it constructs as solely phallic in nature—as
its primary way of conceiving and representing power, while obscuring
the fact that this alleged primacy is not a simple fact of "nature" but
is derived from its culture's tendentious dispositions of gender and
sexuality. Whitman repeatedly threatens the maintenance of the
paternal phallus as the unrepresentable ground of patriarchal representational programs in his writing. He threatens it by means of his "literal" representation of the male organ as one body-part among others,
rather than as *the* primary part, in (for example) the figure of the
"semitic [that is, seminal] muscle" in the 1855 Preface and "Poem of
Many In One"/"By Blue Ontario's Shores," or in his reference to his
penis in "Bunch Poem"/"Spontaneous Me" as "[t]his poem drooping
shy and unseen that I always carry, and that all men carry." Such
representations expose the fact that the penis is *not* identical with and
is in some important ways discontinuous with the symbolic entity—the
phallus—derived from it.

The phallus is represented in "Drum-Taps" by means of an entire
repertory of signs, including signs of the dominant paternal phallus but
also of the phantasmatic maternal phallus and the child-phallus.[3] It
could be argued that I am unnecessarily imposing Freudian terms on
an innocent nineteenth-century text by insisting on interpreting the
main repertory of signs in the 1867 edition as representing a fantasy
of the circulation of the phallus among figures of the restricted family—father, mother, and child; but I maintain that a highly phallicized
thematics of the erection and exposure of signs of power is central not
only to "Drum-Taps" but also to Whitman's culture's most public representations of political power and heroism, such as the heroic-nude
sculptures and outsize columns or "Washington monuments" that
proliferated in American cities during the antebellum period. This
thematics of erection and exposure could not be "safely" or innocently
isolated from phallic associations in the nineteenth century any more
than it can in the twentieth. Whitman's writing stands in adversary

relation to this public representational program, in which the phallus's "natural" and rightful association with paternal/patriarchal authority goes unchallenged.

Besides its intensification of issues of sexuality and gender, the other main consequence of the "closeness to the body" of the writing in "Drum-Taps" is that it frequently produces uncanny relations—in the writing, as in the reading. Freud theorized the uncanny in a 1919 essay in relation to such issues as the threat of castration and related anxieties about inanimate objects or bodies "coming to life" and watching us, or somehow gaining control of events or of other objects and bodies.[4] The uncanny has obvious relations to Whitman's general use of liminality in writing to project his physical presence through the text ("I spring from the pages into your arms," as he writes in one such moment in the 1860 "So long!"). Such effects are intensified in "Drum-Taps," where uncanny relations between author and reader and between figures and objects in the poems themselves multiply. These relations arise because "Drum-Taps" not only directly engages a thematics of phallic domination and exposure but also foregrounds one—the other side of the oedipal coin—of bodily suffering and possible "castration" and death, which are manifested as war injuries in relation to men and childbirth in relation to women. It also frequently represents human figures watching recently dead bodies (as in the case of the "Mother of All," "[p]ensive on her dead gazing"), bodies that have until very recently been alive and are consequently on a borderline between being alive and being dead in the eyes of the observer, as in the case of the speaker of "A Sight in camp in the day-break grey and dim," who uncovers the faces of three recently dead men and with surprise "recognizes" the third—as "Christ himself."

Near the end of "Song of the Banner at Day-Break," the figure of the Poet salutes the eponymous war-pennant of that poem as "Divider of day-break" (that is, divider of the light of day from the preceding darkness of night, *and* divider of the light of the dawn sky, of the ostensibly indivisible originary field of vision). Here, the text at least momentarily ignores some of the achievements of the third edition with regard to negotiating differences to take up again the thematics of dividing and crossing a hitherto unitary gaze and a similarly unitary field of vision that predominates in the second edition, in such key texts of that version of *Leaves of Grass* as "Broad-Axe Poem" and

"Sun-Down Poem"/"Crossing Brooklyn Ferry." In the fourth edition, division and reunion are often represented as being simultaneous moments, but moments in high tension with each other nonetheless. Like the war-pennant in "Song of the Banner," a number of the other major signs of the "Drum-Taps" poems paradoxically mark a point or place in the text as one of both division and (re)union. The 1867 text's strong tendency not to represent division without representing (re)union at the same moment derives from the central political conflict Whitman strives to come to terms with in this poetry: the catastrophic division by the violence of war during 1861–1865 of what he continues to insist on representing as the indivisible Union of the thirty-six United States.

I want now to demonstrate how the uncanny phallic thematics of the fourth edition is deployed in one of the most elaborate of the "Drum-Taps" poems.

"Man's desire and babe's desire": "Song of the Banner at Day-Break"

A representative text from the 1865 *Drum-Taps* and the fourth (1867) edition such as "Song of the Banner at Day-Break" raises some of the same kinds of questions I have considered in connection with the second (1856) edition, in such texts as "Broad-Axe Poem," "Bunch Poem," and "Poem of Women." These questions concern the relations of the range of subject-positions these poems construct and of the voices which enunciate these positions to various political and cultural phenomena such as patriarchy and the paternal phallus, to castration, to the maternal body and phallus, to state power and state violence and the possibility of resisting and opposing them. Such concerns are primary to the fourth edition as they had been to the second. In the 1865–67 version of *Leaves of Grass*, the kinds of recursive powers that had enabled the writing of the intervening edition of 1860 are largely suspended under the pressure of the war and its aftermath.

Some version of "Song of the Banner at Day-Break," the fourth poem in *Drum-Taps*, seems to have been written as early as late 1860, when the "Banner at Daybreak" volume, which appears to have taken its prospective name from the poem, was announced as forthcoming.

"Song of the Banner" frequently strikes a markedly hysterical tone, as in its opening lines:

> O a new song, a free song,
> Flapping, flapping, flapping, flapping, by sounds, by voices
> clearer,
> By the wind's voice and that of the drum,
> By the banner's voice, and child's voice, and sea's voice, and
> father's voice,
> Low on the ground and high in the air,
> On the ground where father and child stand,
> In the upward air where their eyes turn,
> Where the banner at day-break is flapping.

The focus between "Low on the ground" and "high in the air" in this opening stanza is mobile, as is the location of the imputed source of the sound of the "Flapping, flapping, flapping, flapping" which is constitutive of the "new song" the poem both announces and is. In its opening stanza one hears a babble of voices, the wind's, the drum's, the banner's, the child's, the sea's, and the father's. Both the poem's point of view and its location of the sources of the utterances continually oscillate along a vertical axis. These imputed sources are to begin with not one or two or even three voices, but six: two human (child and father), two natural (wind and sea), and two military (drum and banner). The figure of the Poet, who speaks the poem's first eighteen and many of its subsequent lines, circulates among these varying points of view, "weav[ing] . . . and twin[ing]" them into his "song" (line 13).

Frederik Schyberg, in his description of the poem—one of the very few favorable accounts of it in the critical literature of the past fifty years—normalizes the polyvocality of this poem by calling it a "cantata."[5] The term is only partly adequate because it tends to collapse the numerous, frequently shifting sources of the poem's enunciation into the relatively simple, two-dimensional space of the cantata, which consists of soloist(s) and chorus arranged in a stable foreground-to-background relation to each other. Although "Song of the Banner" is one of Whitman's most ambitious attempts to produce in poetry some of the effects of opera and related dramatic forms of vocal music, the poem cannot entirely be assimilated to these forms because it continuously destabilizes the conventions of dramatic narrative and performance which constitute opera and its related musical sub-genres.

Rather than presenting its chief figures—Child, Father, Poet, and War-Pennant—in stable figure-to-ground relations to each other and to the reader, "Song of the Banner" continuously moves through these subject-positions, one after the other. Eventually the Poet's position comes to subtend two of the other positions, the Banner's and the Pennant's on the one hand and the Child's on the other, as he gradually articulates the "new" and "free song" of "war and defiance" which the Banner and Pennant "sing" and which the figure of the Child apprehends and passionately responds to.

However, for approximately the first half of the poem, the problem of "where to listen" remains inseparable from the problem of "where to look," for the "flapping" which the poem both *is* and *is about* is simultaneously a sight and a sound. The first stanza begins, "O a new song, a free song, / Flapping, flapping, flapping, flapping, by sounds, by voices clearer," and it ends with a directing of the Father's and Child's (and by implication the reader's) view upward, to gaze at "the banner at day-break . . . flapping." From the first words each of them utters, the Child's gaze remains directed upward, while the Father's becomes fixed resolutely forward for the rest of the poem:

CHILD

Father, what is that in the sky beckoning to me with long
    finger?
And what does it say to me all the while?

FATHER

Nothing, my babe, you see in the sky;
And nothing at all to you it says. But look you, my babe,
Look at these dazzling things in the houses, and see you the
    money shops opening . . . .

The intensity of either figure's gaze, one upward and the other forward, is nearly deliriant, and the rest of the poem traces out some of the political implications of these rival gazes. That neither figure's gaze is directed at the other may remind the reader of issues raised earlier about the second edition, especially the significance of the two gazes in "Sun-Down Poem." In "Song of the Banner," however, these gazes are not crossed. This text's privileging of gazing as a perceptual mode is in keeping with its initial dismissal of "book-words" as a vehicle of meaning: the banner only "flaps," but its visual *and* aural "flapping" is somehow extremely moving to the Child as well as to the Poet, who "translates" the thrilling "flapping" back into language-in-the-form-of-"book-words." The antiliterary impulses which underlie the *Leaves of Grass* project also manifest themselves here:

> Words! book-words! what are you?
> Words no more, for hearken and see,
> My song is there in the open air—and I must sing,
> With the banner and pennant a-flapping.

Content to seize on material textuality—actual printed books—as a medium for disseminating what he insisted on calling his actual physical presence to the reader at the beginning of his project (that is, in the 1855 poems), Whitman radically revised this idea as early as 1856 in "Sun-Down Poem" ("Crossing Brooklyn Ferry"), in which conditions of absence and distance between poet and reader are provisionally overcome by his imagining the possibility of a paradoxically prospective-retrospective vision capable of linking himself to posterity with the directness of a mutual gaze. This gaze cannot actually be exchanged because of the temporal separation of its respective directors: it has to be mediated by the spectacle of sunset on the waters of the East River, in which the gazes of both nineteenth-century poet and ("A hundred years hence") twentieth-century reader can fix themselves and in a sense find each other in the imaginary visual space of the poem. The fantasy of passing through the printing press "body-and-soul" to reemerge into direct physical contact with the reader impels a representative 1855 poem like "Come closer to me" (later "A Song for Occupations"). A competing fantasy impels "Sun-Down Poem"/ "Crossing Brooklyn Ferry": that of unmediated access between poet and reader through the projection between them of a mutual gaze in which both parties cannot actually be physically participant because they live in different centuries. These fantasies of presence are recast in the third (1860) edition as the recursive capacity, shared by printer's type and the "real body," for "returning impressions indifferently," for being turned into text and then breaking down into something relatively elusive or fugitive from semantic organization which is nonetheless capable of reemerging as text. In doing so, this "substance," which is neither simply corporeal nor simply spiritual, but a compound of both ("the real body"), also becomes capable of figuring new kinds of relations of embodiment, as I have discussed in relation to the "Calamus" poems.

The dynamic relationship between powerful tendencies toward both disintegration and recursivity in the third *Leaves of Grass* is extended and modified in the fourth. In the 1867 volume, to which "Drum-Taps" (1865) is the principal new addition, the dialectical movement among the first four editions with regard to the contest for primacy between the experience of reading words versus that of looking at nonverbal phenomena (the motions of air, light, water, one's own and other people's bodies) oscillates again toward the pole of the gaze directed away from the book and toward other objects. Here, in "Song of the Banner," text-making is represented as being preparatory to a more primal activity, which is the Poet's answering or "compet[ing] [w]ith" the simultaneously visual and aural "flapping" of the banner. The third and final prefatory stanza of the poem concerns the Poet's means for "compet[ing] [w]ith" the banner:

I'll weave the chord and twine in,
Man's desire and babe's desire—I'll twine them in, I'll put in life;
I'll put the bayonet's flashing point—I'll let bullets and slugs whizz;
I'll pour the verse with streams of blood, full of volition, full of joy;
Then loosen, launch forth, to go and compete,
With the banner and pennant a-flapping.

The specific term for language ("verse") in this stanza is combined with a whole series of other terms for what may seem at first to be an inchoate field of human impulses and perceptions—"desire" ("Man's" and "babe's"), "volition" and "joy" ("pour[ed]" in "with streams of blood") combined with the striking sight of "the bayonet's flashing point" and the no less striking sound of the "whizz" of bullets. "[W]eav[ing]" and "twin[ing]" this highly various series of phenomena will, according to this passage, "loosen" and "launch forth" the poem not merely to represent but "to go and compete" actively with the Banner and Pennant's "flapping."

In order to see how these disparate elements constitute the text and in what sense the text is designed to "compete with" the sight and sound of the banner, it is necessary to notice how these elements—"streams of blood," kinetic impulses of the body and the self ("volition" and "joy"), sights and sounds of battlefield violence—interact through the remainder of the poem. After the three prefatory stanzas, the poem proper begins with a metrically irregular quatrain in which the Poet "translates" the Banner and Pennant's "flapping" into words. The Banner "says":

> Come up here, bard, bard;
> Come up here, soul, soul;
> Come up here, dear little child,
> To fly in the clouds and winds with us, and play with the
>   measureless light.

The Child—never gendered in the poem—directs its response not directly to the Banner but to the Father:

> Father, what is that in the sky beckoning to me with long
>   finger?
> And what does it say to me all the while?

The Father responds:

> Nothing, my babe, you see in the sky;
> And nothing at all to you it says. But look you, my babe,
> Look at those dazzling things in the houses, and see you the
>   money-shops opening;
> And see you the vehicles preparing to crawl along the streets
>   with goods:
> These! ah, these! how valued and toil'd for, these!
> How envied by all the earth!

The Child hears the Banner's appeal, but the Father does not; his eyes are fixed not on the sky or the Banner but on the commercial pageant of the city streets—to the exclusion of other possible foci: he tells his child that it sees "Nothing" and that the Banner is saying "nothing at all."

The Father's stern insistence on the value of the mundane "goods" before them in contrast with the Child's attraction to the Banner's song which the Father cannot or will not hear recalls the oblique triangular structure of address of Goethe's celebrated ballad *Erlkönig*, which Whitman may have known as "The Erl-King" in the widely reprinted translation of Sir Walter Scott, one of his favorite poets as a youth. He also may have known the ballad in Schubert's extraordinary (and extraordinarily dramatic) musical setting for solo voice and piano.[6] Whitman rarely took a predecessor's text as a model for a poem of his own, but the palimpsestic relation of "Song of the Banner at Day-Break" to *Erlkönig* is striking, as a look at the first three stanzas of Scott's translation will make apparent:

> O who rides by night thro' the woodland so wild?
> It is the fond father embracing his child;
> And close the boy nestles within his loved arm,
> To hold himself fast, and to keep himself warm.

> "O father, see yonder! see yonder!" he says;
> "My boy, upon what dost thou fearfully gaze?"
> "O, 'tis the Erl-King with his crown and his shroud."
> "No, my son, it is but a dark wreath of the cloud."

> THE ERL-KING SPEAKS
> "O come and go with me, thou loveliest child;
> By many a gay sport shall thy time be beguiled;
> My mother keeps for thee full many a fair toy,
> And many a fine flower shall she pluck for my boy."

Like the Erl-King, the Banner would have the Child come away "[t]o fly in the clouds and winds with us, and play with the measureless light," while the Father in both poems insists on the unreality of the apparition that would spirit the Child away.

   If Whitman were recalling Goethe's/Scott's ballad, part of his revision of it from what he would have called a "feudal" to a "democratic" text might have been to introduce as he does the supplementary figure of the poet into the dramatic Child-Father-Banner situation. The poet whom Whitman adds to "Song of the Banner" is as "dangerous" as we have learned to expect such supplements to be: 88 (almost two-thirds) of the text's 146 lines are spoken by him. He is "dangerous" insofar as he, among all the figures in it, most nearly dominates this otherwise largely decentered poem. The thirty-two lines of Goethe's ballad and of Scott's translation of it are much more nearly equally distributed among its four speakers: the Erl-King himself speaks ten lines; the boy and the narrator eight apiece; and the father six. The narrator of *Erlkönig*/"The Erl-King" speaks only the opening and closing quatrains of the poem, ushering in the scene of the father riding through the night, his child in his arms, and narrating their climactic homecoming:

> Sore trembled the father; he spurr'd thro' the wild,
> Clasping close to his bosom his shuddering child;
> He reaches his dwelling in doubt and in dread,
> But clasp'd to his bosom, the infant was dead.

At least for the American reader unacquainted with the folk traditions from which Goethe's poem derives, no readily discernible politics informs the spiriting away of the child from his father by the erl-king. In contrast, the Poet in Whitman's poem elaborates the broad political significance of the conflict he perceives between the Child, who wants to follow the Banner (and even to become the Banner), and the Father, who wants to preserve the status quo of the American 1850s, especially as it was serving to enrich the financiers and industrialists of the northeastern cities, even if doing so involves denying the meanings the Child and the Poet attribute to the flapping Banner.[7] "Demons and death then I sing," the Poet says (at the beginning of his next-to-last "aria" in the poem), revealing a second way he is "dangerous," as he incites the reader to share his enthusiasm for war in the same way the Banner is inciting the Child.

Those trained only to read "book-words" (line 9), which are degraded by people like the Father in the poem into being mere commercial words, can hear only nonsense in the song of the Banner and of songs like it, including "The Song of the Banner," but for those capable of understanding such nonverbal "songs," they are overfull of meaning:

CHILD

> O father, it is alive—it is full of people—it has children!
> O now it seems to me it is talking to its children!
> I hear it—it talks to me—O it is wonderful!
> O it stretches—it spreads and runs so fast! O my father,
> It is so broad, it covers the whole sky!

In these lines the Pennant manifests its meaning not only as phallus but as maternal phallus and maternal body. "[I]t is full of people—it has children!" is the first line that associates the pennant with the maternal body. But it is also a maternal "phallus" and not simply a maternal "body" (as the rest of the stanza indicates) because "it stretches—it spreads and runs . . . / It is so broad, it covers the whole sky!" In other words, it manifests both a primacy as sign—to "erect" itself over all—and a power as primal sign to tend to obliterate other signs—to "cover[ ]" them, at least temporarily.

The Pennant continues to "unfold" its meanings for the Child here in the sense in which Whitman used the term in the 1856 "Poem of Women" (later "Unfolded Out of the Folds"). In the Child's eyes, the Pennant's flaps and folds become signs of the power of the mother's body and the potency of the maternal phallus. My interpretation of the Pennant in "Song of the Banner" as maternal phallus is indebted to Derrida's interpretation of "Nietzsche's umbrella" as "hermaphroditic spur (*éperon*)," "a phallus which is modestly enfolded in its veils, an organ which is at once aggressive and apotropaic, threatening and/ or threatened."[8] The doubleness this "spur" exudes is precisely the doubleness that marks Whitman's early war poetry, both dreading and welcoming war ("at once aggressive and apotropaic, threatening and/or threatened"). Signs of sexual doubleness ("a phallus . . . modestly enfolded in veils") proliferate in the poems of the fourth edition to an unprecedented degree. In these poems perhaps more than any others of Whitman's one repeatedly encounters signs of a sexuality—a feminine and a maternal one—that is represented as being fiercely menaced by others and whom it in turn menaces. In this edition the "mother of all" is repeatedly represented as being threatened by her (male) enemies, but for each of these vulnerable figures there is a counter-figure elsewhere in the text, such as the figure of the fully phallicized "Mother! with subtle sense severe, with the naked sword in your hand" of "By Blue Ontario's Shore" (line 260).

In the asemantic "flapping" of the Pennant as maternal phallus/body the Child sees and hears that "it is alive—it is full of people—it has children! / . . . it is talking to its children!" The chief of its powers is that of "talking to its children" through channels other than the verbal/linguistic ones the Father in the poem employs—through the visual and tactile contact and exchanges between mother and child and their respective bodies which Kristeva calls the "semiotic."[9] The Child's intense apprehension of the flapping Banner's meaning here mounts to fully delirious proportions ("it talks to me"), and the Father is disgusted and distressed with what he sees as the extravagant non-sense of the Child's response. He once again tries to recall it to the "solid" world of city streets and houses, and of semantically ordered language, which he inhabits and admires:

> Cease, cease, my foolish babe,
> What you are saying is sorrowful to me—much it displeases me;
> Behold with the rest, again I say—behold not banners and
> pennants aloft;
> But the well-prepared pavements behold—and mark the solid-
> wall'd houses.

In response to this, the "Banner and Pennant" urges the Poet (the "bard, out of Manhattan") to assume the role of the mother to "[s]peak to our children all" in the nonsemantic ("semiotic" in the Kristevan sense) language(s) of the "hum" of "factory-engines . . . where our miners delve the ground" and the "hoarse . . . rumbles" of Niagara Falls "where our prairie-plows are plowing." The figures of mining and plowing, conventional ones for sexual penetration of the female body, firmly anchor the "hum" and "rumbles" that the poet is ordered to reproduce in his poetry in their imputed origin in the maternal body. In keeping with the prelogical status of the kinds of unconscious fantasies of the maternal body and phallus of which it is the sign in the poem, the Banner admits its own inability to say *why* it should be raised above every other thing as it instructs the Poet in how to "[s]peak to our children" in a way that they will find irresistible: "For what are we, mere strips of cloth, profiting nothing, / Only flapping in the wind?"

"Profiting nothing" is a phrase upon which much in this text turns: both terms are key ones, for the negation of the single-minded de-votion to "profit," to the uninterrupted expansion of peacetime bourgeois-capitalist development, which the Father represents, is a principal effect of the poem. The Poet responds to the Banner's ques-tion about its and the Pennant's avowed worthlessness in an elaborate speech in which he declares that he "hear[s] and see[s] not strips of cloth alone." In hearing and seeing the Banner and Pennant, he says, he "hear[s] the tramp of armies," "drums," "trumpets," and the sounds lift him aloft to a point where he takes a bird's-eye view of "the precious results of peace": "numberless farms" and "populous cities, with wealth incalculable." "Sweeping the whole," he says, still speaking from his aerial perspective, "I see the countless profit." But the "countless profit" he sees is different both from the scene of amassed social wealth the Father urges the Child to attend to as they stand in the urban street and from the "no-profit" ("profiting nothing") the Banner and Pennant see when they look at themselves and see "mere strips of cloth." What the Child and then the Poet sees is that the signs of national wealth one sees from on high, from the Banner's and Pennant's perspective, constitute a phenomenon of a different order from the signs of riches the Father sees in the "goods" and "solid-wall'd houses" that fill the city streets.

Alongside the "starry banner" of the American flag, which has come to represent the pursuit of material production for its own sake, the Poet would raise

> . . . overall, (aye! aye!) my little and lengthen'd pennant
> shaped like a sword,
> . . . [I]ndicating war and defiance . . . .

Traditional republican iconology had tended to represent the "higher" or heroic values it imputed to its ideal leaders in the readily recognizable phallic forms of classical temple architecture, heroic-nude sculpture, and outsize columns, such as the mammoth "Washington monuments" that were being erected in Baltimore and Washington, D.C., in the 1840s and 1850s. In "Song of the Banner," Whitman challenges the colossal sign of the phallus and the particular forms of social and political domination it represents by opposing to it two other kinds of phallic signs: the maternal phallus, in the figure of the Banner that "stretches . . . spreads and runs so fast . . . [and] covers the whole sky," and the child-phallus, the "little and lengthen'd pennant shaped like a sword," a scandalous sign "indicating war and defiance" against those who would maintain the peacetime status quo whatever the consequences, along with their representational regime of patriarchal phallic monuments.

In comparison with signs of the paternal phallus, which have traditionally taken highly reified forms—they were literally hypostatized in monumental stone in Whitman's culture—signs of the maternal phallus and the child-phallus are relatively unstable and elusive (that is, liminal). The reason for this is *not* that what I am calling the maternal phallus and the child-phallus are not really or significantly related to the phallic realm and might more usefully be called or thought of as something else, but that under the patriarchal constraints of the oedipal system these phantasmatic figures are derived from the paternal phallus and are never fully separated from or independent of it in the unconscious fantasies in which they figure. I have said that the male organ is itself not simply identical with the phallus, but has the relation to the phallus of bodily organ to the symbolic entity directly derived from it. There is, however, some "overlap" in the oedipal system between penis and paternal phallus, one of partial identity between real object and symbolic entity. In contrast, maternal phallus and child-phallus are derived from symbolic entity (the paternal phallus) rather than from bodily organ—and at one and two removes, respectively, even from that, as I shall explain.

Notions of a maternal phallus and a child-phallus arise from unconscious fantasies (most intense in infancy or early childhood) about the mother's appropriating the phallus, which she "lacks," from the father—by retaining it in her body after intercourse. Held in her body, this maternal phallus phantasmatically becomes the "baby" or "babies" which the maternal body has the power of producing. Once produced, this progeny retains some of its imaginary character as phallus, so that in a sense the child "is" rather than "has" a phallus; hence the term "the child-phallus," as opposed to the "child's phallus," which would suggest that the child could fully assume the phallic position. In the oedipal scheme, it cannot, since one cannot be said to "have" a phallus as long as in some sense one "is" a phallus.

In these fantasies the figure(s) of the mother and her body are still powerful ones, not having yet been subordinated to the circuits of oedipalized male-heterosexual desire in which "woman" *is* in some sense identical with the phallus and is therefore by definition one who herself "lacks" the phallus. A text like "Song of the Banner" draws much of its considerable energy from its remobilization of infantile fantasies of maternal power, and of maternal power as representing some kind of alternative to paternal power—before the "lack" that defines the figure of the mother in the oedipal system is imposed on her. That the filial position may also redefine itself in terms derived from, *but not irremediably subordinate to,* paternal power and its chief sign, the paternal phallus, is a condition enabled by the reactivation of the fantasy of the maternal phallus.

Once the Pennant has manifested its meaning of child-phallus in the figure of the "little and lengthen'd pennant," the Child's response to it becomes uncontrollably intense, and the Father is forced to stop denying the Pennant's presence (he has previously referred to it as "Nothing") and to acknowledge its terrible counter-significance for the order he is defending:

CHILD

O my father, I like not the houses;
They will never to me be anything—nor do I like money;
But to mount up there I would like, O father dear—that
    banner I like;
That pennant I would be, and must be.

FATHER

Child of mine, you fill me with anguish;
To be that pennant would be too fearful;
Little you know what it is this day, and henceforth forever;
It is to gain nothing, but risk and defy everything;
Forward to stand in front of wars—and O, such wars!—what
    have you to do with them?
With passions of demons, slaughter, premature death?

Whitman's reordered republic requires two signs at this point in the development of his political critique in *Leaves of Grass:* the stars-and-stripes (the "Banner") to stand for its history from the Revolution to the mid-nineteenth century, and now alongside it the scandalous and defiant "Pennant" as a countersign to the dominant tendency of allowing commercial politics to displace all other political activities in the United States of the 1850s. In the concluding sections of the poem, the Banner is associated with the figure(s) of the mother and the maternal phallus and the Pennant with the figure(s) of the Child and the child-phallus.

The Child's phrase "that banner I like" ("I like not the houses . . . / . . . nor do I like money; / But . . . that banner I like") delicately balances the related issues of desire and identity in this text. The Child's words indicate its awareness that it both "likes" and is in some sense (but not entirely) "like" the Banner, the traditional sign for the nation, whereas the Child's identification with the new sign for the nation's intense arousal in response to political crisis is more nearly total—it has, in fact, the nature of a compulsion: "that banner I like," *but* "That pennant I would be, would be, and must be." "Liking" or being "like" the Banner is voluntary and leaves the Child's identity intact and essentially unchanged, but "becoming" and "being" the Pennant involves a thoroughgoing transformation of identity on the Child's part. On the symbolic register, the Child can both "like" and be partially "like" the Banner, the sign of the maternal phallus, but he must become identical with the Pennant, sign of the child-phallus, of his own derivative relationship to both paternal and maternal phallus in the oedipal system. On the political register, in the role the Child achieves by the poem's end, as exemplary subject and exemplary citizen, it (that is, the ungendered Child) enacts the poem's premise that while peacetime patriotism is at most a partial pursuit, wartime patriotism is total, all-consuming, demanding that one "risk and defy everything" (in the pacifist Father's words), "demons, slaughter, premature death[.]"

The disjunction between the two states of "liking" the Banner and "having to be" the Pennant as this text represents them is absolute. The Father's question to the Child ("[W]hat have you to do . . . / With passions of demons," and so forth) goes unanswered; the two figures pass out of the poem at this point, the Father (one suspects) to retire into "the solid-wall'd houses" and the Child to follow the Pennant. The respective gazes of the two figures never shift: the Father keeps his eyes resolutely forward, and the Child upward. Gazes are never exchanged in this text; the Child looks up and the Poet looks down, but they do not look *at* each other.

I want to consider for a moment how the respective gazes in "Song of the Banner" compare with other significant representations of the gaze in Whitman's writing. One may, for example, make some connections between the figures of the Child in this poem and the boy in "The Child's Champion." Instead of being rescued from a "demon" (the drunken sailor) and drawn "upward" into domestic bliss with his rescuer, as the boy Charles is in Whitman's early tale, the Child in "Song of the Banner" is represented as being drawn irresistibly away from domestic security in the "solid-wall'd houses" of the paternal realm and upward into direct contact with the demonic in the form of the violence of warfare. "Song of the Banner," though, does not itself go on to represent, but only briefly to anticipate, what that contact will be like and what its effects on the Child will be.

Similarly, the Father's overvaluation of "houses" and "money-banks" may remind the reader of the figure of the woman who "owns the fine house by the rise of the bank" and "hides handsome and richly drest aft the blinds of the window." Her gaze is represented as literally transporting her out of the "interior" scene of her sequestered and isolating prosperity into the scene of open-air freedom of the twenty-eight bathers. Again, if one compares the respective trajectories of Father and Child in "Song of the Banner," what is strikingly different about the later poem is that in contrast to the woman in the "twenty-eight bathers" episode, the Father's gaze leads him nowhere, and though the Child's gaze *does* lead it away from the scene of oppressive prosperity, this text represents only the beginning and not the completion of its passage into or through the "other" realm into which it feels compelled to follow the "pennant of war."

What impels "The Song of the Banner at Day-Break" is a fantasy of war both as a recovery of the forsaken and/or prohibited pleasures and terrors of reunion with the maternal body and as a catastrophic pederastic utopia, "launch[ed]" by the poet in the form of the child's exchange with (one should perhaps rather say *for*) the "little and lengthen'd" phallic pennant of war. Lest I seem to be reducing the Civil War to an internalized and miniaturized "psychological conflict" rather than acknowledging its enormous complexity as a political and historical phenomenon, I would emphasize at this point that what I am describing is not anything so grandiose as "the psychological reasons for the Civil War" but rather the logic of a symbolic (re)construction in a literary text of one kind of response to an early phase of the war. In assessing the degree to which factors which are often reduced to "psychic" or "psychological" ones—although I would argue that they too are political rather than "merely private" phenomena—such as an unconscious yearning for reunion with a maternal body can be said to have figured significantly in Whitman's attempts to grasp the meaning (or some meaning) of the war symbolically, it may be useful to remember that for many persons like him who were not committed abolitionists, the war was fought not so much "to end slavery" as it was for the purpose of "preserving the Union"—a goal which was highly susceptible to elaboration in symbolic and phantasmatic terms, including some derived from powerful early experiences of separation from and reunion with the mother's body.

In the poem's last ten lines, the possible conflicts between the range of meanings associated with the Banner and those associated with the Pennant—conflicts successfully held at bay for most of the poem—reassert themselves. As becomes clear in the poem's closing lines, the two flags represent ideas of national self-enlargement or self-engrossment that are ultimately incompatible with each other and cannot be reconciled with each other even in the limited symbolic space of the text. The poet heralds the banner (that is, the stars-and-stripes) for its "cluster of stars, (ever-enlarging stars)," by which he means that its *field of stars is continually increasing in number, rather than "enlarg*ing" in the sense in which he "enlarges" himself or his identity in this final section, by erection or "dilation." The maternal phallus "enlarg[es]" itself not by the dilation of erection (as the paternal phallus does) but by that of gestation and parturition: it produces not merely a temporarily "raised" body-part but, rather, more bodies. In doing so, it manifests its ambiguous status as a phallus which is a consequence of its phantasmatic derivation from the paternal phallus.

The dichotomy between self-enlargement by erection versus self-enlargement by gestation and parturition has its equivalent for Whitman on the level of the history of the gradual self-enlargement of the United States. Political incorporation by annexation is the means by which the country had increased and would continue to increase the geographical scope of its territory during Whitman's lifetime. Once the "manifest destiny" which impelled and allegedly justified this expansionist political practice was fulfilled and all of North America was incorporated into the United States, Whitman imagined that the ideal site would have been established on which the great spiritual project that he identified with America's utopian potential could be completed and fulfilled in the expansion-by-dilation of the American people. The signs of his concern with revising the sex-gender system which was coming to prevail in this country during the first dozen years of the career of *Leaves of Grass* can be understood at least in part as representing a series of permutations, of experimental reassignments on his part, of men's, women's, and children's potential relations to what Whitman perceives as the inevitably phallic, but not necessarily paternal-phallic, foundations of the social order. For reasons that "Song of the Banner at Day-Break" makes clear on the level of the symbolic register, the historical moment in which Whitman could imagine that the conflagration of the Civil War was to be ardently desired, insofar as it would be a watershed event in the transition from the process of geographical nation-enlargement that he was witnessing to the process of mass-spiritual "dilation" among Americans that he was prophesying, was in actuality a quite short-lived one. It would be as brief, in fact, as the corresponding moment in the career of *Leaves of Grass* when the figures of the maternal phallus and the child-phallus could serve as signs of the utopian potential of war. Whitman soon decided that the reality of the "relentless war" far exceeded the sign-repertory available to him or any other writer for representing either its horrors or the heroism of its millions of victims.

"Holes in the Real": Wounds in the Text

We have seen that "Song of the Banner at Day-Break," a representative text from *Drum-Taps* and the fourth (1867) edition, raises some of the same questions that the poetry of the second (1856) edition raises. "Pioneers! O Pioneers!", one of the most popular of the *Drum-Taps* poems and one which has generally been held in almost as low critical esteem as "Song of the Banner," manifests its intertextuality with "Broad-Axe Poem" in its opening lines:

> Come, my tan-faced children,
> Follow well, in order, get your weapons ready,
> Have you your pistols? have you your sharp-edged axes?
> Pioneers! O pioneers!

In its seventh stanza the poem represents the kind of ostensibly beneficent rapine carried out on the land which is the primary contradictory action represented earlier in "Broad-Axe Poem":

> We primeval forests felling,
> We the rivers stemming, vexing we, and piercing deep the
> mines within;
> We the surface broad surveying, and the virgin soil upheaving,
> Pioneers! O pioneers!

The poet's intensely ambivalent feelings toward what he here represents as a corporate activity in which he unhesitatingly joins manifest themselves a little farther on, in stanza 10:

> O resistless, restless race!
> O beloved race in all! O my breast aches with tender love for all!
> O I mourn and yet exult—I am rapt with love for all,
>   Pioneers! O pioneers!

Only a slight lexical supplement is required to transform the "restless" race of mid-nineteenth-century Americans—a quality which bears largely negative connotations in traditional Christian codes of conduct, which generally equated repose with sanctity and "restlessness" with worldliness and resistance to sanctification—to the "resistless" race which is either or both "irresistible" (that is, unbrookable by any outside force) or "lacking in resistance" to its own compulsions to keep moving and keep developing new means of domination by physically transforming the North American landscape and the peoples who inhabit it.[10] The success at domination enjoyed by his own "resistless, restless race" makes the speaker "mourn and yet exult" at the same time. He figures his relationship to the other members of his race as a masochistic one, in which he "aches with tender love for all" and is "rapt with love for all"—which is to say, he is himself in turn only a slight lexical shift away from being in some sense "raped" with/by the "tender love" he attributes to himself but not to his fellow "pioneers," for the "western youths" with/by whom he is "rapt" are "full of manly pride and friendship" for each other (stanza 2), but they are not "rapt" with the kind of "tender love" which makes them seem irresistible ("resistless") to the poet-speaker.

As in "Song of the Banner," the poet in "Pioneers! O Pioneers!" resists his culture's privileging of the paternal phallus. But here, rather than being able to imagine what is for him the utopian possibility of circulating a fraternal phallus, as he has in "Calamus" (most explicitly in "Calamus" no. 4, "These I, Singing in Spring": "Interchange it [the calamus-root], youths, with each other! Let none render it back!"), the poet-speaker makes a defensive move against the paternal phallus with which he is "rapt" by saluting a maternal phallus which he associates with the alleged inevitability of war, in contrast with (as in

"Song of the Banner") the peacetime pursuits (commercial production or westward expansion) which he represents as being carried on under the aegis of the paternal phallus:

> Raise the mighty mother mistress,
> Waving high the delicate mistress, over all the starry mistress,
> (bend your heads all,)
> Raise the fang'd and warlike mistress, stern, impassive,
> weapon'd mistress,
> Pioneers! O pioneers!

Again as in "Song of the Banner," the American Civil War which is about to erupt or has recently erupted ("has the hour come?" the speaker asks in stanza 14 of "Pioneers") is going to be fought under the sign of the "mighty mother mistress," in contrast with the Revolutionary War, which according to "The Centenarian's Story" in *Drum-Taps* was triumphantly fought under the sign of the paternal phallus, as in the emblematic scene from the poem in which Washington reads the Declaration of Independence to his assembled army: "By his staff surrounded, the general stood in the middle—he held up his unsheath'd sword, / It glittered in the sun in full sight of the army." In 1860–61, it is the "star[s]" of the flag transformed into the "fangs" of the "mighty mother mistress" of war that "glitter," as in the lines Whitman added to "Starting from Paumanok" in 1867 which replicate the lines about the unfurling of the sign of the "fang'd and warlike mistress" in "Pioneers": to the 1860 lines (in "Starting from Paumanok," stanza 20 [1860 ed.] or section 6 [1867 ed. and after]), "And I will make a song for the ears of the President, full of weapons with menacing points, / And behind the weapons countless dissatisfied faces," he adds:

> And a song make I of the One form'd out of all,
> The fang'd and glittering One whose head is over all,
> Resolute, warlike One including and over all;
> (However high the head of any else, that head is over all.)

The Civil War over, the "mighty mother mistress" returns to her previously ungendered, altogether undifferentiated form as the "One," the Union. It had taken the threat of the dissolution of the Union to make it seem identical to the poet not only with femininity but with maternity, and specifically threatened or menaced, and threatening and menacing, maternity. As the War actually began to be fought, instead of merely being anticipated with mixed dread and joy, it soon became the occasion of bloodshed and death on a scale unprecedented in the United States. The naive excitement and the equally naive hope that the war would soon be concluded with minimal bloodshed with which Whitman and many others had greeted the war soon gave way to widespread feelings of shock, grief, and guilt. Whitman's poetry registers this transformation through its changed representation of the sign of the maternal phallus under which the violence of the war was to be justified; it soon begins to "droop." Near the end of "The Centenarian's Story," we read:

> Rank after rank falls, while over them silently droops the flag,
> Baptized that day in many a young man's bloody wounds,
> In death, defeat, and sisters', mothers' tears.

Both the hoisting (in the poetry of the early period of the war) and drooping (in the poetry about actual combat and death) of the signs of the maternal phallus and the child-phallus are repeated from poem to poem in *Drum-Taps* and the fourth edition. The disintegration of the poet's previously bellicose attitude under the stress of witnessing intense human suffering on a massive scale manifests itself on the material level in the return of the figure of the pennant of war in the revisionary form of "bandages," "clotted rags," "the clotted lint" which "The [Wound-]Dresser" removes from "[t]he crushed head," "[t]he neck of the cavalry man," "the stump of the arm, the amputated hand," the "wound in the side, deep, deep," "the perforated shoulder," "the foot with the bullet-wound," "[t]he fractured thigh, the knee, the wound in the abdomen." To list all these wound-sites is to call attention to the way section 3 of "The Dresser," in which all these references occur, revises the catalogs of the parts of the human body that Whitman had previously carried out in poems like "I Sing the Body Electric" (1855), as in the passage which appeared as section 9 in the fourth and subsequent editions where body parts are lovingly and exhaustively nominated for some thirty lines.[11]

What is to be done in the text of *Drum-Taps* with the devastated, dismembered, or disintegrating bodies which fill it?[12] The war pennant under which this text was inaugurated is ripped apart into bandages and rags for the wounded in poems like "The Dresser"; in the face of death, it reappears transformed into another fabric, the army blanket, the nondescript and homely shroud of the battle dead, as in "A Sight in Camp in the Daybreak Gray and Dim":

> A sight in camp in the daybreak gray and dim,
> As from my tent I emerge so early sleepless,
> As slow I walk in the cool fresh air the path near by the
>   hospital tent,
> Three forms I see on stretchers lying, brought out there
>   untended lying,
> Over each the blanket spread, ample brownish woolen blanket,
> Gray and heavy blanket, folding, covering all.

Uncovering the first form, the poet sees the face of an old man fallen in battle; uncovering the second, he sees the face of a very young boy; uncovering the third, he sees "a face nor child nor old, very calm, as of beautiful yellow-white ivory." "Young man, I think I know you," the poet says, "I think this is the face of the Christ himself." One may well suspect that some of the uncanny force which the uncovering of the third form in the poem possesses arises not so much from the poet's assertion that the face of the third man is that of "Christ himself" but from the possibility that the poet recognizes the third dead face because it is his own. In the same way in which he had previously "enfolded" other men and their faces and bodies into his texts alongside his own ("You shall stand beside me and look into the mirror with me," 1855 Preface), the speaker-subject of *Drum-Taps* poems like this one repeatedly finds himself being enfolded—now in death— with his dead comrades. Some of the intensity with which he gazes at the faces of his dead comrades arises from the impossibility of his ever himself being able to gaze on his own dead face. As with the imaginary prospective-retrospective gaze which links poet and posterity in "Crossing Brooklyn Ferry," the poet finds a focus for a gaze in the face of this "Christ-figure" which links him in his own present—and, potentially, the reader in his or her own present—with the dead face or body he will someday become. In this poem, uncovering the faces of the newly dead brings the speaker face to face with death—not only with theirs but also with his own at least as yet deferred death—with a discomfiting literality. The text of this poem itself reveals as it conceals or "blankets" its uncanny relation to the poet who enunciates it; at the same time it conceals and reveals its uncanny and liminal relation to a number of the other *Drum-Taps* poems. Is the first dead form, the "gaunt and grim" old man, a double of "the centenarian" who tells "The Centenarian's Story"? Similarly, is the second dead form, whom the poet calls "my child and my darling" (in the very accents of the Erl-King), "sweet boy with cheeks yet blooming," a double (ghost or corpse) of the Child in "Song of the Banner at Day-Break"?

Although no conclusive case can be made that any of these dead figures in "A Sight in the Camp" is in any determinate sense a double of other, similar, living figures in *Drum-Taps*, the uncanny liminality that pervades this and other *Drum-Taps* poems is one of the essential means by which these texts traverse the limits between rival forms of the phallus, between mutilation and healing, between recovery and death. The awful vision that the speaker sees in "Broad-Axe Poem," that of "the European headsman," "masked, clothed in red, with huge legs and strong naked arms," bears an uncanny resemblance to the instrument of his bloody calling—"(Whom have you slaughtered lately, European headsman? / Whose is that blood upon you, so wet and sticky?)." In 1856, the poet unsuccessfully tries to hold this phantasmatic figure at bay by imputing him to an absolute past, to European, pre–New World, historical violence. "I see the blood washed entirely away from the axe," the poet says of the American present (in 1856), but this disinfecting distinction between bloody and violent European past on the one hand and "clean" and secure American present on the other will not hold.

Such a distinction is of course entirely untenable in the aftermath of the Civil War; American history has become as deeply bloodstained as European history ever was, and this development cannot be kept from *Leaves of Grass*, so to speak. Thus the later poems of *Drum-Taps* take on the macabre quality of themselves becoming textual equivalents of the bloody bandages and rags the "Dresser" carries to and from the Civil War wounded. The poet writes in "Lo, Victress on the Peaks," a poem which first appeared in the "Sequel to Drum-Taps" of 1865–66, after the assassination of Lincoln: "No poem proud I, chanting, bring to thee—nor mastery's rapturous verse." Looking back at the poetry of earlier periods, including his own earlier work, he calls his most recent production, "But a little book, containing night's darkness, and blood-dripping wounds, / And psalms of the dead" ("Lo, Victress on the Peaks").

When Whitman incorporated *Drum-Taps* and its sequel into the fourth edition of *Leaves of Grass*, he revised the lines I have just quoted to read, "No poem proud, . . . / But a *cluster* containing night's darkness and blood-dripping wounds" (my emphasis), in keeping with the reclassification of "Drum-Taps" from "a little book" (the 1865 *Drum-Taps*) to what he called a "cluster"—that is, a group of poems linked in theme, one of the major divisions of the *Leaves of Grass* poems, beginning with the third (1860) edition (for example, "Enfans d'Adam," "Calamus," "Chants Democratic"). With the incorporation of "Drum-Taps" into *Leaves of Grass*, Whitman began to make a distinction which would remain crucial throughout the rest of his career between what he seems to have considered two different ways of revising the volume that had become his life-project. Instead of incorporating "Drum-Taps" directly into the fourth edition of *Leaves of Grass* as a "cluster," Whitman made it the first of what he at that point began to call "annexes" to his volume: relatively small, occasional collections of his verse which he integrated into *Leaves* by adding them intact at the end of the volume, rather than integrating them into the text by means of his earlier "organic" model of inserting them or, as he might say, "dilating" them directly into the preexisting text (that is, the previous edition of *Leaves*). *Drum-Taps*, published in 1865, was added as the first "annex" to *Leaves of Grass* in the 1867 addition, and then incorporated into the volume as yet another of its "clusters" in 1871. Subsequent collections of Whitman's verse like "Songs Before Parting" followed the same route of incorporation, first as appended "annexes" and then as "clusters" more closely integrated into the preexisting text, often by dissemination or dispersal through the text (the poems in "Sequel to Drum-Taps," for example, were eventually distributed among "Drum-Taps" and other clusters). After Whitman settled on his final arrangement of the *Leaves of Grass* poems in 1881, he relegated later poems to two lengthy final "annexes," "Sands at Seventy" and "Good-Bye My Fancy."

No doubt practical considerations played a part in Whitman's use of the "annex" method beginning in the 1867 edition, instead of (or, in subsequent editions, in combination with) the "cluster" method of extending the text; rather than thematically integrating new work on its first appearance, he added it in the form of an appendix and gradually worked out its place in his larger scheme. I want to argue that the two terms "annex" and "cluster" have symbolic significance, too. They bear a relation to each other which is analogical to the relation between the two different ways of "enlarg[ing]" the nation which emerge near the end of "Song of the Banner at Day-Break": the "ever-enlarging" field of the banner, the "stars-and-stripes," which represent the *annexation* of new territories, in contrast with what the poet in that text speaks of as the "dilation" of his own "limbs" and "veins" with "[t]he blood of the world." Between the "organic" procedure (Whitman's term) which the third edition initiates, the "cluster" method of organization, and the "annex" method beginning with the fourth edition, occurred what Whitman saw for the rest of his career as the "baptism in blood" (to use the terms of "The Centenarian's Story," "Baptized that day in many a young man's bloody wounds") of the *Leaves of Grass* project and, more broadly, of American history.[13]

Drum-Taps and its sequel could not simply be incorporated into the next edition of *Leaves of Grass* as a new "cluster" because the national history, the massive experience of state violence on the part of soldiers and their families and friends, out of which it is written remained at least for a time (1867–1871) literally and figuratively unassimilable to the larger *Leaves*. Perhaps still too close to this violence to sentimentalize or otherwise move to defend himself and his readers from it in 1867, Whitman had by 1871 seen the "holes in the real" (to use Lacan's phrase for the effect on the subject of the death of others) occasioned by the suffering and death of thousands with whom he had entered into affective contact during the war recede far enough so that he could write the tentative lyric "Delicate Cluster," a key document in the transformation of *Drum-Taps* from unassimilable "annex" to assimilated "cluster":

> Delicate cluster! flag of teeming life!
> Covering all my lands—all my seashores lining!
> Flag of death! (how I watch'd you through the smoke of battle
>   pressing!
> How I heard you flap and rustle, cloth defiant!)
> Flag cerulean—sunny flag, with the orbs of night dappled!
> Ah my silvery beauty—ah my woolly white and crimson!
> Ah to sing the song of you, my matron mighty!
> My sacred one, my mother!

The speaker of this eight-line lyric reassumes the subject-position of the Child of "Song of the Banner" at the moment when the war pennant reveals itself to be the maternal phallus ("flag of teeming life! / Covering all my lands," the "flap" and "flap[ping]" symbolic object and the "rustl[ing]" skirts, "cloth defiant," which reveal as they conceal it). Coming to this relatively simple and in some ways simplistic little 1871 text after looking at the complex qualities of a number of the 1865 poems may perhaps make the years following the Civil War seem a regressive moment in Whitman's career. In order to counter this impression, I want now to consider, in the light of my discussion to this point of some of the central concerns of *Drum-Taps,* the other "annex" which Whitman added to the 1867 *Leaves,* "Songs Before Parting." This "annex" is largely taken up with his rewriting of the 1856 poem, "Poem of Many In One," as "As I Sat Alone by Blue Ontario's Shore" (later "By Blue Ontario's Shore").

Dilating on Death: "By Blue Ontario's Shore"

Of all Whitman's poems, "By Blue Ontario's Shore" registers perhaps most fully the scope of his revisionary practices in the first four editions of *Leaves of Grass.* He seems to have revised it more frequently and more thoroughly than any other text, and consequently it provides a primary example of the palimpsestic nature of his writing in the first twelve years of his career. Much of the poem incorporates material from the 1855 Preface, which Whitman had recast as verse for the second (1856) edition and entitled "Poem of Many In One." Redistributed into forty-nine verse paragraphs of widely varying lengths, a second version of the poem appeared in the third (1860) edition as the first of the twenty-one "Chants Democratic." Whitman substantially altered the text for the final time in the fourth (1867) edition by reentitling it "As I Sat Alone by Blue Ontario's Shore" and intercalating in it a series of parenthetical apostrophes, a number of them addressed to a figure called alternatively "Mother" or "Democracy," concerning the meaning of the Civil War.

In its first two appearances as a poem (in 1856 and 1860), the text begins as a straightforward self-announcement of nationalist ambitions:

> A nation announcing itself,
> I myself make the only growth by which I can be appreciated,
> I reject none, accept all, reproduce all in my own forms.

The "proof" of the "breed" that constitutes this nation is then put forward in a set of terms which are identical with those in that other 1856 text, "Broad-Axe Poem." Here, just as in "Broad-Axe," sheer "nativity" has made this people "powerful and tremendous," "executive" and "[self-]sufficient": "We wield ourselves as a weapon is wielded."

Retaining these lines nearly unaltered in the 1867 version, Whitman prefaces them with an opening section which qualifies the unbridled "executive" power and "sufficien[cy]" of this American "breed" and which also situates the poet in a new set of political and historical relations to this text, through an encounter between himself and the figure of a "Phantom, gigantic, superb," a sort of national muse:

> As I sat alone, by blue Ontario's shore,
> As I mused of these mighty days, and of peace return'd, and
>   the dead that return no more,
> A Phantom, gigantic, superb, with stern visage, accosted me,
> *Chant me the poem*, it said, *of the range of the high Soul of Poets,*
> *And chant of the welcome bards that breathe but my native air—*
>   *invoke those bards;*
> *And chant me, before you go, the Song of the throes of Democracy.*

Appended to these new opening lines is the first of the poem's newly inserted parentheses:

> (Democracy—the destined conqueror—yet treacherous lip-
>   smiles everywhere,
> And Death and infidelity at every step.)

Such are the "throes of Democracy" of which this poem in its now (1867) definitively revised version is to be "the Song." These "throes" include not only those in which "Democracy" has struggled against the "treacher[y]" and "infidelity" of her recent would-be betrayers, but, as we shall see in the text's successive parentheses, the "throes" of labor and childbirth which become this text's chief figure for the war-process that has preserved and has been at least for a time identical with "Democracy," and the chief products of war/"Democracy": "peace return'd, and the dead that return no more." The war has produced peace, but it has destroyed many lives; in giving birth to ("return[ing]") peace, "Democracy" has at the same time given death to countless persons. Between the now-fulfilled desire for the return or rebirth of peace on the one hand and the never-to-be-fulfilled desire for the return of many of the persons who have died in the struggle to restore peace on the other, there is in "As I Sat Alone by Blue Ontario's Shore" a troubling disjunction that can never be repaired. The text takes as one of its primary functions the continuous troubling of this disjunction which not only will not go away but also will not manifest itself in terms less paradoxically disparate than that of a figure simultaneously giving birth and death to the "breed" that has contradictorily survived/not survived the Civil War. What has been bought at the incalculable cost of the similarly incalculable loss of tens of thousands of lives? Whitman's attempts to answer this question take the contradictory form that only the highest political ideals, called "democracy" or "union," could have been "worth" such a cost, but insofar as this "cost" is incalculable, there is no way of rendering "cost" and "value" ("democracy," "union") commensurate. It is as if for Whitman there could in retrospect be no common terms between the terrible cost that the political conflict eventually exacted and the idle hope he and many of his contemporaries had initially entertained that "the union could be preserved" without sacrifice of much life.

In contradistinction from the "breed" of such earlier texts as "Broad-Axe" and this poem in its "Poem of Many In One" version, one that is aggressively self-reliant, there is in the second section of this text ("A nation announcing itself"), in the parenthesis added to this section, a second "breed" that is threatened with total loss, destruction, and darkness; this "breed" seems to be composed of poet, "mother," and "sisters":

(O mother! O sisters dear!
If we are lost, no victor else has destroyed us;
It is by ourselves we go down to eternal night.)

Poet, "mother," and "sisters," as survivors of the war and mourners for its dead, are somehow threatened with still further loss and destruction. What is the relationship between this threatened "breed" to the unthreatened one, "powerful and tremendous," which also inhabits this text? The poem's next parenthesis suggests that the former (poet, "mother," and "sisters") endure travail that the latter "breed," "executive" and "self-pois'd," does not:

(With pangs and cries, as thine own, O bearer of many
  children!
This chant all wild, to a race of pride I give.)

"What we are we are," say the "breed" of section 2, and "nativity is
answer enough to objections." This version of "nativity" appears pain-
less and disengendered. In contrast with it the poet produces his
"chant" and the "mother" her progeny "[w]ith pangs and cries." The
"chant" of the poet and the "pangs and cries" of poet and mother are
as "wild" as the "race" the mother engenders is "proud." As in "Broad-
Axe Poem," the poet seems to align himself with the figure of the
child-bearing woman in the "throes" of a situation that is simultaneously life-threatening and life-producing, rather than with the figure
of the "proud race" of men who form a closed circle of unthreatened
power.

   Although the poet includes himself in both groups in the 1867
poem's opening (for example, both he and the "proud race" of men
and he and the "mother" and "sisters" threatened with destruction are
"we" in different parts of section 2), the poem's seventh section, at
twelve lines the longest of the parentheses interpolated into the 1867
version of the poem, presents a very different kind of vignette of
political power and victory in relation to gender from the 1856 ones
of "Broad-Axe" and "Many In One." In the new section 7, a victorious
figure of indeterminate gender who is hailed as "Libertad" ("Libertad!
from the conqueress' field return'd") stands with

   (. . . clench'd and lifted fist,
   And your foot on the neck of the menacing one, the scorner,
     utterly crushed beneath you;
   The menacing, arrogant one, that strode and advanced with his
     senseless scorn, bearing the murderous knife;
   Lo! the wide-swelling one, the braggart, that would yesterday
     do so much!
   To-day a carrion dead and damn'd, the despised of all the
     earth!
   An offal rank, to the dunghill maggots spurn'd.)

Here (to invoke the terms of the second line of the poem) "peace
return[s]" with a literal vengeance, and of "the dead that return no
more" we are shown not the piteous figures of some of the righteous

dead of the war but only a single villainous figure who has recently been "menacing, arrogant," "senseless," and "murderous," and who is now "dead and damn'd" and "despised." "[T]he wide-swelling one" who perpetrated the recent breech of peace has been reduced to "carrion" and "offal" and ignominiously left on "the dunghill." What is striking about the terms of this vignette in relation to the other parentheses about the war experience interpolated into the poem is that in this one, some of the key terms associated with either of the two "breeds" who populate the poem—the "proud" (male) "race" in the main body of the poem and the threatened "breed" of poet and female figures who populate its parenthetical apostrophes—get transferred from one of these groups to the other. For example, "the wide-swelling one" here is not the pregnant mother or mother-to-be but the "menacing, arrogant" male, and instead of standing "proud" and inviolate, he has been defeated, humiliated, and executed for his treachery. In this lengthy parenthesis, a crucial set of Whitman's terms for "separate spheres" of gender powers and political powers in general become definitively destabilized: male political "pride" and power can be not only a positive value, an American (male) birthright, it can also be "murderous" "arrogance"; "wide-swelling" can be not only the physical sign of rightful pride (in men) and of incipient maternity (in women) (the two primary forms of political power by gender, according to Whitman), it can also be the sign of "the braggart" inflated with treachery—now female as well as male. "I chant a new chant of dilation or pride," Whitman had written in 1855 in what was to become section 26 of "Song of Myself"; in 1867, "As I Sat Alone by Blue Ontario's Shore" presents an elaborate exploration of the nature of the range of possible relations, from glorious to ignominious ones, between these two modes of "swelling" or (self-) inflation. That the section's motion will be a gradual one from the heights to the depths is signaled in its opening words, "Lo! high," and signaled again in relation to the "lo[w-lying]" figure of the executed and despised "braggart," "Lo! the wide-swelling one," who has become "dung[ ]," the opposite of the most highly esteemed of bodily products, a newborn infant.

Section 11 represents the other longest new interpolation in the poem; the last nine of its fifteen lines form a parenthetical apostrophe to the "Angry cloth" of the war pennant of "Song of the Banner at Day-Break":

(Angry cloth I saw there leaping!
I stand again in the leaden rain, your flapping folds saluting;
I sing you over all, flying, beckoning through the fight—O the
  hard contested fight!
O the cannons ope their rosy-flashing muzzles! the hurtled balls
  scream!
The battle-front forms amid the smoke—the volleys pour
  incessant from the line;
Hark! the ringing word *Charge!*—now the tussle, and the
  furious maddening yells,
Now the corpses tumble curl'd upon the ground,
Cold, cold in death, for precious life of you,
Angry cloth I saw there leaping.)

As in "Song of the Banner," the "flapping folds" of the "[a]ngry cloth"
the poet here stands "saluting" are in one sense those of the maternal
phallus, the signs of which are not simply the projectile shape of the
paternal phallus but "flap[s]," "folds," and fabric ("cloth"). Is it the
cloth that is "angry," one may wonder about these lines, or is it the
speaking subject who is, projecting his anger at himself and his fellows
for welcoming the war onto the flag, along with the imaginary double
sexuality he has imputed to it? It may well be the speaker rather than
the cloth that is "angry" here, because in this extended parenthesis
the poet rewrites "Song of the Banner at Day-Break" in the aftermath
of the eventual defeat of the forces that he had previously imagined
rallying under the double aegis of the maternal phallus and the child-
phallus in the first years of the war. Although violence had been a
central concern of "Song of the Banner"—the poem is in a sense a
hymn to the subversive powers of violence—sexual violence as such
had been suppressed in the "enthusiastic" lyrics of the early period of
the war. In contrast, sexual violence erupts in postwar compositions
like this parenthesis. When "[t]he cannons ope their rosy-flashing muzzles" and "the hurtled balls scream," the reader may see and hear a
scene of castration (paternal-phallic cannons flaring and "balls" flying);
the reader may also see the "natural" corporeal violence of the
"ope[ning]" or dilation of the female genitals in childbirth and the
"scream[ing]" of the mother in travail and of the newborn infant. Such
an interpretation of the parenthesis in section 11 is supported by the
parenthesis in section 17, where (paternal-) phallic instruments of

warfare, cervical dilation and childbirth, and a (maternal-) phallic cloth capable of "covering the world" are all conjoined in a single vignette representing an uncanny vision:

> (Democracy! while weapons were everywhere aim'd at your
> breast,
> I saw you serenely give birth to children—saw in dreams your
> dilating form;
> Saw you with spreading mantle covering the world.)

I have already pointed out (in the parenthesis in section 4) the poet likening his poem ("the song of the throes of Democracy," as he calls it in section 1) to the cries of the mother in labor ("With pangs and cries, as thine own, O bearer of many children! / This chant all wild, to a race of pride I give"). Beyond the commonplace usage of conception, pregnancy, and the travail of childbirth as figures for the writing and bringing through the press of a book, a number of political and sexual-political meanings arise from Whitman's elaboration of these corporeal figures in "As I Sat Alone by Blue Ontario's Shore." What takes on something like definitive form in this text is a connection or alignment Whitman has been working to effect in a series of texts throughout the first four editions of *Leaves of Grass*, beginning with a set of passages in the 1855 *Preface* and "I celebrate myself." This connection is one between a set of figures of the dilation of various bodily orifices and organs (mouth, lungs, penis, cervix, anus) and what he sees as a corresponding set of forms of political and sexual-political liberty and power.[14]

In section 6, Whitman brings a number of passages from the 1855 Preface together and in doing so concentrates in the relatively brief compass of its forty lines a plethora of his terms for the figuration of various forms of political liberty as bodily dilation. The term "plethora" is a precise one for Whitman's rhetorical practice in characteristic passages like this one, for the word means not simply an "abundance" as it is commonly figuratively used to mean but specifically "a bodily condition characterized by an excess of blood and marked by turgescence and a florid complexion; a superfluity; being in a state of distension, swollenness, tumidity." Sexual connections of various kinds are conflated with childbirth to yield a "superfluity" of meanings linking bodily, particularly sexual and reproductive, organs and processes with political power, as in lines 6–13, where figures from passages near the beginning and end of the 1855 Preface (pp. iv and xi, respectively) are brought into striking juxtaposition. No longer the poet himself but a representative "west-bred" boy or man is spoken of as "incarnating this land,"

> Attracting it Body and Soul to himself, hanging on its neck
>   with incomparable love,
> Plunging his semitic [changed to "seminal" in 1871 and after]
>   muscle into its merits and demerits,
> Making its cities, beginnings, events, diversities, wars, vocal in
>   him,
> Making its rivers, lakes, bays, embouchure in him,
> Mississippi with yearly freshets and changing chutes—
>   Columbia, Niagara, Hudson, spending themselves lovingly in
>   him,
> If the Atlantic coast stretch, or the Pacific coast stretch, he
>   stretching with them north or south,
> Spanning between them East and West, and touching whatever
>   is between them . . . .

Rather than simply becoming "fluid," as the ideal of the 1855 edition would have him do, the representative figure here enters into a complex series of relations with others—with other persons, and with the cities, rivers, and coasts that physically constitute the nation—which are transacted through various dilated bodily orifices or organs. Instead of emphasizing fluidity and *its* desirable properties, "As I Sat Alone by Blue Ontario's Shore" foregrounds other capacities of several parts of the body: their open or dilated quality and their fleshliness. This is not so much the case in the phallus which the "west-bred" male "[p]lung[es]" into the body of the land, for it is "dilated" only in the sense of being distended without being open, but rather in his throat, in which "its cities, beginnings, events, diversities, wars" become "vocal in him," and in his throat and/or anus in which the rivers which "embouchure in him" "spend[ ] themselves lovingly in him."

Rigid hierarchizing distinctions between bodies and body parts fostered by patriarchal cultures like Whitman's (male over female; the phallus over other sexual organs; associations of shame and disgust with the anus; the general proscription of "sodomy"—that is, oral-genital, anal-genital, oral-anal contact) are partially broken down in passages like section 6: such supposedly fundamental distinctions as male/female and inside/outside are transgressed as the "west-bred" male is here represented as making love to the land by penetrating it with his "semitic muscle" and, three lines later, having love made to him by the rivers "spending themselves lovingly in him." He is "surrounding" at the same time he is surrounded (six lines later): "His spirit surrounding his country's spirit, unclosed to good and evil, / Surrounding the essences of real things." In section 6, as in much of the rest of the poem, Whitman is concerned not only with male-homoerotic relations but also with the dilative capacities of women's bodies per se, for example, in pregnancy and childbirth ("the Union" in section 6 is spoken of as being both "impregnable" and the product of "the gestation of new States"), as well as with the dilative capacities women's and men's bodies share, such as the capacity to dilate the throat in utterance, in speech, "chant," or song. All these may serve as terms in which the hitherto relatively stable gender distinctions which defined the "two breeds" of Whitman's earlier poetry, the "proud race" of men and the women out of whose bodies this "breed" is "unfolded," can be broken down. In some of the new poetry of 1867 such as section 6 of this poem, male and female bodies are represented as having more "in common" than they have seemed to have in Whitman's earlier poetry. In emphasizing the dilative capacity of both male and female bodies, Whitman discovers a set of relatively noninvidious terms in which to attempt to break down reifications of masculine and feminine corporeality *without* making the particular properties of men's and women's bodies identical with each other—as he had, for example, at the beginning of the second edition, in "Unfolded Out of the Folds," where male bodies are female bodies simply turned "wrong side out."

Despite the programmatic breaking-down in this text of the earlier editions' more conventional genderings of the human body, other kinds of conflicts arise between bodies which are not primarily matters of gender, although they are by no means unrelated to it. It is not primarily men and women or their bodies that are in direct conflict with each other, but the bodies of the being-killed and the being-born. These figures encounter each other in such uncanny and disturbing passages as the one quoted previously which represents "Democracy" lying in the midst of a wartorn battlefield, dilated and giving birth at bayonet-point: "(Democracy, while weapons were everywhere aim'd at your breast, / I saw you serenely give birth to immortal children, saw in dreams your dilating form . . .)."

At a comparably crucial moment in the third (1860) edition, in "Leaves of Grass. 1" ("As I Ebb'd with the Ocean of Life"), the climax of the poem had erupted through parentheses, which I have called the typographical sign of utterance through "dead lips": "(See! from my dead lips the ooze exuding at last! / See—the prismatic colors, glistening and rolling!)." We have seen how Whitman uses parenthetical interpolations in "By Blue Ontario's Shore" as a method of repeatedly "dilating" the text not only to incorporate new material but to signal that these additions are being made as responses to what Whitman sees as an unprecedented, and in some highly significant ways, irresolvable crisis; here, the parentheses which enclose these additions mark the historical and political disjunctures which separate them from the rest of the text. His claims for the "democratic" equality of all parts of the human body, female as well as male, and all forms of sexual behavior, have never been more radical and uncompromising or more elaborately articulated than they are in the revisionary text of the 1867 "As I Sat Alone by Blue Ontario's Shore." It is important to emphasize at this point that parts of human bodies are being declared *politically* equal, all equally deserving of recognition and representation, and not merely equivalent or identical with each other. Whitman acknowledges the paradoxical sameness-in-difference and difference-in-sameness that joins and disjoins bodies. He does not declare all their parts "the same," that is, he does not concur in his culture's tendency simultaneously to privilege and to bar from literal representation one body-part, the phallus.

It is perhaps the sharpest irony of a career scored by such ironies that it is in the same text that we find one of Whitman's most successful attempts to render male and female bodies and their respective parts politically equal that we also find Whitman's most disturbing representations of the piteous vulnerability of the human body being ravaged in the naked and inescapable grip of state power.

It has become a commonplace observation on the part of Whitman's biographers that only in the tragic atmosphere of the Civil War hospitals, among their diseased, wounded, and dying inmates, did he find a social setting in which he could express his homoerotic desires with any degree of fullness,[15] as he nursed and befriended dozens of other men in extraordinary circumstances which permitted—even in a sense required—that he share with them a whole range of otherwise largely proscribed kinds of physical and emotional intimacies: dressing, undressing, bathing, bandaging, lifting, hugging, kissing, and holding hands with them; counseling them, reading to them, and writing letters for them; distributing "treats" (candy, ice cream, glasses of milk, chewing tobacco) among them; standing by them during frequently traumatic medical or surgical procedures; sitting by them during physical crises; in the event of their death, notifying their families. Despite the time-honored, and homophobic, critical-biographical convention of valorizing Whitman's alleged "sublimation" of "pathological" homoerotic desire into "lofty" self-sacrifice and self-abnegation in his Civil War hospital service, it is possible to read "Drum-Taps," as several critics have recently noticed in print, as a direct continuation and extension of the male-homoerotic political project inaugurated in "Calamus," in such poems as "As I Lay with My Head in Your Lap Camerado," "As Toilsome I Wander'd Virginia's Woods," and "O Tan-Faced Prairie-Boy."[16]

The male-homoerotic political program of *Leaves of Grass* is extended into its postwar form in the fourth edition and especially in "Drum-Taps." To my knowledge, no one has yet addressed the question of why maternity becomes so prominent in this program after the Civil War, but it may be useful to do so, for maternity pervades the "Drum-Taps" poems with an intensity we have learned to associate with the "return of the repressed." This last phrase is not a casual designation, for the signs of maternity which otherwise figure so significantly in the successive editions of *Leaves of Grass* are generally absent from the third edition and are conspicuously repressed in "Calamus," where, in all forty-five of the poems constituting that "cluster," the mother is invoked only once, in passing, in a couple of lines: "O mother! have you done much for me? / Behold, there shall from me be much done for you." These lines, along with a substantial part of the text in which they appear ("Calamus" no. 5, "States!") were eliminated from all subsequent editions of *Leaves* after the one in which they first appeared. From eighteen of its discarded lines, adding only three new lines to it, Whitman fashioned the "Drum-Taps" poem

"Over the Carnage Rose Prophetic a Voice," which undertakes to assure the "Sons of the Mother of All" that all will be well despite the mass "carnage" of the war; the resounding affirmations of the "Calamus"-style "prophe[cies]" which the "voice" delivers sound somewhat hollowly in their new historical context: "[A]ffection shall solve the problems of freedom yet, / Those who love each other shall become invincible."

One thing that becomes clear in the extension of the "Calamus" project into "Drum-Taps" and its *Sequel* (1865–66, including Whitman's elegy for Lincoln, "When Lilacs Last in the Dooryard Bloom'd," and seventeen other, mostly quite short, poems) is the persistence of a determinate relation in Whitman's writing between male-homoerotic subject-positions and a conception of maternity as a uniquely powerful albeit liminal state poised on the borderline between life and death. This relation is thoroughly obscured in "Calamus," which takes a utopian male-homoerotic politics as its primary object. It is foregrounded in "Drum-Taps," in which—after initially embracing a utopian position derived not from fantasies of the heady prospects of male "fluidity" but from similarly heady fantasies of the antipatriarchal power proceeding from the maternal phallus—Whitman at least partially abandons his utopian aspirations for his poetry to try to come to terms with the recent dystopian realities of mass violence and death, and to produce terms for them which will link them to his ongoing project of cultural revision without falsifying either history or the project. As I argued earlier, based on the evidence of "Song of the Banner" as well as on a number of other "Drum-Tap" poems, Whitman's Civil War experiences intensified his belief that although the foundations of culture were inherently phallic in their organization, they were *not* inherently paternal-phallic. In "Song of the Banner" and at other moments in his Civil War poems he invites the reader to imagine living under what he presents as the counter-aegises of the maternal phallus and the child-phallus.

Such moments occur frequently in "Drum-Taps" and in the poetry of the fourth edition overall; in fact, the generalizing and hierarchizing phrase "over all" is one of the key terms of this poetry, and one of the key terms in which maternity manifests itself in it, as in the previously quoted lines added to the 1860 "Proto-Leaf" ("Starting from Paumanok") for the 1867 edition:

The fang'd and glittering One whose head is *over all;*
Resolute, warlike One, including and *over all;*
(However high the head of any else, that head is *over all.*)

                                                  [my emphases]

I have argued that in such passages what is being insistently "held over everyone's head" is the aegis of the maternal phallus, and that one of the main ongoing projects in Whitman's war poetry is an exploration of an unconscious fantasy of the maternal phallus as support and guarantor of the child-phallus and as alternative aegis to the paternal phallus of patriarchy (that *all* phallic aegises are inherently patriarchal and oedipal is a possibility that hardly manifests itself in Whitman). According to this fantasy, although the powers of the child-phallus in isolation are highly circumscribed, when it is placed alongside the maternal phallus it can (perhaps successfully) challenge the dominance of the paternal phallus.

One of the principal meanings represented by the maternal and child-phalluses in their dual alliance against the paternal phallus is that of feminine support for male-homoerotic desire and behavior— "feminine" specifically in its oedipalized form of "maternity." Such a relationship had been at least implicit in *Leaves of Grass* from its inception in the 1855 Preface, where "the sweet milk of the nipples of the breasts of the mother of many children" (1855 ed., p. xii) is said to "solve readily" with the "freshets and . . . chutes" which the "beautiful masculine Hudson . . . embouchure into" the American "bard" (p. iv), and in "I celebrate myself," where the eponymous leaves of grass that figure in what was to become section 6 of that text are said to "transpire from the breasts of young men" as they do from "mothers' laps." The most elaborate representation of maternity as a support for male-homoerotic desire and behavior in all of Whitman occurs in the episode from "I wander all night in my vision"/"The Sleepers" discussed in Chapter 2, in which the speaker retails the anecdote of his mother as a young woman falling in love with an itinerant Indian woman who mended rush-bottom chairs. In that extended passage, the figure of the mother affirms with her narrative of her own homoerotic desire for a stranger the value of the male-homoerotic ethos in which the son-speaker moves elsewhere in the poem, as, for example, when he represents himself at the center of a "gang of blackguards with mirth-shouting music and wild-flapping pennants of joy."

As I mentioned earlier in this discussion, figures of maternity, almost entirely absent from "Calamus" and the third edition, abound in the fourth. The remarkable intensity and affective saturation of much of Whitman's poetry representing the suffering of sons and mothers in the Civil War has often been attributed to the intensity and depth of his personal experiences in the course of his hospital work, in which his complex feelings toward his soldier-patients were channeled into what was for him an emotionally laden relationship of nurturance which tended in his culture to be constructed as a maternal one.

When Whitman's literary executors set about publishing some of his correspondence soon after his death, they produced two volumes. One, entitled *Calamus*, brought together many of his letters to Peter Doyle. The other, entitled *The Wound Dresser*, is composed of many of his letters to his mother during the Civil War. In making these collections, the executors acted on an acutely sharp perception among them that Whitman's love letters to Doyle and his accounts to his mother of his intense involvement with the Civil War soldiers who came under his care were not only perhaps the most revealing and compelling of Whitman's letters, they were also the writing which bears most interestingly on the poetry of "Calamus" and "Drum-Taps," and therefore to a considerable degree on the *Leaves of Grass* project as a whole.

The prominence of the figure of the mother in Whitman's writing has commonly been attributed—homophobically—to his allegedly inadequate relations with women other than his own mother and to what many critics have characterized as "a close, perhaps abnormally close, relationship" with her.[17] I would like to inflect the question away from whether Whitman's personal relationship with his mother lay within the bounds of what some of his twentieth-century critics consider "normal" onto broader grounds. In the concluding section of this chapter, I shall discuss in the context of the poem "When Lilacs Last in the Dooryard Bloom'd" the possible import for Whitman's culturally revisionary project of the relationship he keeps reconfiguring in "Drum-Taps" as mother-and-son, maternity-and-male-homoeroticism, and maternal-phallus-and-child-phallus.

Uncanny Survivals: The Erotics of "When Lilacs Last in the Dooryard Bloom'd"

"When Lilacs Last in the Dooryard Bloom'd" has been one of the chief textual sites on which critics have recently focused de-(homo)eroticiz-ing, de-historicizing, and de-politicizing readings of Whitman's Civil War poetry. Near the end of his study of the history of the English elegy, for example, Peter M. Sacks provides a sketch of how he would go about reading Whitman's famous elegy in relation to the English-language elegy tradition. Sacks begins his comments by rightly recog-nizing that the poet of "Lilacs" charges himself in writing the poem with the complex and difficult task of mourning and elegizing Lincoln without "reestablish[ing] fatherhood" in the text, without reinstating "the kind of figure traditionally essential to elegiac consolation," "a highly differentiated, totemic [male] figure of authority and justice."[18] The potential compatibility of Sacks's notion of there being a marked antipaternal element in "Lilacs" with my reading of the fourth edition overall as Whitman's most highly concerted assault on the dominance of the paternal phallus in his culture's sign-system should be evident. But our readings diverge when he places what he interprets as a gesture of "sexual renunciation" (the poet's "break[ing]" off of the sprig of lilac as a self-castrative gesture) at the center of his projected reading of the poem. Sacks prefaces his discussion of this gesture by commenting on the general necessity in interpreting elegy of the reader's being "alert to the issue of the mourner's sexuality," but the only sexual "issue" he then alludes to in his discussion of "Lilacs" is the general one of what he calls "the castrative work of mourning." But, I would argue, there are other kinds of sexuality in play in "Lilacs," and in mourning practices in general, besides simply "castrative" ones.

In describing the nature of the "sexual renunciation" he sees at the heart of the poem, Sacks argues that in order to make what Whitman calls the "tally," the "association of the lilac with his own childhood and with a part of his own body" which "serves as the sexual renunci-ation that in turn provides" the self-surpassal the elegist seeks, he must accept the "disruption of his erotically dyadic fantasies" and "accept[ ] instead . . . a triadic relationship such as that between himself and the two companion forms of death [who appear in section 15 of the poem] or that between himself, the bird [the hermit thrush], and the dark mother [death]."[19] These are of course not the only triads that figure importantly in the poem; there is also that of the lilac, the "drooping star in the west," and the "thought of him I love" (Lincoln)—the "trinity" the poet salutes in section 1 and which in a sense the whole poem mourns and celebrates.

I want to interrogate the assumption of some commentators on "Lilacs," including Sacks, that the disruption and displacement of the dyad by the triad in the poem is an unmistakable sign of de-eroticization.[20] In describing the inevitable opening up of the supposedly erotic dyad into less erotic or nonerotic forms of triadic relationship in this poem, Sacks writes, "Whitman has moved beyond the moment of sexual sacrifice to a more socialized, less erotic vision of relationship."[21] In the context of my preceding discussions of modes of relationship in Leaves of Grass, there are a number of questions to be raised about the assumptions underlying such a judgment. Foremost among them is, given the marked emphasis on triadic relationships in "When Lilacs Last in the Dooryard Bloom'd," on what grounds does one assume that Whitman has hitherto conceived of relationship or erotic relationship as fundamentally dyadic? Although it is true that (male) specularity plays a crucial role in the poetry of the first edition, and doubling is in one sense a dyadic relationship, in another important sense it is not: the "double" is a phantasmatic, oxymoronic "other-self," not a real "other." It is not "the couple" (neither "homosexual" nor "heterosexual" nor parental) that emblematizes relations in the first Leaves of Grass; it is the "fluid" self immersed in the circuits of desire. It is the oedipal triangle in a variety of configurations that emblematizes the second and fourth editions. In the third it is the exemplary split subject of "Calamus" struggling to negotiate identity and difference, sometimes between himself and another person, but more often between himself and the liminal, collective "other" of a political community which is largely inchoate and which the writing itself is designed to call into existence. Throughout the Leaves of Grass project, the mode of relation that remains predominant is the uncanny one the successive texts are designed to produce between author and reader. Although from the viewpoint of the privatized reader this relation may appear to be dyadic, from the point of view of the author and the text it is not, because the author makes his appeal through

each successive text to an undecidable number of readers simultaneously. "You up there! You, whoever you are," are Whitman's cus-
tomary terms for directly addressing the reader, and although he may
sometimes claim to desire to "leap into" the "arms" of the reader (as
in the 1860 "So long!"), the generality of the terms ("whoever you
are") suggests that he conceives of the relationship as being broader
and more general than a simply specific and individual one between
himself and one other reader. The focus in the author's relations with
his readers is on the "streams" of feeling passing between them, rather
than on a dyadic relationship with any one reader. And rather than
representing a relational norm in Whitman, the erotic pairings depicted in a number of the "Calamus" poems (for example, "When I
Heard at the Close of the Day," or "We Two Boys Together Clinging")
are exceptional. They are also highly problematic in the broader context of the project, because they are alternately represented as being
so satisfying that they isolate the erotic subject from all but one other
person, or so painful that they isolate him altogether.

What is perhaps most important to notice about the whole range of
modes of relationship represented in *Leaves of Grass* is that the social
and the sexual are usually not oppositional categories in them, nor is
the social conceived of as being essentially nonerotic while the erotic
is consigned to the restricted orbit of what the culture considers the
sexual. It is the effect of the entire project not only to eroticize the
social realm but also to socialize the culture's construction of the erotic
as the highly anxiogenic realm of the intimate, the private, the shame-
ful, the concealed, the destructive.

Without mounting a full-scale reading of "Lilacs" of my own, I want
to conclude by discussing some of the features of its representation of
the ongoing erotic program(s) of the *Leaves of Grass* project that make
it a text consonant in many ways with other characteristic texts of the
fourth edition, rather than the grand gesture of "sexual renunciation"
some critics have taken it to be. It is not my intention to reduce a
rich and complex text to a schematic representation of the phallic;
however, I think it is important to notice the ways in which this poem
continually invokes a particular erotic and sexual-political vocabulary.
I would interpret the poem's references (sections 3 and 7) to the
speaker's gesture of breaking the sprig of lilac from the bush to place
on the coffin, for example, not only as a self-castrative gesture, as

Sacks does, or as a castration of the maternal phallus, but as a central element in the text's repertory of signs drawn from infantile erotic experience. Holding and being held, holding and releasing ("loosing"), and a traumatic rupture between the phases of each of these processes—"breaking"—are the key terms in which the erotic drama of this text is enacted—or, to be more precise, they are the chief terms in which the drama of the speaker's coming to terms (to the degree that he does) with the death of Lincoln and all the losses of the war that Lincoln's death is made to represent is related to the "drama" of the origins of sexuality in the individual subject.

Beginning with the "cruel hands" that "hold [the speaker] powerless" in section 2—a figure which Harold Bloom reads as a "concealed reference" to a "failed" masturbatory act in which an initially auto-erotic response has not helped relieve the speaker of his grief[22]—the text continuously relates its "working through" of grief to the speaker's touching, holding, and handling of parts of his own body and of the maternal body and being held and handled in turn, chiefly by the figure of the "Dark Mother," but also by the "fallen star" and by the hands of the two ghostly comrades with whom he "passes" into the swamp to hear the hermit thrush's song.

The "solitary," "hermit" thrush, "withdrawn to himself, avoiding the settlements," inhabiting "the swamp," living "in secluded recesses," "[s]ings by himself a song," and, given the elaborate solo positioning of the "shy and hidden bird" (itself a readily recognizable phallic equivalent of the penises, "drooping shy and unseen," said to be "lurking" in the 1856 "Bunch Poem"/"Spontaneous Me"), it is unsurprising that his "solitary" song is one of autoerotic pleasure. But in presenting the figure of the bird in section 4, the poem immediately makes clear the traumatic psychic origins of all forms of sexuality, including the autoerotic; the bird's song is not simply pleasurable but is said to be the "Song of the bleeding throat," and "Death's outlet song of life." Thus sexuality itself is not simply pleasurable; violent desires and aggressive impulses, some of them directed at the self, are as much constitutive parts of it as are the experiences of "sweet love" which the bird evokes in his song, the "gliding near" of the mother "with soft feet," and the pressure of her "sure-enwinding," "cool-enfolding" arms (section 16).

The figure of a "Dark Mother," "Death," is the mother in her familiar role in the poetry of the fourth edition, as the uncanny figure the hermit thrush of "Lilacs" salutes in its song, amidst her other sobriquets, as the "strong Deliveress." "Deliveress" suggests both midwife and woman giving birth, but the "strong Deliveress" "delivers" death. Can the figure be said to be a killer—that is to say, does any of the guilt for the death of Lincoln and the countless other war dead adhere to her? Not as the poem presents the figure, I would say, since the "Dark Mother" not only "delivers" death but herself *is* death. As a "mother," she is of course also an at least erstwhile giver-of-birth, so her roles are several and are complexly disjunct from each other in some ways: she gives birth, brings death, somehow *is* death. She also occupies the crucial position of being the first erotic object for the subject besides (in this case) his own body. I would want to relate the erotic primacy of the maternal figure in this poetry to the "breaking" off or shattering that both requires and permits the subject of the poem (and to some degree the reader along with him) to move among realms that are in some ways highly disjunct: those of infantile experience, initiation into sexuality, the death of others, loss and mourning, and the prospect of one's own death.

In the face of the overwhelming grief and guilt he shared with many of his contemporaries over the terrible losses of the war, Whitman does not simply renounce sexuality by making melancholy and self-castrative gestures in his poetry. As psychoanalytic theory long ago made clear, melancholic and self-castrative impulses are themselves behaviors with strong erotic components, however conflicted they may be. Far from renouncing or "moving beyond" sexuality in "When Lilacs Last in the Dooryard Bloom'd," Whitman relaunches a self through a poetic congeries of the defiles of signified desire through which he has launched his earlier models of the self in the earlier editions of his book. In its intertwinings of the entry of the subject into sexuality with the recognition of death, "Lilacs" links the political and historical catastrophe of the Civil War and the assassination of Lincoln with what Whitman represents as the recapitulation of the catastrophe in the psychic career of each of his readers, of every subject who enters the culture. The figures who "fly the flight of the fluid and swallowing soul" in the first edition "pass" (a key word in "Lilacs," especially in the climactic section 19) through *Leaves of Grass* again in this poem, through the "floods" (of light) of section 11, the "copious" pouring motion with which the speaker spreads flowers on the coffins of all the war dead in section 7, again in the light "bathing all" and "enveloping man and land" in section 12, in the "liquid and free," "wild and loose" song of the hermit thrush in section 13, but most of all in "the loving, floating ocean," "the flood of bliss" in which Death is said to "[l]ave[ ]" the dead. Figures the reader may recognize from the "Paumanok" poems of the third edition ("Out of the Cradle Endlessly Rocking" and "As I Ebb'd with the Ocean of Life") also seem to repass (or be repassed) through the text, "[d]own to the shores of the water," "[t]he ocean shore, and the husky and whispering wave," "the rising and sinking waves," in sections 15 and 16. The speaker of "Calamus" no. 1 ("In paths untrodden, down by the margins of pond-waters") seems uncannily to walk again in "Lilacs," here appropriately accompanied by two ghostly companions, pursuing the hermit thrush down "the path by the swamp in the dimness" (section 15), "[i]n the swamp, in secluded recesses," "withdrawn" from the world of the cities, as the "Calamus"-singer says he is.

In the figure of the "Dark Mother" the reader reencounters the liminal figure of the mother-who-gives-birth-to-death first seen in the only slightly earlier "Drum-Taps" poems and in Whitman's revisions of his earlier poetry for the fourth edition (most notably in "As I Sat Alone by Blue Ontario's Shores"). This figure represents an extreme of sorts in Whitman's writing. His most powerful figure for femininity, she is also his most misogynistic figure: through her, he equates death with femininity and particularly with maternity. The shattering incursion of death into all the characteristic scenes from his earlier poems that are recapitulated in "When Lilacs Last in the Dooryard Bloom'd" recasts these scenes in fundamentally different forms from his earlier versions. But it is specifically with his representation of maternity that Whitman finally lodges death, so to speak, in the fourth and subsequent editions, and the conjunction of the two figures itself represents a foreclosure of possibilities of further lines of critique—for example, into the misogynistic implications of "lodging" death with maternity or femininity—to which the *Leaves of Grass* project may be said to have at least in part succumbed. Never having imagined it as being situated anywhere but in the midst of the history which it both laments and celebrates, Whitman would perhaps not be as bothered as many of his readers may be to consider how in some ways the *Leaves of Grass*

project as he commenced it and partially carried it out in the first
dozen years after 1855 was itself to prove, like the man who wrote it,
both an uncanny survivor and a piteous casualty of the ravages of the
Civil War.

THE VISIONARY and utopian project that Whitman had initiated in
the first *Leaves of Grass,* and that he went on to explore through the
labyrinthine paths of the several editions that ensued on the first,
reached its limits in the fourth edition. Rather than seeing Whitman
as simply abandoning his radical project at this point in his career, as
some critics have done, I would argue that he had in a sense completed
that project, and that if he had not exhausted its possibilities—it had
been, after all, an undertaking by design limitless, unbounded—he
had discovered the very limitations of any project thus conceived. The
two editions of his poems that he fashioned in the last decades of his
life, as well as the great outpouring of prose he produced during the
same period, indicate that he felt in the aftermath of the Civil War
that newly emergent political realities demanded quite different strategies and practices from the kinds I have analyzed in this book.
   The monitorily entitled "Deathbed Edition" of *Leaves of Grass* issued
by Whitman and his circle in the last months of his life was intended
by him to supersede all previous editions, but in the century since his
death a series of scholars and critics of his work have declined to
accept this dramatic gesture as genuinely final or definitive. Indeed,
the archaeology of Whitman's production of his major text has been
one of the most notably thriving branches of the critical literature on
Leaves of Grass, at least since the days of Emory Holloway's early
researches into the genesis of the poems in the early part of this century. Only a few years before issuing his Deathbed directive about his
"final intentions," in what would appear to be quite a different mood,
Whitman had written the following words in his 1887 preface, "A
Backward Glance O'er Travel'd Roads": "Difficult as it will be, it has
become . . . imperative to achieve a shifted attitude . . . towards the
thought and fact of sexuality, as an element in character, personality,
the emotions, and a theme in literature. I am not going to argue the
question by itself; it does not stand by itself." Nearing the end of
another century, pressured by quite different historical and political
imperatives from those Whitman and his contemporaries faced, those

of us engaged in working to achieve in our society "a shifted attitude . . . towards the thought and fact of sexuality" are frequently forcibly reminded that, as Whitman knew, "the question . . . does not stand by itself." For those who are interested in better understanding the effects of sexuality's having been centrally instantiated in our culture, *Leaves of Grass* remains a work of crucial importance. Its discoveries are still of interest to us, and its challenges still largely unfulfilled.

Notes

Index

Notes

Introduction

1. The two major texts which champion one or the other of the various editions of *Leaves of Grass* are Malcolm Cowley's Introduction to his reprint, *Walt Whitman's "Leaves of Grass": The First (1855) Edition* (New York: Viking Press, 1959), pp. vii–xxxvii; and Roy Harvey Pearce's Introduction to his facsimile edition of the third (1860) edition (Ithaca, N.Y.: Cornell University Press, 1961), pp. vii–li. Gay Wilson Allen's description of the basic differences between the various editions is useful, if somewhat impressionistic. See "The Growth of Leaves of Grass" in his *The New Walt Whitman Handbook* (New York: New York University Press, 1975), pp. 67–159.

2. Fredson Bowers inaugurated the close study of Whitman's revisions with his scrupulous reconstruction of the composition of the third edition, *Whitman's Manuscripts: "Leaves of Grass" (1860), A Parallel Text* (Chicago: University of Chicago Press, 1955). The most thorough work on the transition from one of the editions of *Leaves of Grass* to another is Arthur Golden's two-volume study of Whitman's revisions of the third (1860) edition in preparation for the fourth (1867), *Walt Whitman's Blue Book: The 1860–61 "Leaves of Grass" Containing His Manuscript Additions and Revisions* (New York: The New York Public Library, 1968). Sculley Bradley, Harold W. Blodgett, Arthur Golden, and William White edited the three-volume *"Leaves of Grass": A Textual Variorum of the Printed Poems* (New York: New York University Press, 1980).

3. References to Whitman's prose are to the Library of America edition, *Whitman: Poetry and Prose* (New York, 1982), except where otherwise noted. This passage appears on p. 671 of that volume.

4. Ibid., pp. 1010–1011n.

5. Ibid., p. 1011n.

6. Ibid.

7. I am indebted to Allen Grossman's important essay on Whitman's and Lincoln's politics for the fundamental insight that Whitman's poetics is founded

in his belief in the power of his writing to distribute "affectionate presence." See Grossman's "The Poetics of Union in Whitman and Lincoln: An Inquiry toward the Relationship of Art and Policy," in *The American Renaissance Reconsidered: Selected Papers from the English Institute, 1982–83,* ed. Walter Benn Michaels and Donald E. Pease (Baltimore: Johns Hopkins University Press, 1985), pp. 183–208; see especially pp. 188–191 on the significance of presence in Whitman's poetry.

8. The fullest treatment of the relation of Whitman's writing to literary theories of metonymy is in C. Carroll Hollis, "Metonymy in Whitman and in *Leaves of Grass,*" in *Language and Style in* Leaves of Grass (Baton Rouge: Louisiana State University Press, 1983), pp. 154–203.

9. *Whitman: Poetry and Prose,* p. 669.

10. My work is indebted to a number of contemporary historians whose work resoundingly vindicates Whitman's words about sexuality "not stand[ing] by itself." Chief among these works are the following: John D'Emilio, "Capitalism and Gay Identity," in *Powers of Desire: The Politics of Sexuality,* ed. Ann Snitow, Christine Stansell, and Sharon Thompson (New York: Monthly Review Press, 1983), pp. 100–113; Carroll Smith-Rosenberg, *Disorderly Conduct: Visions of Gender in Victorian America* (New York: Oxford University Press, 1985); Christine Stansell, *City of Women: Sex and Class in New York, 1789–1860* (New York: Knopf, 1986); and Jeffrey Weeks, *Sex, Politics and Society: The Regulation of Sexuality since 1800* (New York: Longman, 1981).

11. See Michel Foucault, *The History of Sexuality,* vol. 1: *An Introduction,* trans. Robert Hurley (New York: Random House, 1978), especially part 2, "The Repressive Hypothesis," pp. 15–49.

12. *Whitman: Poetry and Prose,* p. 1011n.

13. Although the book neglects to consider either the homosocial or sexual dimensions of its subject per se, Sean Wilentz's *Chants Democratic: New York City and the Rise of the American Working Class, 1788–1850* (New York: Oxford University Press, 1984) is the most important study to date of the artisanal and working-class social and political milieu in which Whitman grew up. Other important recent studies which take up (among other matters) changes in the process of socializing young people in the antebellum United States are Joseph F. Kett, *Rites of Passage: Adolescence in America 1790 to the Present* (New York: Basic Books, 1977); Anthony F. C. Wallace, *Rockdale: The Growth of an American Village in the Early Industrial Revolution* (New York: Norton, 1978); Paul E. Johnson, *A Shopkeeper's Millennium: Society and Revivals in Rochester, New York, 1815–1837* (New York: Hill and Wang, 1978); Mary P. Ryan, *Cradle of the Middle Class: The Family in Oneida County, New York, 1790–1865* (Cambridge: Cambridge University Press, 1981); and W. J. Rorabaugh, *The Craft Apprentice: From Franklin to the Machine Age in America* (New York: Oxford University Press, 1986). In thinking about the successive editions of *Leaves of Grass* in the historical context of how modes of relation between men were redefined in the United States between 1840 and 1867 (that is, during the first half of Whitman's career), I have profited from Eve Kosofsky Sedgwick's brilliant analysis of the ways in which a series of eighteenth- and nineteenth-century English literary texts register remarcations over time of the boundaries between a set of historically

specific forms of male homosociality and homophobia. See her *Between Men: English Literature and Male Homosocial Desire* (New York: Columbia University Press, 1985).

14. Foucault's suggestive pages on the historicity of homosexuality in *The History of Sexuality*, vol. 1, have been highly influential; passages on p. 43, where he discusses the question of the emergence of the "homosexual" as "personage" and "species," and on pp. 101–102, where he considers the complex consequences of the proliferation of discourses of "homosexuality" in the nineteenth century, have frequently been invoked in recent historical work on same-sex identities and relations. For fuller discussions of male-homosexual identities and the related kinds of social formations that preceded them in premodern and early-modern Western history, see Alan Bray, *Homosexuality in Renaissance England* (London: Gay Men's Press, 1982); Jeffrey Weeks, *Coming Out: Homosexual Politics in Britain from the Nineteenth Century to the Present* (London: Quartet Books, 1977), and *Sex, Politics, and Society*; Ed Cohen's *Talk on the Wilde Side: Towards the Genealogy of a Discourse on Male Sexuality* (New York: Routledge, forthcoming); and Jonathan Ned Katz, Introduction to *A Gay/Lesbian Almanac* (New York: Crowell, 1982).

15. For the text of Symonds's letter, see Herbert M. Schueller and Robert L. Peters, eds., *Letters of John Addington Symonds* (Detroit: Wayne State University Press, 1969), III. For the text of Whitman's response, see Edwin Haviland Miller, Jr., ed., *Walt Whitman: The Correspondence* (New York: New York University Press, 1969), V. The primacy of male-male sexual gestures (affectionate and otherwise) in Whitman's thinking about his own and his readers' relation to his major themes is clear in an exasperated statement he is said to have made about Symonds in the very month before their climactic exchange of letters. In response to the English author's sending him a copy of his essay, "Democratic Art, with Special Reference to Walt Whitman," the poet is reported by Horace Traubel to have snorted that he doubted whether Symonds had yet "gripped 'democratic art' by the nuts, or L of G either"—the implication clearly being that Whitman saw himself as having done precisely that in his own writing.

16. Although he does not use the clinical phrase, "homosexual panic" is, for example, biographer Gay Wilson Allen's verdict about where Whitman's six illegitimate children came from: "Whitman doubtless believed that the fiction of his illegitimate children would allay any suspicion that Symonds might have concerning the normal heterosexuality of the poet of *Calamus.*" See Allen's *The Solitary Singer: A Critical Biography of Walt Whitman* (New York: Macmillan, 1955), p. 536. Eve Kosofsky Sedgwick has considered the implications of "homosexual panic" for the writing of a number of Whitman's contemporaries, especially Henry James, in her "The Beast in the Closet: James and the Writing of Homosexual Panic," in *Sex, Politics, and Science in the Nineteenth Century Novel: Selected Papers from the English Institute, 1983–84*, ed. Ruth Bernard Yeazell (Baltimore: Johns Hopkins University Press, 1986), pp. 148–186.

17. On the difference between the social and political expectations that British and American readers brought to *Leaves of Grass* during Whitman's lifetime, see the "Coda" to Sedgwick's *Between Men*, especially pp. 205–206, where she argues concerning Whitman's British readings of his work that "the cultural

slippage of the Atlantic crossing meant that the sexual-ideological packages sent by the Kosmic American were very different from the ones unpacked by the cosmopolitan Englishman."

18. For the exchange between Stoddard and Whitman, see Miller, ed., *Whitman: Correspondence*, II, 97–98.

19. Originally published in San Francisco in *The Overland Monthly*, edited by Bret Harte, "South Sea Idyl" was reprinted in 1873 along with others of Stoddard's stories in a volume called *South-Sea Idyls*. Winston Leyland has recently edited a new one-volume collection of Stoddard's stories in which "South Sea Idyl" appears under the title "Chumming with a Savage: Kana-Ana." The collection is entitled *Cruising the South Seas: Stories by Charles Warren Stoddard* (San Francisco: Gay Sunshine Press, 1987).

20. Speaking of Whitman's representations of *"the body"* in *Leaves of Grass* as critics have commonly done has the unfortunate and misleading consequence of tending to neuter Whitman's conspicuous gendering of many of the bodies that fill his texts. Given Whitman's privileging of male-homoeroticism in the political program of *Leaves of Grass* from its inception in 1855, it is important to recognize that when he writes about a "body" or "bodies," these are frequently implicitly or explicitly gendered male. When this is the case with a given Whitman text, I have acknowledged the (male-)gendered character of the body or bodies it represents by introducing the parenthesis "(male)" before the term "body." This is not by any means to suggest that "the body" is *always* male in Whitman unless it is explicitly gendered female, but in the male-homoerotic fantasy of perfect "fluidity" and "specularity" of bodies and identities that impels the first (1855) edition of *Leaves of Grass* and is the subject of my two opening chapters, it is crucial to note that the mergings being represented are same-sex ones between males.

21. Wilentz, *Chants Democratic*, provides invaluable information about Whitman and the working-class political milieu of his youth. Floyd Stovall provides a useful guide to Whitman's early (that is, 1840s) political activism and related journalism in Chapter 3, "Journalist and Politician," in *The Foreground of "Leaves of Grass"* (Charlottesville: University of Virginia Press, 1974), pp. 31–46. Chapter 2 of Allen's *Solitary Singer* provides a standard account of Whitman's youthful politics (pp. 41–66). A representative selection of Whitman's political journalism from 1846 to 1848, when he edited the Brooklyn *Daily Eagle*, appears in *The Gathering of the Forces*, ed. Cleveland Rogers and John Black, 2 vols. (New York: Putnam's, 1920).

22. Harry Hayden Clark, ed., *Thomas Paine: Representative Selections* (New York: Hill and Wang, 1961), pp. 199, 200.

23. *The Creation of the American Republic 1776–87* (Chapel Hill, N.C.: University of North Carolina Press, 1969), p. 613.

24. Ibid., pp. 613–614.

25. *The Machiavellian Moment: Florentine Political Thought and the Atlantic Republican Tradition* (Princeton, N.J.: Princeton University Press, 1975), p. 521.

26. Ibid., p. 518.

27. *Walt Whitman: Poetry and Prose*, p. 1318.

28. Ibid., pp. 798–799.

29. Quoted from Ronald G. Walters, *Primers for Prudery: Sexual Advice to Victorian America* (Englewood Cliffs, N.J.: Prentice-Hall, 1974), pp. 161–162.

30. Stephen Nissenbaum, *Sex, Diet, and Debility in Jacksonian America: Sylvester Graham and Health Reform* (Westport, Conn.: Greenwood Press, 1980), p. 27.

31. Ibid., p. 25.

32. Ibid., chap. 2, pp. 25–38.

33. See Madeleine B. Stern, "The Long and the Short of It: Whitman's *Leaves of Grass*," in *Books and Book People in Nineteenth-Century America* (New York: Bowker, 1978), pp. 157–161.

34. For information about Trall, see Harold Aspiz, *Walt Whitman and the Body Beautiful* (Urbana, Ill.: University of Illinois Press, 1980), pp. 44–45.

35. Dixon authored *A Treatise on Diseases of the Sexual System* (New York, 1855 [9th ed.]). For more information on Dixon and his association with Whitman, see Aspiz, *Body Beautiful*, pp. 59–61.

36. For Dixon's prestigious position in the professional establishment of his time, see Martin Kaufman, "Edward H. Dixon and Medical Education in New York," *New York History* 51 (1970), 394–409.

37. Dixon, *Treatise on Diseases*, pp. 232, 238, 234.

38. Besides the aforementioned studies of modes of socialization in antebellum America by Wilentz, Kett, Wallace, Johnson, Ryan, and Rorabaugh, several studies which specifically treat the Jacksonian male-purity movement and its aftermath require notice. Of these, the most useful is Carroll Smith-Rosenberg, "Sex as Symbol in Victorian Purity: An Ethnohistorical Analysis of Jacksonian America," *American Journal of Sociology* 84 (supplement, 1978), S212–S247. Smith-Rosenberg provocatively considers contrastingly positive representations of male sexual pleasure in mid-nineteenth-century American popular writing in her "Davey Crockett as Trickster: Pornography, Liminality, and Symbolic Inversion in Victorian America," in *Procreation or Pleasure? Sexual Attitudes in American History*, ed. Thomas L. Altherr (Malabar, Fla.: Robert E. Krieger, 1983). G. J. Barker-Benfield surveys the American male-purity movement through its representative ideologue the Reverend John Todd in part III of *The Horrors of the Half-Known Life: Male Attitudes toward Women and Sexuality in Nineteenth-Century America* (New York: Harper and Row, 1976), pp. 135–174.

39. David Cavitch's *My Soul and I: The Inner Life of Walt Whitman* (Boston: Beacon Press, 1985) is a recent example of the strong privatizing trend in Whitman studies. Cavitch ignores Whitman's elaborate and rich relations to Jacksonian vernacular culture (as many critics before him have done) in favor of treating the poet as an isolated figure. Having effectively detached Whitman from his broad social milieu and historical context, Cavitch concludes his book with the highly reductive and pathologizing thesis that Whitman's "conflicts with his parents [are] the main issues in his creative life" (p. 139).

40. Barker-Benfield's "spermatic economy" hypothesis has been highly influential on studies of nineteenth-century male writers; Joel Porte's reading of the "spermatic economy" which informs Emerson's writings is a good example of the literary-critical appropriation of Barker-Benfield's model. See Porte's *Representative Man* (New York: Oxford University Press, 1979), pp. 259–267. Some of the limitations of Barker-Benfield's model as a tool for literary interpretation are

evident in Harold Aspiz, "Walt Whitman: the Spermatic Imagination," *American Literature* 56:3 (October 1984), 379–395.

41. Smith-Rosenberg, "Davey Crockett as Trickster," in Altherr, ed., *Procreation or Pleasure?*, p. 44.

1. Rendering the Text and the Body Fluid

1. "Fluidity" has long been a commonplace term in Whitman criticism for describing both the "flowing" language of his writing and the rapid and metamorphic shifts of identity it represents. The term is a key one in my discussions of Whitman's poetry, especially with regard to what I interpret as his initial enthusiasm in the 1855 *Leaves of Grass* for the idea of the commutability and interchangeability of identity among males, and the discomfort he soon began to manifest with the notion—as early as the second (1856) edition, I shall argue. The most perspicacious critic of "fluidity" in Whitman's writing has been D. H. Lawrence, whose account in *Studies in Classic American Literature* of the centrality of "merging" in *Leaves of Grass* is unfortunately extremely distorted by homosexual panic.

2. For the publication history of "The Child's Champion," see the headnote to the text prepared by Thomas L. Brasher for his edition of *Walt Whitman: The Early Poems and the Fiction* (New York: New York University Press, 1963), pp. 68–79.

3. Citations to "The Child's Champion" are to Brasher's edition. Page-number references to this edition of the tale will be included parenthetically in the text.

4. Freud's major statement on the constitutive role psychic censorship plays in mental productions is to be found in *The Interpretation of Dreams*. The passage quoted in the text occurs in James Strachey's translation of that work (New York: Basic Books, 1965), p. 537.

5. *Introductory Lectures on Psychoanalysis*, trans. and ed. James Strachey (New York: Norton, 1966), p. 139.

6. Milton Hindus, ed., *Walt Whitman: The Critical Heritage* (London: Routledge and Kegan Paul, 1971), p. 23.

7. *Walt Whitman: Poetry and Prose*, p. 667.

8. *Walt Whitman: The Correspondence*, V, 73.

9. *Literature, Obscenity, and Law* (Carbondale, Ill.: Southern Illinois University Press, 1976), pp. 18–19.

10. The passage occurs in *The Rights of Man*; I quote it from Clark, ed., *Thomas Paine*, 101.

11. Patterson discusses "the stress on the difficulty of understanding" in a literary text as "a sign of the hermeutics of censorship" in *Censorship and Interpretation: The Conditions of Writing and Reading in Early Modern England* (Madison: University of Wisconsin Press, 1984), p. 243.

12. Citations to the first (1855) edition of *Leaves of Grass* are to Richard Bridgman's facsimile edition of the text (San Francisco: Chandler, 1968). The passage quoted here occurs on p. 15. Since Whitman's own ellipsis dots are ubiquitous in the 1855 *Leaves of Grass*, I have reproduced them without any

spacing between them (....) to indicate that the passage in the text contains such punctuation. When I intend ellipsis dots to indicate my own omission of words or phrases from a quoted passage, I have included spaces between them (. . . .). Subsequent references to page numbers in the facsimile of the first edition will be included in the text.

13. Robert K. Martin, *The Homosexual Tradition in American Poetry* (Austin: University of Texas Press, 1979), p. 21.

14. Martin's survey in the opening pages of his book of the overwhelmingly homophobic character of what was taken to represent mainstream Whitman criticism for most of this century had an important initial effect on the redirection of that discourse toward somewhat less oppressive ways of characterizing the pervasive male-homoeroticism of *Leaves of Grass*. Some of the same material originally appeared as "Whitman's 'Song of Myself': Homosexual Dream and Vision," *Partisan Review* 42:1 (1975).

15. Another passage in *Leaves of Grass* (in 1855 and all subsequent editions) of comparable importance to the "twenty-eight bathers" which represents (among other things) lesbian desire occurs in the poem Whitman later retitled "The Sleepers." I shall discuss this passage later in this chapter.

16. Sculley Bradley and Harold W. Blodgett, eds., *Walt Whitman: Leaves of Grass*, Comprehensive Reader's Edition (New York: New York University Press, 1965), pp. 32–33.

17. Edward F. Grier, ed., *Walt Whitman: Notebooks and Unpublished Prose Manuscripts*, vol. I (New York: New York University Press, 1984), p. 77.

18. In *Beneath the American Renaissance: The Subversive Imagination in the Age of Emerson and Melville* (New York: Knopf, 1988), David S. Reynolds has persuasively linked *Leaves of Grass* with a wide range of popular discourses of the antebellum period, including not only the temperance movement but also the discourses of other major social movements, such as general moral reform, anti-Catholicism, and abolitionist oratory. Reynolds's work, which appeared after I had finished writing this chapter, supports the kinds of connections I argue for among Whitman's "pre-literary" writing, *Leaves of Grass*, and popular discourses, as when Reynolds writes, "As early as 1842, the year he produced his best-selling temperance novel *Franklin Evans*, he had illustrated his awareness that in America moral fanaticism could be *exploited* as an avenue to the tabooed" (p. 105). See pp. 103–112 for Whitman's relation to reform rhetoric, and also pp. 309–333 and 507–523.

19. "A Child Is Being Beaten," in *Sigmund Freud: Sexuality and the Psychology of Love*, ed. Philip Rieff (New York: Collier, 1963), p. 108.

20. Brasher, ed., *Walt Whitman: Early Poems and Fiction*, p. 186.

21. Ibid., p. 243.

22. Ibid., p. 57.

23. "The Shadow and Light of a Young Man's Soul," *Union Magazine* (June 1848); reprinted in Brasher, ed., *Walt Whitman: Early Poems and Fiction*, p. 330.

24. See Brasher's collation of Whitman's various accounts in later life of his motives for writing *Franklin Evans*, in Brasher's headnote to the novel in his edition of the *Early Poems and Fiction*.

25. Wilentz, *Chants Democratic*, pp. 306–314. Paul E. Johnson analyzes the

class antagonisms apparent in the Rochester, New York, temperance movement around the same time in *Shopkeeper's Millennium*, pp. 79–83.

26. Brasher, ed., *Walt Whitman: Early Poems and Fiction*, p. 127.

27. Wilentz, *Chants Democratic*, p. 312.

28. *Essay on the Necessity of Correcting the Errors Which Have Crept into the Washingtonian Temperance Movement* (New York, 1846), p. 6; quoted in Ian R. Tyrrell, *Sobering Up: From Temperance to Prohibition in Antebellum America, 1800–1860* (Westport, Conn., 1979), pp. 163–164; and in Wilentz, *Chants Democratic*, p. 309.

2. Fluidity and Specularity in the Whitman Text

1. See Roy Harvey Pearce's valuable study of American intellectual and cultural history, *Savagism and Civilization: A Study of the Indian and the American Mind* (Baltimore: Johns Hopkins University Press, 1953; rev. ed., 1965), especially chap. 4, "The Idea of the Savage," pp. 105–134.

2. The entry occurs in an Emerson journal of 1842; it is quoted in Edwin Haviland Miller, *Walt Whitman's Poetry: A Psychological Journey* (Boston: Houghton Mifflin, 1968), p. 148. See also David Leverenz, "The Politics of Emerson's Man-Making Words," *PMLA* 101:1 (January 1986), 38–56.

3. Ralph Rusk, *The Life of Ralph Waldo Emerson* (New York: Scribner's, 1949), p. 292.

4. Luce Irigaray identifies and critiques what she calls "a complicity of long standing" between certain repressive, patriarchal forms of rationality and the privileging of "a mechanics of solids alone" over a complementary "'mechanics' of fluids." See her essay "The 'Mechanics' of Fluids" in *This Sex Which Is Not One*, trans. Catherine Porter with Carolyn Burke (Ithaca, N.Y.: Cornell University Press, 1985), pp. 106–118.

5. Both pictures are reproduced in a 1969 article in *Art Quarterly* which argues that the Krimmel drawing served as a source for Mount's painting. See Donald D. Keyes, "The Sources for William Sidney Mount's Earliest Genre Paintings," *Art Quarterly* 32:3 (Autumn 1969), 258–268. The Mount painting is reproduced on p. 258 of Keyes's article and the Krimmel on p. 264.

6. Whitman's early writing on Mount, among other contemporary painters, is reprinted in *The Uncollected Poetry and Prose of Walt Whitman*, ed. Emory Holloway (New York: Peter Smith, 1932).

7. Matthiessen discusses resemblances between Whitman's and Mount's work in *American Renaissance: Language and Expression in the Age of Emerson and Whitman* (New York: Oxford University Press, 1939), pp. 321–322.

8. Mary Kelley surveys the historical consequences for women writers of what she calls "literary domesticity" in *Private Woman, Public Stage: Literary Domesticity in Nineteenth-Century America* (New York: Oxford University Press, 1984). Kathryn Kish Sklar's *Catharine Beecher: A Study in American Domesticity* (New Haven: Yale University Press, 1973) is an important study of one of the chief ideologues of the first phase of the domesticity movement. Jeanne Boydston, Mary Kelley, and Anne Margolis, eds., in *The Limits of Sisterhood: The Beecher Sisters on Women's Rights and Woman's Sphere* (Chapel Hill: University of North Carolina

Press, 1988), provide valuable material for comparative purposes between different phases of the cult of domesticity as represented in the respective writings of Catharine Beecher and her younger sister Isabella Beecher Hooker; see, for example, pp. 13–14 and 184–186. Finally, Mary Ryan gives a perspicacious account of the high degree of congruity in sentimental-domestic ideology between what it posited as the "proper sphere" of home-centered "influence" for women versus the corresponding "sphere" of commercial "self-making" for men, in "Varieties of Social Retreat: Domesticity, Privacy, and the Self-Made Man," in her *Cradle of the Middle Class: The Family in Oneida County, New York, 1790–1865* (Cambridge: Cambridge University Press, 1981), pp. 146–155.

9. My model for the role specularity plays in the construction and projection of male desire in Whitman derives in obvious ways from Jacques Lacan's "The Mirror Stage as Formative of the Function of the I," in *Ecrits: A Selection,* trans. Alan Sheridan (New York: Norton, 1977), pp. 1–7. For a provocative critique of the political limitations of this aspect of Lacanian theory in relation to antebellum American cultural formations, see Michael Warner's essay "Thoreau's Bottom" (forthcoming).

10. Whitman's pieces on Dr. Colyer's troupe's performances are reprinted in Holloway, ed., *Uncollected Poetry and Prose,* pp. 191–193.

11. Ibid., p. 191.

12. Reprinted in Hindus, ed., *Walt Whitman: The Critical Heritage,* p. 45.

13. See Alan Sinfield's account of this in his recent volume on Tennyson in the *Rereading Literature* series (Oxford: Basil Blackwell, 1986).

14. June Jordan's "For the Sake of a People's Poetry: Walt Whitman and the Rest of Us" originally appeared in her book *Passion* (Boston: Beacon Press, 1980). It has been reprinted in *Walt Whitman: The Measure of His Song,* ed. Jim Perlman, Ed Folsom, and Dan Campion (Minneapolis: Holy Cow! Press, 1981), pp. 343–352. The same collection presents responses to Whitman's poetry in the form of poems and essays by a number of other women writers, including Muriel Rukeyser and Denise Levertov. For a provocative critique of Whitman's techniques of appealing to readers, see Doris Sommer, "Supplying Demand: Walt Whitman as the Liberal Self," in *Reinventing the Americas: Comparative Studies of Literature of the U.S. and Spanish America,* ed. Bell Gale Chevigny and Gari LaGuardia (Cambridge: Cambridge University Press, 1986), pp. 68–91.

15. Gilchrist's early article, "A Woman's Estimate of Walt Whitman," is reprinted in Thomas B. Harned's 1918 volume of letters between Gilchrist and Whitman. The "too great waves" passage I quote in the text occurs on p. 56 of Harned's collection.

16. Hindus, ed., *Critical Heritage,* pp. 46–47.

17. The twenty-two-year-old Henry James, in his early, unfavorable review of Whitman's *Drum-Taps,* seems to have registered some of this subliminally: he attacks the poet (with more perspicacity than he is likely to have realized) for playing in his poetry what James calls "the little nursery game of open your mouth and shut your eyes." The review is reprinted in Hindus, ed., *The Critical Heritage,* p. 113.

18. Karen Sánchez-Eppler provides an excellent discussion of the relation of Whitman's poetry to the language of slavery and abolition in her essay "To Stand

Between: A Political Perspective on Whitman's Poetics of Merger and Embodiment," *ELH* 56:4 (Winter 1989), 923–949.

3. Dividing the Text and Crossing the Gaze

1. Because to my knowledge no facsimile of the second (1856) *Leaves of Grass* has ever been published, line number references to poems new to that edition have for the reader's convenience been made to the *Variorum* edition, vol. 1. As in previous chapters, page-number references to the 1855 edition are to the Chandler Publishing Company facsimile.

2. "Make it [the broad-axe] the American emblem preferent to the eagle," Whitman writes in a notebook from the period when he first drafted parts of "Broad-Axe Poem." See Grier, ed., *Walt Whitman: Notebooks and Unpublished Prose Manuscripts,* I, 299.

3. Lewis Hyde, for example, writes, "As in those churches in which sex is tolerated only as an instrument of procreation, it is a persistent quirk of Whitman's imagination that heterosexual lovemaking always leads to babies. His women are always mothers. No matter how graphically Whitman describes 'the clinch,' 'the merge,' within a few lines out pops a child." See his *The Gift: Imagination and the Erotic Life of Property* (New York: Random House, 1983), pp. 185–186.

4. Except for James E. Miller, Jr.'s, "The 'Broad-Axe': Arising Shapes," in *A Critical Guide to "Leaves of Grass"* (Chicago: University of Chicago Press, 1957), pp. 90–103, the principal full-length critical interpretations of the poem have mostly been psychoanalytic. See Alvin H. Rosenfeld, "The Eagle and the Axe: A Study of Whitman's 'Song of the Broad-Axe,'" American Imago 25:4 (Winter 1968), 354–370; Stephen Black, *Whitman's Journeys into Chaos: A Psychoanalytic Study of the Poetic Process* (Princeton, N.J.: Princeton University Press, 1975), pp. 151–157; and Dorothy M.-T. Gregory, "The Celebration of Nativity: 'Broad-Axe Poem,'" *Walt Whitman Quarterly Review* 2:1 (Summer 1984), 1–11.

5. Linda Peavy has related the opening lines of "Song of the Broad-Axe" to Anglo-Saxon riddle forms in her article "Wooden Flesh and Metal Bone," *Walt Whitman Review* 20 (December 1974), 152–154.

6. Whitman seems to use the word "bowels" in two senses. One of these is in its older sense of meaning "the innermost recesses of the body, the seat of deep feelings" (that is, something like what has long since come to be called ordinarily the "heart"), as in the proverbial phrase "the bowels of compassion," which he quotes facetiously in an early letter I shall discuss later. The other sense is the modern colloquial one of "bowels" meaning not "innermost" but "lowermost" cavity of the torso, the lower intestine. The overlap of the two senses in English (or American) ordinary usage in the nineteenth-century allows Whitman (as we shall see in the discussion of his use of the phrase "bowels of compassion") to suggest a comically grotesque *and* (I shall argue) sexually significant downward dislocation of the "seat" of deep feelings from the "bowels" (that is, "heart") to the "bowels" ("lower intestine").

7. Grier, ed., *Whitman: Unpublished Manuscripts,* I, 73.

8. The central elements of this chain (that is, feces = baby = gift) are described in Freud's *Three Essays on the Theory of Sexuality,* trans. James

Strachey (New York: Avon, 1965), p. 82. Norman O. Brown discusses the whole "magic-dirt complex" in *Life against Death: The Psychoanalytic Meaning of History* (Wesleyan, Conn.: Wesleyan University Press, 1959), p. 300.

9. Quoted in Arthur Golden, "Nine Early Whitman Letters, 1840–1841," *American Literature* 58:3 (October 1986), 352–353.

10. Ibid., p. 353n.

11. Ibid., p. 353.

12. Naomi Schor, "Mother's Day: Zola's Women," *Diacritics* 5:4 (Winter 1975), 16. The passage on Barthes on the "symbolic axis of castration" to which Schor is referring occurs on p. 35 of the English translation of *S/Z*, trans. Richard Miller (New York: Hill and Wang, 1974).

13. See Richard Klein's discussion of some of the implications for cultural theory of Melanie Klein's researches into the content and dynamics of persistent albeit unconscious infantile fantasies in his article "In the Body of the Mother," *Enclitic* 7:1 (Spring 1983), 66–75. The phrase quoted in the text occurs on p. 69.

14. The psychoanalytic theory of the infantile fantasy of the retention by the mother of the father's phallus(es) in her body, and of the child's fantasy of appropriating them by ravaging the maternal body, was first developed by Melanie Klein in such works as *The Psycho-Analysis of Children* (1932). Klein's influential general theory of pre-oedipal subjectivity has been revised, among other places, in Julia Kristeva's work, particularly in her *La révolution poétique* (Paris: Seuil, 1974) and in the first half of *Pouvoirs de l'horreur* (Paris: Seuil, 1980).

15. Kenneth Burke interprets "Crossing Brooklyn Ferry" as successfully performing an act of "transcendental bridging" in his essay "Acceptance and Rejection," *Southern Review* 2 (1936), 604 (later incorporated into his *Attitudes toward History* [1937]). Stanley K. Coffman, Jr.'s, essay, "'Crossing Brooklyn Ferry': A Note on the Catalogue Technique in Whitman's Poetry," *Modern Philology* 51 (1954), 225–232, has been the most frequently cited of formalist-structuralist accounts of the poem. Coffman's essay has often been used to support, although it does not itself explicitly argue, the popular hypothesis that the catalogs in "Crossing Brooklyn Ferry" are artistically superior to most of the other catalogs in Whitman's poetry, which are allegedly random, disorganized, and otherwise insufficiently related to the formal structure of the text. As I repeatedly try to show in my discussions of Whitman's poetry, his catalogs often have social and political significances that simply may not register as values on the formalist aesthetic level.

16. Blodgett and Bradley, eds., *Walt Whitman: Leaves of Grass* (Comprehensive Reader's Edition), pp. 158–159n.

17. *A Critical Guide to "Leaves of Grass,"* p. 80.

18. Quentin Anderson makes his "sociopathic" reading of Whitman's purposes in writing "Crossing Brooklyn Ferry" crucial to his attack on the poet for allegedly undermining what Anderson sees as the foundations of society: the acceptance of one's place in the network of existing social, particularly familial, roles. See "The World in the Body," in *The Imperial Self* (New York: Knopf, 1971), pp. 119–165. David Cavitch alleges that "Crossing Brooklyn Ferry" is a product of the poet's melancholy isolation and his yearning for stasis in the face of an ever-changing world in *My Soul and I*, pp. 106–113. M. Wynn Thomas brings some of what he calls "the darker or richer" hues of "Crossing Brooklyn Ferry" into focus,

treating the recurring "intimations of bafflement" in the text as real barriers to reading it as simply celebratory. See his *The Lunar Light of Whitman's Poetry* (Cambridge, Mass.: Harvard University Press, 1987), pp. 92–116.

19. The phrase quoted in this sentence is from Thomas, *The Lunar Light*, p. 96. See also Cavitch, *My Soul and I*, p. 107.

20. Jacques Lacan, "Of the Gaze as *Objet Petit a*," in *Four Fundamental Concepts of Psychoanalysis*, ed. Jacques-Alain Miller, trans. Alan Sheridan (New York: Norton, 1978), p. 81.

21. Thomas discusses the poem in the context of the Luminist movement in his *The Lunar Light of Whitman's Poetry*.

22. Anderson, *The Imperial Self*, p. 79.

23. Henry Nash Smith, "Walt Whitman and Manifest Destiny," in *Virgin Land: The American West as Symbol and Myth* (Cambridge, Mass.: Harvard University Press, 1950), pp. 44–48. The passage quoted in the text occurs on p. 48. Annette Kolodny has influentially revised the kinds of assumptions and conclusions Smith reached in *Virgin Land* in two works of her own: *The Lay of the Land: Metaphor as Experience and History in American Life and Letters* (Chapel Hill: University of North Carolina Press, 1975), and *The Land before Her: Fantasy and Experience of the American Frontiers, 1630–1860* (Chapel Hill: University of North Carolina Press, 1984).

24. *Letters from Paumanok* (1851), reprinted in Holloway, ed., *Uncollected Poetry and Prose of Walt Whitman*, p. 258.

4. The Politics of Nature and the Decomposition of God

1. The autograph manuscript of this note is in the Trent Collection in the Duke University Library. Richard M. Bucke published it in his collection *Notes and Fragments* (1899).

2. Edwin Haviland Miller, ed., *Walt Whitman: The Correspondence* (New York: New York University Press, 1961), I, 44.

3. Whitman was of course far from unique in cherishing scriptural ambitions for his writing: his hope of producing some kind of new American Bible that would reorient the spiritual and moral life of the nation was one he shared with a number of his contemporaries, as recent work by Jane P. Tompkins and Lawrence Buell has demonstrated in the cases of Harriet Beecher Stowe and other American authors of the mid-nineteenth century. See Tompkins, "Sentimental Power," in her *Sensational Designs*, pp. 122–146, and Buell's chapter on the rewriting of scripture as an American literary practice in his *New England Literary Culture*. Rather than taking over such fundamental aspects of Judeo-Christian scriptural tradition as its pervasive soteriological or apocalyptic strains—as, for example, Stowe and Julia Ward Howe did in some of their most popular writings of the 1850s and 1860s—Whitman in the "New Bible" of the third edition of *Leaves of Grass* attempts to launch a gospel of immanence grounded in the text's extensive interrogations of the categories of the natural and the real.

Two undated manuscript notes of Whitman's—presumably from early in his career and quite possibly from circa 1857 when he was most interested in conceiving of *Leaves of Grass* as a scripture—take up the desirability of founding new

American religions and writing new scriptures for them. In the first of these he writes, "Theological inferences once thought orthodox may be demolished by the scientific and historical inquiries of our times, but the collect of the Bible as a traditional poem various in its sources and times, remains the most instructive, suggestive, even artistic memorial of the past" (Trent Collection, Duke University Library, quarto 35). At the end of a second, longer note headed "Founding a new American Religion (?No Religion)," Whitman writes, "There are [those] that specialize a book, or some one divine life, as the only revelation. I too doubtless own it whatever it is to be a revelation, a part, but I see all else, all Nature, and each and all that to it appertains. The processes of time[,] all men, the universes[,] all likes and dislikes and developments, —a hundred, a thousand other Saviours and Mediators and Bibles" (Trent Collection, ms. 64).

4. Quoted in Gay Wilson Allen, *The Solitary Singer: A Critical Biography of Walt Whitman* (New York: Grove Press, 1955), p. 232.

5. Citations to *Leaves of Grass* in this chapter are to Roy Harvey Pearce's facsimile of the 1860 edition (Ithaca, N.Y.: Cornell University Press, 1961), except where otherwise noted. Further citations to this edition will be noted in the text.

6. For my understanding of the three senses in which the word "type" functions in the 1860 *Leaves*, I am indebted to Frank Kermode's analysis of the similarly multiple significance of the term in Hawthorne's writing. See Kermode's *The Classic: Literary Images of Permanence and Change* (Cambridge, Mass.: Harvard University Press, 1983), pp. 89ff. Kermode writes, "[F]or centuries it was believed that God had provided two books, the Bible and Nature, and that Nature too was inscribed with divine hints—the plants bore each a sign indicating its use, just as history revealed God's will to men. Before those times were effectively over the characters of printing had come to be called types; each was inscribed with the letter which was its function" (p. 92). As Kermode says, it was Jonathan Edwards who first extended typological interpretation to natural, and not merely scriptural, phenomena (ibid., p. 90). See Edwards's *Images or Shadows of Divine Things*, ed. Perry Miller (New Haven: Yale University Press, 1948). Miller first argued that there was a determinate relation between Edwards's habit of reading types out of nature and Emerson's and other nineteenth-century American writers' perception of the natural world as a collection of spiritually emblematic objects in his essay "From Edwards to Emerson." See also Ursula Brumm, "Jonathan Edwards and Ralph Waldo Emerson," in her *American Thought and Religious Typology*, trans. John Hoaglund (New Brunswick, N.J.: Rutgers University Press, 1970), pp. 86–108. The collection edited by Sacvan Bercovitch, *Typology and Early American Literature* (n.p.: University of Massachusetts Press, 1972) is a standard source for the study of typology in the context of American colonial writing. A more general collection is Earl Miner, ed., *Literary Uses of Typology from the Late Middle Ages to the Present* (Princeton, N.J.: Princeton University Press, 1977); this volume includes Karl Keller's essay, "Alephs, Zahirs, and the Triumph of Ambiguity: Typology in Nineteenth-Century American Literature" (pp. 274–314), in which Keller gives a rather cursory series of readings of Whitman texts as rooted in typological habits of mind (pp. 290–294).

The primary structure of typological interpretations is to relate divine "promises" made at one point in history to their subsequent fulfillment at a later point, and especially to relate figures and events from the pre-Christic era (for example, the arrival of the Israelites in the Promised Land) to their supposed fulfillment in the salvific actions of Christ (for example, his death and resurrection). There is of course an extensive critical literature on the allegedly determinate effect of the typologizing practices of Puritan writers on a body of long-lived conceptions of America as a "chosen" nation with a divinely sanctioned historical mission, and as part of this there is a considerable literature on the consequences of such a politics of sacralized nationalism for a number of American Renaissance writers, Whitman among them. Whitman's emphasis throughout his writing career on the promissory character of American history raises many questions about the relation of his thinking to typological traditions. Several critics have related Whitman's mode of presenting himself—or more precisely "his self," with emphasis on his representative selfhood rather than on his own personal identity—to the presentation in typological tradition of "antitypes," human figures who represent the fulfillment in history of a promise prefigured in other persons in earlier times.

While it is possible to relate some of Whitman's representations (perhaps most notably those in the 1855 *Leaves*, especially in the Preface) of the poet's participation in the unique historical role of the nation to the dynamics of promise and fulfillment, typal prefiguration and antitypal figuration, that characterize typologizing interpretations of scripture and history, Whitman foregrounds a less overtly historical and teleological aspect of typological tradition in the third edition. This is the tradition of typological allegorizing, the interpretation of natural phenomena as signs of spiritual truths, which was introduced into typological tradition by Philo of Alexandria and practiced most influentially for American writers by Samuel Mather (*Scriptural Types*, 1666) and Jonathan Edwards (*Images and Shadows of Divine Things*). The importance of this hermeneutic mode for American Renaissance texts like Emerson's "Nature" and for transcendentalist theories of nature in general has been widely remarked. Whitman's means of revising this tradition, especially with regard to its privileging of a spiritual, transcendent realm over a natural, immanent one, are perhaps most clearly evident in the 1860 "Leaves of Grass. 1"/"As I Ebb'd."

7. "Type" seems to have had a quite short-lived career as meaning "species or genus" in discourses of evolution. The *O.E.D.* definition of the term in this sense (8.b.) cites examples only from the 1840s and 1850s; this suggests that the term manifested the particular range of multiple meanings (theological type, printer's type, species threatened with extinction) it has in the 1860 text for only about twenty years before the text's appearance, and not for long thereafter.

8. In a series of ironic reversals in the 1856 "Poem of The Propositions of Nakedness," Whitman had written, "Let shadows be furnished with genitals! Let substances be deprived of their genitals!" This poem was retitled "Respondez!" in the 1871 *Leaves of Grass* and then canceled in its entirety in subsequent editions.

9. Attempting to substantiate the major claims of the third edition by articulating the notions of politics and religion in which they are grounded involves the third edition in a paradox of the kind Kenneth Burke has described in a section of *A Grammar of Motives* as the "Paradox of Substance." Looking back over the career of the notion of "substance" in several mainstream Western philo-

sophical discourses, Burke argues that the term has generally done double duty, to mean "main part, real being, essential component" while retaining some of its literal etymological meaning of "base, bottom, prop, support, stay; hence, metaphorically, that which lies at the bottom of a thing, as the groundwork, subject-matter, argument of a narrative, speech, poem"—in other words, both the person, text, thing itself *and* the underlying support which sustains it or imbues it with sense. Burke finally relates the paradox of substance to the confusion of the demarcation of inner and outer spaces in which the notion of substance involves us: "[T]hough used to designate something *within* the thing, *intrinsic* to it, the word etymologically refers to something *outside* the thing, *extrinsic* to it." See Kenneth Burke, "The Paradox of Substance," in *A Grammar of Motives* (Berkeley: University of California Press, 1962), pp. 21–23. As in the *Leaves of Grass* project as a whole, the process of substantiation carried out in the third edition involved both further elaborations and clarifications of a substance that was in one sense "already there" (intrinsic) in the first and second editions, in however "inchoate" a state Whitman by 1860 may have come to feel it had existed in those texts, but that in another sense needed to be added to those texts (extrinsic) in order to produce the new *Leaves of Grass*, which would be "shored up" with a more fully articulated version of its politics and religion than had previously been the case.

10. The phrase "both God's books" is from Kermode, *The Classic*.

11. Quoted in Karen E. Rowe, "Prophetic Visions: Typology and Colonial American Poetry," in *Puritan Poetry and Poetics: Seventeenth-Century American Poetry in Theory and Practice*, ed. Peter White (University Park, Pa.: Pennsylvania State University Press, 1985), p. 48.

12. Gay Wilson Allen's "Walt Whitman and Stoicism," in *The Stoic Strain in American Literature: Essays in Honor of Marston LaFrance*, ed. Duane J. MacMillan (Toronto: University of Toronto Press, 1979), pp. 43–60, is typical of the simplistic notion of the significance of stoicism for Whitman's writing: "Although in some lines of *Leaves of Grass* the poet may sound like a neighing centaur, in the larger context of his total writings he was an ethical didacticist, with a high regard for *virtue* in the stoic sense" (p. 43).

13. David E. Hahm, *The Origins of Stoic Cosmology* (n.p.: Ohio State University Press, 1977), p. 3.

14. Quoted in ibid., p. 15. Whitman rehearses a form of Chrysippus's famous paradox ("When I say the word *chariot*, a chariot goes through my mouth!") in the 1860 "Proto-Leaf": "See! steamers steaming through my poems!" (1860 ed., p. 21). Michel Serres, the leading theorist of Hellenistic-style nature-theory in our own time, has noted the primacy of criteria of conjunction and separability in stoic and epicurean nature-theory as a whole; see his "Lucretius: Science and Religion," in *Hermes: Literature, Science, Philosophy*, ed. Josue V. Harari and David F. Bell (Baltimore: Johns Hopkins University Press, 1982), p. 112.

15. See Bernice Slote et al., *Start with the Sun*.

16. *Collected Prose*, p. 1101.

17. Quoted in Harold Bloom, *Poetry and Repression: Revisionism from Blake to Stevens* (New Haven: Yale University Press, 1976), p. 250. Bloom gives a capsule history of Whitman's expressed attitudes toward Emerson on pp. 250–251.

18. Burke, *A Grammar of Motives*, p. 178.

19. Ronald Schleifer, "Literality and Printing in Whitman," *Arizona Review* 22:3 (Fall 1984), 41–53.

20. "Extinction" is R. W. B. Lewis's term for the anxiety that impels the powerful new writing of the 1860 "Paumanok" poems, particularly "As I Ebb'd."

21. Freud, "Psychoanalytic Notes on an Autobiographical Account of a Case of Paranoia" [The "Schreber case"], in *The Standard Edition of the Complete Psychological Works of Sigmund Freud*, vol. XII, ed. James Strachey, trans. Alix and James Strachey (London: Hogarth Press, 1958), p. 71.

22. Kristeva, *Revolution in Poetic Language*, p. 254.

23. The idea that all historical religions and their presiding deities shared certain common characteristics, including, in the modern era, obsolescence and decay, was of course not original to Whitman; it was a commonplace of the Enlightenment critique of institutionalized religions. It was the informing idea, for example, of the French savant Constantin Volney's 1791 *Les ruines, ou méditations sur les révolutions des empires*, a book of which Whitman's freethinking father owned a translation and which Whitman claimed to have reread frequently during his youth.

24. See Allen, *Solitary Singer*, p. 238, for this possibility.

25. Irigaray, *Speculum*, p. 79. See also Toril Moi, *Sexual/Textual Politics: Feminist Literary Theory* (New York: Methuen, 1985), p. 137.

26. The central Freudian text for male homosexuality and paranoia, as I shall discuss later in this chapter, is Freud's 1911 study of Schreber's *Memoirs of My Nervous Illness*, S.E. XII, 3–82.

27. The emphasis in both texts on phenomena like "mocking" birds, "corpse poison," and a decomposed and persecutory deity confirms my conjecture that the third edition locates itself on the cultural terrain of paranoia. According to Freud, paranoid imaginings themselves tend to have a decomposing effect on psychic constructions: "Paranoia decomposes just as hysteria condenses," he asserts in the Schreber case (ibid., p. 49). This process of decomposition, he goes on to say, "is . . . designed to prevent the occurrence of unduly powerful impressions" (p. 50n.).

28. Jardine, *Gynesis*, p. 98.

29. Kristeva, *Revolution in Poetic Language*, p. 156.

30. Jacques Lacan, "The Direction of the Treatment and the Principle of Its Power," in *Ecrits: A Selection*, trans. Alan Sheridan (New York: Norton, 1977), p. 265.

5. "The Blood of the World"

1. See Asselineau, *The Evolution of Walt Whitman: The Creation of a Personality* (Cambridge, Mass.: Harvard University Press, 1960), pp. 308–309, n. 103: a volume of poems by Whitman to be called "Banner at Daybreak" was advertised as being "in preparation" in the back pages of William Van O'Connor's *Harrington* and in two issues of the abolitionist paper the *Liberator*, November 2 and 9, 1860.

2. "The Eighteenth Presidency!" is reprinted in *Walt Whitman: Poetry and Prose*, pp. 1307–1325.

3. An essential text for the theory of the relation of the phallus to representation is Lacan's "The Signification of the Phallus," in *Ecrits: A Selection*, trans. Alan Sheridan (New York: Norton, 1977), pp. 281–291. Compare Jacqueline Rose's translation of the same material as "The Meaning of the Phallus," in her and Juliet Mitchell's *Feminine Sexuality: Jacques Lacan and the Ecole Freudienne* (New York: Norton, 1982), pp. 74–85. For an overview of recent feminist critique of Lacan's theory of the phallus, see Kate Linker, "Representation and Sexuality," in *Art After Modernism: Rethinking Representation*, ed. Brian Wallis (New York: The New Museum of Contemporary Art, 1984), pp. 391–415; see especially pp. 393–401.

4. "The 'Uncanny,'" trans. Alix Strachey, reprinted in *Studies in Parapsychology*, ed. Philip Rieff (New York: Collier, 1963).

5. Frederik Schyberg, *Walt Whitman*, trans. Evie Allison Allen (New York: Columbia University Press, 1951), p. 191.

6. Whitman claims to have read Lockhart's 1833 edition of Scott's *Complete Poems* "thoroughly" and repeatedly, in a footnote to "A Backward Glance o'er Travel'd Roads" (*Walt Whitman: Complete Poetry and Selected Prose*, p. 665n.) Whitman specifically mentions enjoying Scott's "copious revisions" of his poems; perhaps the experience contributed to his own revisionary habits.

7. On the transformation of American society as a consequence of shifts in scale in American economic activity beginning circa 1850, see Carroll Smith-Rosenberg, "Bourgeois Discourse and the Progressive Era: An Introduction," in *Disorderly Conduct: Visions of Gender in Victorian America* (New York: Oxford University Press, 1985), pp. 167–181, especially pp. 169–171. Smith-Rosenberg (pp. 325–326, n. 1) cites Robert Wiebe, *The Search for Order, 1877–1920* (New York: Hill and Wang, 1967), as an influential account of the historical shift in leadership in the United States at mid-century and after "from a small-town, commercially based bourgeoisie to a new, far more complex bourgeois economic and social structure." On the changes in the appearance of city streets which give the Father's praise of the signs of wealth in "Song of the Banner" its political point, see also Mary P. Ryan, *Cradle of the Middle Class: The Family in Oneida County, New York, 1790–1865* (Cambridge: Cambridge University Press, 1981): "The streets of the city at midcentury were no longer bordered by a smooth line of small shops and houses. The urban horizon was now broken by more massive commercial and industrial enterprises" (p. 149; see also pp. 151–152).

8. Jacques Derrida, *Spurs: Nietzsche's Styles*, trans. Barbara Harlow (Chicago: University of Chicago Press, 1979), p. 129.

9. Kristeva discusses the relation of the infant's experience of the presymbolic "semiotic" in relation to the mother's body in *Desire in Language*, ed. Leon S. Roudiez, trans. Thomas Gora, Alice Jardine, and Leon S. Roudiez (New York: Columbia University Press, 1980), pp. 141, 241–242, and elsewhere.

10. The speaker of one of the *Drum-Taps* poems himself claims to be "restless" and to "make[ ] others so" in "As I Lay with My Head in Your Lap, Camerado."

11. Of this phenomenon in *Drum-Taps*, Debra Fried has observed, "[W]hat in earlier volumes was a repeating catalogue of celebratory plenitude shades into the stiff stammer of epitaph: the parade of life becomes a funeral march. That is, one may read the progress of Whitman's canon, as the song of myself is hoarsened

into whispers of heavenly death, as the transformation of his repetitive habits from the rapture of fullness to the numbness of stasis and loss." (See her article on elegy in *ELH* 53:3 [Fall 1986], 631 n. 13.) I disagree with Fried's point here insofar as it depends on a highly restricted notion of what constitutes "Whitman's canon." In my own project of attempting to read out some of the dialectical relations that can be discerned among the first four editions of *Leaves of Grass*, one of the tendencies in Whitman criticism I have been most interested in opposing is the common one that there is a univocal "progress" (usually downward after 1855 or 1860) to be read out of his career. Such arguments commonly depend on restricting the "canon" to the more "rapturous" (to use Fried's terms) moments of Whitman's early poems and then to the "hoarser" or "number" (to use Fried's term) moments of subsequent poems which thematize "stasis and loss." The net effect has been repeatedly to reduce the career of *Leaves of Grass* to an allegory of the poet's life that is reductive of the actual historical complexities of the career and of the relationships between writing and politics which it embodies.

12. Herbert Levine deals with the general figure of union/disunion in "Union and Disunion in 'Song of Myself,'" *American Literature* 59:4 (December 1987), 570–589. The "three-part plot" of "Union, Disunion, and Reunion" he proposes for the structure of "Song of Myself," and his general attempt to use "Song of Myself" as a microcosm for Whitman's career as a whole, lead him to make the kinds of reductive allegorizing gestures discussed in the previous note, a consequence of his following the common practice of considering only a restricted canon of Whitman's poems, in this case only *the* canonical one, "Song of Myself."

13. The editors of the textual variorum of *Leaves of Grass* give an excellent, elaborate account of the development of the principles of incorporation by "cluster" and "annex" in the successive editions of Whitman's work, in "Cluster Arrangement in *Leaves of Grass*," vol. 1, pp. lvii–lxxv.

14. The literary consequences of tropes of "dilation" and "deferral" in medieval poetry have been explored by Lee Patterson in "'For the Wyves Love of Bathe': Feminine Rhetoric and Poetic Resolution in the *Roman de la Rose* and the *Canterbury Tales*," *Speculum* 58:3 (July 1983), 656–695. I have found Patterson's demonstration of "how rhetorical structure can bear erotic value" (p. 671) in the texts he considers helpful in thinking about similar relations in the "dilative" rhetoric of the fourth edition of *Leaves of Grass*. See also Patricia Parker, "Dilation and Delay: Renaissance Matrices," *Poetics Today* 5:3 (1984), 519–535; "Shakespeare and Rhetoric: 'Dilation' and 'Delation' in *Othello*," in *Shakespeare and the Question of Theory*, ed. Patricia Parker and Geoffrey Hartman (London: Methuen, 1985), pp. 54–74; and, finally, "Deferral, Dilation, Différance: Shakespeare, Cervantes, Jonson," in *Literary Theory/Renaissance Texts*, ed. Patricia Parker and David Quint (Baltimore: Johns Hopkins University Press, 1986), pp. 182–209. For a discussion of Whitman's use of the term in his writings of 1855 and before, see P. Z. Rosenthal, "'Dilation' in Whitman's Early Writing," *Walt Whitman Review* 20:1 (March 1974), 3–15.

15. Whitman's chief biographers and biographical critics since Schyberg—Allen, Asselineau, Kaplan, and Zweig—have tended to make much of his "sublimation" of his homoerotic desires in his dedication to his work among sick and wounded Civil War soldiers. Emphasizing the pathos of Whitman's "necessary"

(as they see it) sexual self-denial, critics have, with a few exceptions, largely ignored his own accounts of what he saw as the primarily *political* significance for him of his Civil War experiences, as when he writes (in *Specimen Days*), "Those three years [spent in the hospitals] . . . ha[ve] given me the most fervent view of the true *ensemble* and extent of the *States.*" Roger Asselineau quotes this passage in *The Evolution of Walt Whitman* (vol. 1, p. 160) and refers the reader to similar passages from *Democratic Vistas* and from one of Whitman's wartime letters to his mother (September 15, 1863).

16. See, for example, Joseph Cady's "*Drum-Taps* and Nineteenth-Century Male Homosexual Literature," in *Walt Whitman: Here and Now*, ed. Joann P. Krieg (Westport, Conn.: Greenwood Press, 1985), pp. 49–59.

17. The phrase quoted is Myrth Jimmie Killingsworth's characterization of how a "Freudian" might describe Whitman's relationship with his mother. The words occur in Killingsworth's rather superficial survey, "Whitman and Motherhood: A Historical View," in *On Whitman: The Best from "American Literature,"* ed. Edwin H. Cady and Louis J. Budd (Durham, N.C.: Duke University Press, 1987), pp. 245–260. The phrase quoted in the text occurs on p. 256.

18. Peter M. Sacks, *The English Elegy: Studies in the Genre from Spenser to Yeats* (Baltimore: Johns Hopkins University Press, 1985), p. 316.

19. Sack's discussion of "sexual renunciation" in "When Lilacs Last in the Dooryard Bloom'd" occurs on p. 317 of *The English Elegy*.

20. Helen Vendler similarly argues that "[t]he deliberately nonerotic companionship implied by a group of three coincides . . . [in "Lilacs"] with Whitman's imagining this form of association as the appropriate one for the old; any procession of the young would have to be paired off two by two." See her "Reading Walt Whitman," in *The Music of What Happens: Poems, Poets, Critics* (Cambridge, Mass.: Harvard University Press, 1988), p. 135.

21. Sacks, *The English Elegy*, p. 317.

22. See "Whitman's Image of Voice: To the Tally of My Soul" in Bloom's *Agon*. The reference to "cruel hands" occurs on p. 135 of the essay, as reprinted in Harold Bloom, ed., *Modern Critical Views: Walt Whitman* (New York: Chelsea House, 1985).

Index

Throughout this index, *Leaves of Grass* is abbreviated as *LG*. Individual works by Walt Whitman are listed by category under his name.

Adhesiveness, 12–13, 50, 156. *See also* Homoerotic desire, male

Anality, 94–95, 234n6; in "The Child's Champion," 28–29; in 1855 *LG*, 51–52; in "Song of the Broad-Axe," 93; in "By Blue Ontario's Shore," 208

Anderson, Quentin, 113–114

"Annex," as organizing device in *LG*, 199–200

Anti-onanist discourses, 19–25. *See also* Male-purity movement

Asselineau, Roger, 171

Barker-Benfield, G. J., 24–25

Barthes, Roland, 96

Blodgett, Harold W., 48

Bloom, Harold, 218

Bowers, Fredson, 2

Bradley, Sculley, 48

Burke, Kenneth, 140, 238n9

Castration: in 1856 *LG*, 91, 96–98, 104; in "Crossing Brooklyn Ferry," 110; in 1867 *LG*, 206. *See also* Oedipal dynamics; Phallus; Pre-oedipal fantasy

Cavitch, David, 106, 229n39

Censorship: and *LG*, 30; and 1855 *LG*, 37, 52–53. *See also* Self-censorship

Childbirth: as figure for war-process in 1867 *LG*, 202, 206–207, 209, 210, 219. *See also* Maternity, figures for

Child-phallus: in "Drum-Taps" poems, 175–176; in "Song of the Banner at Daybreak," 187–189, 193, 196, 213. *See also* Maternal phallus; Phallus

"Cluster," as organizing device in *LG*, 199–200

Corporeality, 2–4, 7; performative models of, 69–73; Stoic and epicurean theories of appropriated by WW, 128–131, 158; foregrounded in WW's Civil War poetry, 173–174; and "the body" in WW's writing, 228n20. *See also* Embodiment, Politics of; "Real body"

Death, WW's conception of, as constructed entity, 149–150, 163, 165–166, 168–169, 170, 219

Decomposition, as characteristic of writing, 127, 135–138, 142, 150–151, 156–158

Derrida, Jacques, 185

Difference, figures for: in 1856 *LG*, 88–90, 97–98; and principle of "indifference" in 1860 *LG*, 133–134, 156–157, 159–160, 162. *See also* Oedipal dynamics

Dilation, 192–193, 199–200, 201, 205–210

Disencryptment, 158–170. *See also* Homoerotic desire, male

Dixon, Edward H., 22–23

Doyle, Peter, 214

Edwards, Jonathan, 127

Ejaculation, figures for, in 1855 *LG*, 38, 44, 49–50, 60–61

Elegy-rhetoric, 171–173. *See also* War-rhetoric

Embodiment, politics of: of *LG* in general, 14; and male-purity movement, 18–25;

Index

Embodiment (*cont.*)
  of American landscape, 114–119. *See also* Corporeality
Emerson, Ralph Waldo, 30, 59–60, 139–141
Encoding of proscribed discourses within other discourses, 53–58

Fellatio, figures for: in "The Child's Champion," 28; in "Song of Myself," section eleven, 41–42
Female body. *See* Women, representations of
Fetish, 103
Fluidity, principle of, in WW's writing, 7, 14–15, 230n1; and revision, 16–18; in "The Child's Champion," 26–36; as ideal state for males in 1855 *LG*, 36–52; in relation to principle of specularity, 59–77; versus "solidity," 60–62; between women, 86; WW's critique of in 1856 *LG*, 88–89, 110; WW's critique of in 1860 *LG*, 127, 132–133, 138, 162
Freud, Sigmund: on psychic function of self-censorship, 30–32; on beating fantasies, 54; on "magic-dirt complex," 94; on paranoia, 143, 154–155; on uncanny, 176
Fried, Debra, 241n11

Gaze, powers of: in "Song of Myself," section eleven, 41, 43, 164; in "Crossing Brooklyn Ferry," 108–111, 164; in "I Saw in Louisiana a Live-Oak Growing," 163–164; in "Song of the Banner at Daybreak," 176–177, 179–180, 190–191; in "A Sight in Camp in the Daybreak Gray and Dim," 197. *See also* Specularity
Gender identity: transferential character of, in "Song of Myself," section eleven, 39–43, 45; undecidability of, in 1856 *LG*, 115–119; disruption of symmetrical models of, in "As I Ebb'd with the Ocean of Life," 138; in "Song of the Banner at Daybreak," 182; destabilization of, in WW's Civil War poetry, 205; in "By Blue Ontario's Shore," 209; and "the body," 228n20. *See also* Corporeality; Embodiment
Gilchrist, Anne, 71
Golden, Arthur, 2, 94
Graham, Sylvester, 19–21
Grossman, Allen, 225n7

Hand, writer's: uncanny presence of, in "Song of Myself," section eleven, 46

Holloway, Emery, 221
Homoerotic desire, male, 9–15; in "The Child's Champion," 27–30, 32–33; in 1855 Preface, 75–76, 117–118; in "Salut au Monde!," 121; in "Calamus" poems, 160–161, 165–166; in "Drum-Taps" poems, 211–214. *See also* Disencryptment; Lesbian desire
Homophobia, emergence of, in U.S., 9–11; as registered in "The Child's Champion," 33–34; in "As I Ebb'd with the Ocean of Life," 153–154; in "Calamus" poems, 157
Homosexual identity, emergence of, in U.S. and Great Britain, 11; and WW's response to, 12–15; and "paranoia," 157. *See also* Homoerotic desire, male; Lesbian desire; Lesbian identity
Homosociality, male: historical changes in, in U.S., 10–11

Indeterminacy, principle of: 7, 26, 35–36, 38, 46
Irigaray, Luce, 152, 232n4

James, Henry, 233n17
Jordan, June, 71

Kosmos, 16, 68, 75
Kristeva, Julia, 146–147, 157, 185

Lacan, Jacques, 107, 109, 144–145, 165–166, 167, 200
Lesbian desire, representations of: in "The Sleepers," section six, 83–86, 213
Lesbian identity, emergence of, in U.S., 45
Lewis, Felice Flanery, 36
Lewis, R. W. B., 144
Liminality, principle of: in 1855 *LG*, 38, 40, 49–51, 65, 69, 74; in "Crossing Brooklyn Ferry," 109–110; in relation to uncanny, 176, 197
Lincoln, Abraham, 215, 218, 219
Literality, principle of, 26, 35–36, 38, 51–52
Literary, status of, in *LG*, 2, 6, 8, 16
Lowell, James Russell, 150

Male-purity movement: emergence of, in U.S., 19–23; WW's relation to, 24–25. *See also* Anti-onanist discourses
Martin, Robert K., 41, 231n14
Masturbation. *See* Anti-onanist discourses

Index

Maternal phallus: in "Song of the Broad-Axe," 92–93, 103–104; in "Drum-Taps" poems, 175–176, 212; in "Song of the Banner," 184–185, 187–189, 192–193, 200–201, 206–207

Maternity, figures for: in "The Child's Champion," 67–68; in 1856 LG, 91–92; in 1867 LG, 203–205, 211–214, 219, 220; absence from "Calamus" poems, 211

Mather, Samuel, 127

Melancholia, 149–150, 170, 219. See also Mourning, erotics of

Miller, James E., Jr., 105

Mirroring. See Specularity

Mount, William Sidney, 64–65

Mourning, erotics of, 215–220

Native Americans, representations of: in "The Sleepers," section six, 83–86; in "Song of Myself," section thirty-nine, 86–87

Nature: WW's conception of, as political: 132, 158–159, 170; hostility of, in "As I Ebb'd with the Ocean of Life," 143

Nissenbaum, Stephen, 20, 21

Nudity, textualization of, 70. See also Corporeality

Oedipal dynamics: of 1856 LG, 88–92, 98, 100; and infantilization of perspective in 1856 LG, 137; subversion of, in 1860 LG, 145; as revised in 1867 LG, 176. See also Castration; Phallus; Pre-oedipal fantasy

Owen, Robert Dale, 20, 21

Paine, Thomas, 16–18

Paranoia: as "cultural terrain" in "As I Ebb'd with the Ocean of Life," 142–143; and attack on transcendence in 1860 LG, 154–155; explored in "Calamus" poems, 159, 163

Patterson, Annabel, 37

Patterson, Lee, 242n14

Pearce, Roy Harvey, 126

Penis: derivation of symbolic entity of phallus from, 103; difference from phallus, 175; "lurking" in "Spontaneous Me," 218

Phallus, representations of: in "The Child's Champion," 29; in 1855 LG, 51, 116; in 1856 LG, 98, 100–103; in 1860 LG, 148; in 1867 LG, 174–175, 177, 184–193, 206; in heroic-style public architecture, 187. See also Child-phallus; Maternal phallus

Pocock, J. G. A., 17

Politics of Leaves of Grass project, 2–4, 16, 225–226n7

Pre-oedipal fantasy, 103–104

Primal scene: in "Crossing Brooklyn Ferry," 112–113

Print: uncanny presence of, in WW's writing, 72–73. See also Type

Racial difference, representations of: in 1855 LG, 80–87

Rape, male-male: in "The Child's Champion," 28–29; in "As I Ebb'd with the Ocean of Life," 143–144, 153; in "Pioneers! O Pioneers!", 194

Reader relations, 69, 71; in "Crossing Brooklyn Ferry," 109

"Real body," WW's conception of: in 1860 LG, 126–133, 157–158. See also Corporeality; Embodiment; Recursivity

Recursivity: in relation to printer's type, 131–132; as characteristic of both writing and "real body," 134; as modified in 1867 LG, 181. See also "Real body"

Revision, 1, 6; U.S. Constitution as "pretext" for WW's practice of, 16–18; WW's practice of, in LG, 18–19; and self-censorship, 29–32

Reynolds, David S., 231n18

Ryan, Mary P., 233n8, 241n7

Sacks, Peter M., 215–216.

Sánchez-Eppler, Karen, 233n18

Schor, Naomi, 96

Scripture, WW's conception of 1860 LG as new version of, 123–125, 150–152, 236n3

Sedgwick, Eve Kosofsky, 226n13, 227n16

Seduction, authorial, 74, 118

Self-censorship: in revision of "The Child's Champion," 29–32; as formative element in WW's poetry, 34, 52–53; in "Song of Myself," section eleven, 44–45; in revisions of 1855 Preface, 117–118

Sexuality: WW's conception of, as fundamentally political, 4–5, 7–8, 159. See also Embodiment; Homoerotic desire, male; Homosexual identity, emergence of; Lesbian desire; Lesbian identity

Slavery: WW's critique of, in 1855 LG, 80–83

Smith, Henry Nash, 113

Smith-Rosenberg, Carroll, 24–25

Sommer, Doris, 233n14

Specularity, principle of: mediates between fluidity and solidity in 1855 *LG*, 62; in "The Child's Champion," 65–66; and mirroring, 68; as means by which human body is incorporated into printed text or photographs, 69, 73; in 1855 Preface, 74–76; and structure of desire between women, in "The Sleepers," section six, 85; power of, critiqued in "Crossing Brooklyn Ferry," 110–111; replaced in 1856 *LG* by "taking vista," 113

State violence, 99–101, 107, 177, 198, 200, 210

Stoddard, Charles Warren, 12–14

Substance: WW's conception of, in 1860 *LG*, 126–130

Substitution, principle of, 6–7

Symonds, John Addington, 11–13, 36

Temperance, discourses of: "The Child's Champion" and, 29

Thomas, M. Wynn, 106

Tissot, Samuel A. A., 20

Todd, John, 20–21

Tompkins, Jane P., 236n3

Trall, Russell Thacher, 22

Triad as unit of erotic relationship: in "When Lilacs Last in the Dooryard Bloom'd," 216–217

Type/Typology, 125–128, 141–142, 148–151, 237n6. *See also* Print

Uncanny: in "The Child's Champion," 63, 65; in "Crossing Brooklyn Ferry," 108–109; in "A Sight in Camp in the Daybreak Gray and Dim," 197–198; in "By Blue Ontario's Shore," 209; in "When Lilacs Last in the Dooryard Bloom'd," 215–226. *See also* Liminality

Vendler, Helen, 243n20

Warner, Michael, 233n9

War-rhetoric, 172–173. *See also* Elegy-rhetoric

Whitman, Louisa Van Velsor, 214

Whitman, Walt
  LEAVES OF GRASS
    1855 edition, 36–52, 59–87
    1856 edition, 88–122
    1860 edition, 123–170
    1867 edition, 171–221
    "Deathbed" edition, 221

  POETIC WORKS
    "As I Ebb'd with the Ocean of Life," 125–154, 210, 220
    "Broad-Axe Poem." *See* "Song of the Broad-Axe"
    "By Blue Ontario's Shore," 89, 116–117, 201–210
    "Calamus" poems, 158–170
    "Calamus. 1." *See* "In Paths Untrodden"
    "Calamus. 2." *See* "Scented Herbage of my Breast"
    "Calamus. 4." *See* "These I Singing in Spring"
    "Calamus. 8." *See* "Long I Thought That Knowledge Alone Would Suffice Me"
    "Calamus. 9." *See* "Hours Continuing Long, Sore, and Heavy-hearted"
    "Calamus. 15." *See* "Trickle Drops"
    "Calamus. 17." *See* "Of Him I Love Day and Night"
    "Calamus. 20." *See* "I Saw in Louisiana a Live-Oak Growing"
    "Calamus. 25." *See* "The Prairie-Grass Dividing"
    "Calamus. 27." *See* "O Living Always, Always Dying"
    "Calamus. 29." *See* "One Flitting Glimpse"
    "Calamus. 43." *See* "O You Whom I Often and Silently Come Where You Are"
    "Centenarian's Story, The," 195, 196, 200
    "Crossing Brooklyn Ferry," 105–113, 148, 176
    "Delicate Cluster," 200
    "Dresser, The." *See* "The Wound-Dresser"
    "Drum-Taps" poems, 171–201
    "Hours Continuing Long, Sore, and Heavy-hearted," 166
    "In Paths Untrodden," 160, 220
    "I Saw in Louisiana a Live-Oak Growing," 163–166
    "I Sing the Body Electric," 81–83
    "Leaves of Grass. 1." *See* "As I Ebb'd with the Ocean of Life"
    "Long I Thought That Knowledge Alone Would Suffice Me," 166
    "Lo, Victress on the Peaks," 198
    "Of Him I Love Day and Night," 169–170
    "O Living Always, Always Dying," 168–169

Index

"One Flitting Glimpse, Caught through an Interstice," 160–162

"Out of the Cradle Endlessly Rocking," 155, 220

"Over the Carnage Rose Prophetic a Voice," 212

"O You Whom I Often and Silently Come Where You Are," 162

"Pioneers! O Pioneers!", 193–195

"Poem of Many in One." See "By Blue Ontario's Shore"

"Poem of Procreation." See "Woman Waits for me, A"

"Poem of Salutation." See "Salut au Monde!"

"Poem of Women." See "Unfolded Out of the Folds"

"Poem of Wonder at the Resurrection of the Wheat." See "This Compost"

"Prairie-Grass Dividing, The," 167

"Proto-Leaf." See "Starting from Paumanok"

"Salut au Monde!", 120–122

"Scented Herbage of my Breast," 166

"Sight in Camp in the Daybreak Gray and Dim, A," 197–198

"Sleepers, The," 49–50; section six, 83–86, 213

"So Long!", 176, 217

"Song of Myself": section five, 47–49; section six, 97–98, 136, 213; section eleven, 38–47, 159, 160–162; section thirty-nine, 86–87

"Song of the Banner at Daybreak," 177–193

"Song of the Broad-Axe," 92–105, 161, 176, 193, 198, 202, 204

"Starting from Paumanok," 129–132, 156, 158, 195, 212–213

"Sun-Down Poem." See "Crossing Brooklyn Ferry"

"These I Singing in Spring," 167–168

"This Compost," 136–138

"Trickle Drops," 166

"Unfolded Out of the Folds," 77–78, 185

"We Two Boys Together Clinging," 217

"We Two, How Long We Were Fool'd," 151

"When Lilacs Last in the Dooryard Bloom'd," 215–221

"Woman Waits for Me, A," 96–97

"Word Out of the Sea, A." See "Out of the Cradle Endlessly Rocking"

"Wound-Dresser, The," 173, 196

PROSE WORKS

"Backward Glance o'er Travel'd Roads, A," 3, 8, 221

"Child and the Profligate, The." See "Child's Champion, The"

"Child's Champion, The," 26–36, 53–54, 160–162, 190–191

Democratic Vistas, 90

"Eighteenth Presidency!, The," 17, 172

Franklin Evans, 54, 55–56

"Madman, The," 54

"Poetry To-Day in America—Shakspere—The Future," 132

Preface to 1855 LG, 74–75, 89, 151–152, 213

Preface to 1876 LG, 3, 9

Whitman, Walter (father), 20

Wilde, Oscar, 36

Wilentz, Sean, 23, 56

Women, representations of: in "Song of Myself," section eleven, 39–47; in "The Sleepers," section six, 83–86; in 1856 LG, 91–92

Wood, Gordon S., 17

Working-class culture: WW's engagement with, 24; and temperance movement, 56–58

Wright, Frances, 20